Public and Professional Writing

*For Wayne, Freya and Loki, and for my Omi, Rosa Prasser (1912–2004)*

# Public and Professional Writing

## Ethics, Imagination and Rhetoric

Anne Surma

First published in 2005 by
PALGRAVE MACMILLAN
Houndmills, Basingstoke, Hampshire RG21 6XS and
175 Fifth Avenue, New York, N.Y. 10010
Companies and representatives throughout the world.

PALGRAVE MACMILLAN is the global academic imprint of the Palgrave
Macmillan division of St. Martin's Press, LLC and of Palgrave Macmillan Ltd.
Macmillan® is a registered trademark in the United States, United Kingdom
and other countries. Palgrave is a registered trademark in the European
Union and other countries.

ISBN 1–4039–1581–4 hardback
ISBN 1–4039–1582–2 paperback

This book is printed on paper suitable for recycling and made from fully
managed and sustained forest sources.

A catalogue record for this book is available from the British Library.

Library of Congress Cataloging-in-Publication Data

Surma, Anne, 1961–
    Public and professional writing : ethics, imagination and rhetoric /
Anne Surma.
        p. cm.
    Includes bibliographical references and index.
    ISBN 1–4039–1581–4 – ISBN 1–4039–1582–2 (pbk.)
    1. Business writing. 2. Report writing. I. Title.

HF5718.3.S87 2005
808′.06665—dc22                                        2004051406

10  9  8  7  6  5  4  3  2  1
14  13  12  11  10  09  08  07  06  05

Printed and bound in Great Britain by
Antony Rowe Ltd, Chippenham and Eastbourne.

# Contents

# Acknowledgements

An earlier version of parts of Chapter 1, 'Marking the space: writing as ethical, imaginative and rhetorical praxis', appeared as 'Defining professional writing as an area of scholarly activity' (2000), *TEXT*, 4,2, at http://www.gu.edu.au/school/art/text/oct00/surma.htm.

An earlier version of parts of Chapter 2, 'The struggle to relate: writers and readers of corporate and public documents', appeared as 'Professional writing as ethical rhetoric: the Australian Government's response to *Bringing them home*' (2001), *Australian Journal of Communication*, 28,2, pp. 33–46.

An earlier version of Chapter 4, 'Challenging unreliable narrators: writing and public relations', appeared as 'Public relations and corporate social responsibility: developing a moral narrative' (2004), 5,2 *Asia Pacific Public Relations Journal*.

Many wonderful people have, directly and indirectly, supported me through this whole process; without them, the manuscript would never have been completed. I make special mention of just a few stars. Peta Bowden encouraged me to get going with my writing, and has expanded my understanding of the field of ethics. Helena Grehan read and commented painstakingly on drafts, coaxed me patiently through various anxieties and uncertainties, and is still speaking to me. Jim Porter made incisive and thoughtful suggestions on a draft of the whole manuscript. And Peta, Rob Briggs, Kate Fitch, Paul Galea and Jacquie L'Etang each read and offered helpful feedback on various chapters. Sandra Wilson helped steer my course with practical advice and sound judgement. Cheryl Miller and other staff at Murdoch University provided the stable space, the talking and the coffees that sustained me. My students at Murdoch, colleagues and clients and case study participants have all kept me passionate about and motivated by my work. On the home front, Ron and Marie stepped in to look after their grandchildren when they saw me floundering. Pete, my generous brother, created the book's jacket design from a flimsy brief emailed from the other side of the world. Other members of my family, especially Janina, Ella, Gig and George, have cheered me on relentlessly, and believe in this person I still aspire to become. And last and always most, Wayne, Freya and Loki have loved me while I lived on another planet, and make coming down to earth a warm and important place to be. Thank you.

# Preface

In this book I explore public and professional writing produced through diverse modes and genres, for example, corporate and political documents, websites and emails. I also investigate the processes of developing and the impacts of reading such writing in various contexts, for example, within and between workplaces, in the corporate, public and political spheres, and in physical and virtual spaces. Having argued that ethics, imagination and rhetoric are necessarily interwoven in writing that treats as pivotal the relationship between writers and readers, I draw on interviews with writers and critically analyse an international selection of sample texts and case studies to demonstrate the activity, effect and potential value of writing and reading as social practices.

Implicit in my engagement in the chapters below, with sources from the USA and Europe as well as Australia, is a more global, inclusive approach to professional writing. Currently, much of the work in the field comes from the United States: the range and richness of its material is an inspiration to those of us working elsewhere, in variously defined disciplinary soil. Nevertheless, researchers, educators and practitioners in Australia and in Europe are engaging in praxis through important alternative histories and along other, similarly productive paths. As a result, much could be gained from a sharing of our respective approaches to and initiatives in writing. This attempt to transcend geographical boundaries is by no means a simultaneous call to circumvent cultural distinctions. On the contrary, my focus on an ethical and imaginative approach to our rhetorical practices specifically demands a responsibility for attentiveness to other positions. Given the current climate of fear (of the other) palpable around the world, a climate which threatens to obscure the value of diverse texts and textualising processes, we could usefully confer on how we each write and read, and how we might do so otherwise, and reciprocally.

As well, the broader definition for professional writing that I have proposed serves, among other things, to encourage the potential for exchange between specialists whose nomenclature has traditionally kept them apart. In this way, public relations writers, technical writers and political writers, for example, although producing and circulating documents with different discursive functions, in different contexts, are united by the orientation of their rhetoric to the public space, and by their interest in the relationships to be developed with readers. The notions and orders of those differing relationships could stimulate comparative and mutually enriching reflections on why and how we write, and how we might write better for our readers in future.

And finally (provisionally speaking, that is), as the idea of professional writing is transforming, so is the idea of who professional writers might be. As I hope the following pages will highlight, to do professional writing is to negotiate discourses of technology, of politics, of the economy, of business, of law – of relations of power. We would do well to develop the interdisciplinary base of our practice. This is not in order to broaden and bolster the label 'expert' and so gain and sustain the status of the untouchable 'professional'. It is rather in order to understand the ways in which our first and foremost interpersonal, moral and creative social (humanities-centred) practice is not only delimited by but can challenge and change those discourses that preclude us from using our imagination when we write to – and for – one another.

# Introduction

## Professional writing as significant and evolving praxis

Writing in the public realm, in today's knowledge-based economy,[1] can be a hugely powerful and influential activity, particularly when writers write from positions of authority or professional or political power. The privilege of writing in these spaces brings with it responsibilities and obligations to others whom writers address and in whose communities texts circulate. Paradoxically, however, these specifically textual responsibilities and obligations are sometimes ignored by the management of institutions and corporations. While employers typically declare the value and significance of effective communication skills – including writing – in getting the job 'done', there seems to be little explicit acknowledgement of the potential influence of language extending beyond its instrumental function. Cezar M. Ornatowski puts the point succinctly, when he explains that 'effectiveness and efficiency, understood in terms of usefulness to employers, as the basic premises for communicative action appear to leave the communicator no provision, at least in theory, for action that does not "efficiently" further the goals of the institution or interests she serves' (2003, p. 174). It seems, therefore, that words – as forms of ethical action – on page or screen, despite billions of dollars being invested in their (regularly glossy) production, really don't matter after all.

In this book I critique that paradox. I also set out to suggest how and why professional writing can make a vital contribution, through the process of meaningful exchanges between writers and readers, to the development of a fairer and more equitable society.

Today, many of us working and writing in institutions, organisations or corporations produce a range of written discourses – client reports and letters, internal and external emails, websites, policy and discussion documents, and so on. Most of these texts interweave a complex of rhetorics: those of specialist and general knowledges, of information, education and persuasion, of public and community relations, of economics, of law and regulation, of citizenship and morality.[2] As well, with the advent of increasingly sophisticated communication technologies, writing, as a process of and forum for exchange or dialogue between citizens in public and professional spheres, has proliferated.

So, do we write more just because we can, or is it because we have things to say to one another? In other words, why are we writing and for whose benefit? If we represent an organisation or institution (and many writers do) that claims to be a good corporate citizen, is it acceptable that, aside from our expressly marketing endeavours, we write chiefly to serve our own (largely economic) ends? For example, if we are writers of course materials designed for prospective students in the university context, how do we justify our combining of marketing with pedagogical or disciplinary rhetoric? And to which of those rhetorics do we give greater attention or focus?[3] Furthermore, what are the material impacts of our writing on our readers and on others, and are we disinclined to think about those impacts because, as a result of the ways we live and work today, we are less likely to see, and so care about, them? In other words, if we write for a wide or largely anonymous readership (as we may often do when developing website material on behalf of a government institution, or when preparing a corporate document for circulation among diverse stakeholders – employees, shareholders, consumers), our textual and technological contact with our readers can all too easily be treated as an abstract technical function rather than imagined as an interpersonal exchange. As a consequence, are we genuinely interested in understanding *who* our readers are (and *how* our writing might affect them or enable them to respond), apart from such knowledge helping us better to achieve our own writing ends?[4] Are we serious about engaging with the needs and interests of our readers – colleagues, clients and our larger communities – even if that means modifying our texts to achieve a more balanced, productive exchange from *all* interlocutors' points of view?

The field of public relations has played an important role in drawing attention to the importance of addressing a wide range of stakeholders in establishing and sustaining an organisation's viability. But, how often does the rhetorical address of any such powerful body involve a genuine willingness to admit the dissonance of competing stakeholder voices and the attempt to review and revise responses (both textual and pragmatic) to accommodate their differences? For example, Shell, the global group of energy and petrochemical companies, has a 'Tell Shell' page on its website (http://www.euapps.shell.com/TellShell/), which declares its 'commit[ment] to open and transparent dialogue with [its] stakeholders'. Individuals are invited to post their contributions (including criticisms and challenges) to debates on issues such as the role of multinationals in society, the environment and energy and technology.[5] The company also posts its responses to specific comments or questions put by members of the public. Similarly, the UK-wide communications solutions provider, the BT Group (www.btplc.com) periodically carries out email debates and live Internet discussions on topics of interest to its stakeholders, such as the role and responsibilities of business, and communication technologies' influence and impacts on cultures and communities. The company claims that stakeholder dialogue has been used in the selection of non-financial key performance indicators and the selection of communication and education as key themes for its 'social investment programmes', for example. However, more research is required into whether such dialogue serves as a rhetorical game of ping-pong, or whether it contributes to the changes (in attitudes, beliefs and practices) that writers and readers may judge it wise to make in light of others' words.

I have the feeling that we can't be at all confident about the answers to the questions posed above. And that therefore it isn't surprising that many readers approach corporate and public texts with a sense of cynicism or distrust. Readers recognise self-serving rhetoric. We can often read the difference between writers committed to imaginatively engaging with us, despite the inevitably disjunctive positions of writers and readers, and writers lacking such imagination. We look to see ourselves (our identities, discourses, interests, values) engaged within the texts written to us, to see ourselves addressed or acknowledged, so that a space for our potential response is opened up. Thus, in policy documents or reports or news and information texts produced by government, we read to see how we are positioned as citizens. In the brochures or websites describing corporate profiles and activities we look for our representation as stakeholders. And in internal workplace emails or memos, we infer from others' correspondence their view of us as colleagues. From these reading practices we determine whether and how we are encouraged or enabled to respond.

The activities of ethics, imagination and rhetoric, whose intrinsic value for writing praxis I set out to demonstrate as interrelated forms (and see the next section), can be harnessed to help us navigate the demands of diverse writing and reading contexts. None of them reconstructed in their application to particular writing and reading situations, ethics, imagination and rhetoric are *ever* reified entities and, as processes and practices, they are amoebic in their impulse to otherness and transformation. Therefore I hope it will be clear that my study does not attempt to universalise approaches to or reflections on writing. However, even a sustained insistence on raising ethical questions related to professional writing practices and on determinedly working to develop an imaginative rhetoric will not alone resolve all the problems resulting from predominantly market-driven or individualistically-oriented business and political practices. Nonetheless, a key impetus in the writing of this book has been my belief and my dream that such insistence will encourage us to reconsider the order of our priorities.

In the following chapters, I explore and interrogate current and normative writing practices in the public and professional realms. I argue for the ways in which writing as responsible social praxis – one focused specifically on the relationships forged between interlocutors through written texts – could better serve the interests and values of readers, writers and the community. In my discussion, and perhaps unlike many similar previous bodies of work in the field, I assume a broadened scope for professional writing. Thus, public relations, political, workplace and corporate writing, each highly significant in its influence on contemporary public and social life, are all considered. In other words, these writing domains, from which texts are generated by individuals or groups (either acting in the service of or representing institutional or corporate bodies) and addressed to specific or general readers, wield an authority that, as I have mentioned, make writers accountable.

It is at this point worth clarifying briefly the sense of 'public and professional writing' of the book's title and the term's use in the following chapters. (An extended overview of the discipline itself is given in Chapter 1.) First of all, my intention is not to distinguish two different modes of writing through the use of 'public' and 'professional'. On the contrary, I intend that all discussions of professional writing (the shorthand term I use most frequently in the book) retain the sense of this genre's potential reach and impact, not only within but often well beyond its immediate discursive contexts. In other words, professional writing is also public writing. This is perhaps most readily understood when we consider the writing of corporate, organisational or government websites and various public relations texts, for example. But it also applies in the cases of workplace email writing or a company's letters to its clients. Even when writing is exchanged between individuals or between select groups of individuals involved in business- or community-related endeavours – commercial, non-commercial, political, government or non-government – its rhetoric, whether directly or indirectly, has public ramifications. The way in which experts in a particular professional field construct and present advice to clients in letters or reports, for instance, serves to influence (to reinforce or modify) readers' understandings about and their relation to not only the experts in question but the field in which the experts work, that field's relevance to or value for readers and their communities, as well as all interlocutors' respective places and roles in a given culture. It is that capacity for writers' and writing's influence – their power and authority – that, in part, grants them status as 'professional' at all and, inseparable from that, demands of them a social obligation and responsibility to others. Secondly, the term 'writing' (in preference to, say, communication) is used in conjunction with 'public and professional' because of the way in which the status of writing as a noun – a letter, word, text, or even an occupation – is always interwoven with or disrupted by its *productive* significance as a (participial form of) verb – a present or ongoing activity or process. As a participial form, writing also implies agency: *someone* writing, and someone identifying (reading) that writing. Thus writing has a vital interpersonal and social dimension. And finally, and interestingly, the etymological links between public and publish – the latter comes from the Latin *publicare*, to make public – underscores the connection between writing and technologies of communication that allow texts to be made easily, quickly and widely available for readers in the social domain.

As I have hinted above, my research into professional writing practices has consistently uncovered a stubborn tension between the social and human perspective on the one hand and the economic and instrumentalist perspective on the other. This is, crudely speaking, a tension between ethical and rationalist views on the function, objectives and value of professional writing in the public domain. Although in recent years many corporate and political rhetorics have, apparently, dissolved at least some of the friction between expediency and morality in their discursive practice (sometimes by putting the latter squarely in the comfortable service of the former), their antagonism undoubtedly remains. Terms now current in public, professional and political discourse, such as 'corporate citizenship', 'social capital' and 'triple bottom line' indicate the rhetorical partnership between socially and environmentally responsible and financially-driven initiatives. But how far do these rhetorical articulations really coincide with public and professional practice? In other words, are such linguistic terms themselves merely the servants of expediency, or do they represent (textually) an authentic commitment to wrangling with rival material pressures? Is there, then, a demonstrable relationship between social practices and the rhetorics that represent them? In some cases, there certainly might be. For instance, in her fascinating analysis of the 'discursive struggle' that arose between the Royal Dutch/Shell Group and its critics over the corporation's business practices, Sharon Livesey suggests that Shell 'opened itself to such potentially democratizing discursive forms as stakeholder engagement, dialogue, and "social" reports (i.e. reports on corporate social and environmental performance). These discursive moves were both shaped by and constitutive of company action and practice' (Livesey 2001, p. 59).

Each of the chapters offers a (loosely defined) critical discourse analysis of textual material from a range of writing and reading contexts. Critical discourse analysis treats language, particularly public texts, as a form of social practice, and is concerned with the ways in which language organises and mediates (asymmetrical) relations of power between speakers or writers and readers, and the ways in which it naturalises particular ideologies (see Fairclough 1995, 2001).[6] My aim is to question the value of certain writing practices, which purport to communicate with others but which fail to engage with them either meaningfully or productively. Individual case studies try to show that this failure may be the result of writers conceiving readers not as active (as potential writers themselves), but essentially as 'receivers' of already accomplished messages. The case studies also try to show that texts have limited value when writers develop texts uninformed by an understanding of the positions – discursive, social, economic – of their potential readers and of how those positions may affect readers' ability or inclination to engage with and respond to such texts.[7]

## Interviews

Two of the chapters draw on interviews with professionals who write. My approach to interviewing has attempted to model itself broadly on that outlined by Sullivan and Porter in their salutary text, *Opening spaces: writing technologies and critical research practices*. In that text, Sullivan and Porter advocate a research approach to writing with computers which they call 'methodology as praxis' (see Sullivan and Porter 1997, pp. 45–75). In brief, the authors critique traditional research approaches that give primacy to method, that claim to be able to separate methodology from research practice, and that ignore the potential for the reshaping of method according to research practice or specific situation: 'Methodology that is portrayed as a set of immutable principles, rather than as heuristic guidelines, masks the impact of the situation – of the practice – on the study in ways that could unconsciously reinscribe theory's dominance over practice' (Sullivan and Porter 1997, p. 66). They draw on a range of feminist approaches to research practices that challenge the notion of objective or neutral researchers evaluating the activities of participants in a given research situation using a singular or rigid methodology.

Sullivan and Porter thus devise an expansive strategy for research praxis that relies on a range of discipline, theory and method; that constructs new knowledge domains; that is flexible and adaptable to the needs of a particular situation; that is self-reflexive and critical; that admits the vital interdependence of researcher and researched; that understands human emotions as significant to the research process and its 'content'; that acknowledges and discusses the disruptions to the planned research and the tensions inherent in its process; and that explores the political and ethical implications of this work.

The writers I interviewed are professionals for whom writing comprises a significant component of their work, but who would not describe themselves as professional writers. For each of the chapters I was interested in raising questions about the relationship between notions of professional practice and notions of subjectivity in situated contexts, and the connections between both of these and understandings of the function and value of writing as communicative exchange. I therefore felt that, in addition to my own reflections on these matters, and in addition to the work of other scholars on which the chapters would be drawing, the work would be enhanced by the voices of others (all but one of whom were not self-described professional writers).

I decided that the best approach for eliciting this kind of material was to carry out semi-structured interviews with a small number of participants. I imagined that the interviews would be more fluent and more relaxed if I interviewed participants whom I knew, whose work contexts and professional disciplines I was familiar with (though certainly not expert in), and whom I thought would be comfortable abut talking with me. Before carrying out the interviews, I had done some preliminary research and prepared a skeletal framework for the respective chapters. It was on the basis of these frameworks that I devised my interview questions (see below).

I mentioned above that I felt that the incorporation of other voices would 'enhance' my work. In fact, however, the material I gathered from the interviews actively worked to help me redefine a rhetorical structure and a theoretical focus for the two chapters that later emerged. For example, in Chapter 2, I was prompted to investigate further questions relating to expertise and authority as a consequence of interview participants' comments. And in Chapter 5, I was led on a trail to the writing of Richard Lanham and the idea of 'toggling between' looking through and looking at language as a direct result of the views and responses offered by interview participants.

As I hope the (admittedly deliberate and organised) interspersing of the participants' views with my developing discussions indicates, in neither chapter was I interested in making definitive, empirically generalisable or quantifiable claims about particular writing practices in specific contexts. What I was concerned with in both chapters, however, was to try to enact the writing praxis I advocate in the book. I wanted to try to enable other voices, other views, to articulate their different responses, to engage in discussion about writing, and also to reconceptualise writing-related matters in ways that better relate my interests to their own.

From my preliminary research for both chapters, I drafted a series of questions around which to structure the interviews. This task made me realise very quickly the ways in which, as the researcher, my own particular concerns and interests were, to some extent at least, bound to be imposed on interviewees. Perhaps this wouldn't be a problem if our perspectives were shared. But what if – and this was the more likely scenario – the participants didn't share those concerns or interests? What if they perceived (at least some of) my questions as irrelevant to their own ideas about what was or wasn't important in relation to their writing practices? I decided therefore that the interview questions would provide flexible guidelines rather than prescribe the strict format for our discussion. I would use my draft questions as a guide, and modify or adjust them according to the specific drift of the one-on-one interview encounter. This is what I did. However, even then some participants interpreted the questions I was asking differently from the way I had imagined they would: not, I think, because the questions were unclear, but rather because the terms of the question had different resonances for them than they did for me.

Having sought and been granted permission from the relevant management in the different organisations, I approached individuals and requested permission to interview them, on a one-to-one basis. I explained that each interview would last one-and-a-half to two hours. Each prospective participant I approached agreed to be interviewed. Having obtained their agreement, I asked participants to send me, before our interviews, four or five sample reports, letters or faxes (in the case of participants in Chapter 2's study), and a sample of fifteen to twenty emails recently (within the last month) sent or received in the course of their work (in the case of participants in Chapter 5).

The interviews lasted between one and two hours (and most lasted around an hour-and-a-half). All except one (which took place over lunch at a café) were conducted in the participants' workplaces. All interviews were taped.

Participants' interest in or enthusiasm for discussion certainly varied, though each of them appeared happy to talk about writing in relation to their work. In only one case did I feel that the interview process hadn't enabled a participant to talk meaningfully with me. The participant in this case was under considerable pressure to complete some urgent work before going on leave the following day. He had also forgotten, until the last minute, that we had arranged to meet. The interview was, quite understandably, an unwanted distraction, though he insisted on going through with it.

The resulting chapters are proof of the (necessary?) imbalances of power that obtain between researcher and researched. From the interviews I have selected only those comments that suit my purposes for argument, pattern and contrast. While quoted comments are, of course, the participants' own, they are recontextualised in the flow of a discourse that is not their own. In other words, although I described as clearly as I could to each of the interview participants the nature of my research and the locus of my interests, I did not, for example – except in the case of two of the university-based participants who were already familiar with my work – explain that I was taking a postmodern, loosely critical discourse approach to the book project, nor did I define the terms ethics, imagination and rhetoric as I use them. This was partly because I did not want to overwhelm the participants with my own discursive preferences. However, it was also because I felt that as the participants themselves were not regular users of the discourses' associated rhetoric, they might have felt alienated by its use. And they may then have also felt disinclined to talk with me. I am aware, therefore, that the tensions between competing rhetorics that I discuss in this text are clearly not to be regarded as other writers' exclusive 'problems'; they are also very much mine, as a writer of academic texts.

## An ethical, imaginative and rhetorical approach: why it's valuable and why it's a struggle

Assuming the distinctiveness of each writing activity, the significance of agency and the primary value of writing as relational, the first chapter seeks to develop an account of how we can harness ethics, rhetoric and imagination to explore responsible and productive processes for writing texts on the one hand and reading and interpreting those texts on the other. The relation between self and others is central to the notions of ethics, imagination and rhetoric that the chapter explores. That relation is always already in the making – through the writing and reading of texts. For example, when I start a new job I already have a preconceived or hypothesised sense of my relations with my new boss, my new colleagues and my prospective clients. This sense may be one either approximating to, or distanced from, that of my peers. However, depending on the ways in which, in the course of our work, we write to (and, of course, otherwise interact with) each other, those relations will continually shift and change. In the best-case scenario, we will adjust our writing (and other) practices in light of what we learn about one another, as well as about the function and value of our written texts (to our intended and other potential readers).

Similarly, the postmodern approach I take in this book views writing practices as constituting and modifying intersubjective relations. It rejects the possibility of rhetoric and writing simply having the capacity to reflect stable or apparently objective truths. Accepting, as I do, the post-structuralist view of language as a signifying system, in which signs are only definable by their relationship to and difference from other signs, means that rhetoric and writing do not reflect the 'real' world unproblematically, but instead help to construct (a provisional version of) it. This does *not* mean, however, that language floats in the ether, remote from our material everyday lives and experience. Far from it. Linguistic signs may refer to or call up other signs, but together those signs position us in the world (they identify us and allow us to identify ourselves to others through writing). As well, depending on our relative positions of power or status, writing allows us to help determine or influence actions, practices, beliefs and values in the real world – for ourselves, for those we represent, and for others. Rhetoric thus also helps us, as writers, to make sense of – to articulate – our world and to represent what and how it means to be in the world with others. An illustration of this point is given in the range of terms current in public oral and written discourse around the world to describe those people whose arrival in a country is unauthorised. These people are variously described in the media, in government and non-government texts, in discussion and debate as 'asylum seekers' or 'illegal immigrants' or 'illegals' or 'queue jumpers' or 'refugees'. Obviously, each of these labels rhetorically positions such individuals differently, and each assists citizens and governments to define, rationalise and decide appropriate attitudes towards and 'treatment' for them (see Clyne 2002; Gelber 2003). (It is worth noting, however, that the effects on particular individuals of having different labels thus assigned to them are not yet publicly textualised.)

Most important of all, then, is that rhetoric can offer us, as writers, the opportunity to make sense of our world through our ongoing interactions with readers. But of course, like all other forms of interaction in public and professional life, our various written interactions often represent diverse interests, conflicting views, opposing perspectives. The meanings that various texts and discourses generate jostle for prominence: they occupy a contested space in culture. That the meanings generated by texts are contested suggests that for different people – for writers and readers – texts can both mean and do different things. By extension, the impacts that meanings have or the actions they result in will be experienced and felt and responded to in myriad ways. As professional writers, surely then we must make a commitment to imagining what our texts might (variously) mean, what they might do and what they might bring about not only in our terms, but also in the terms – and in the worlds – of others.

This is why I argue for a moral commitment to professional writing. Pivotal is its human dimension: writing is an ethical activity with ethical implications. It is not merely a game of finesse or fun or trickery, or a matter of convention or platitude; nor is it combat for the sake of combat. And nor is writing ever simply a matter of technological expediency, as Steven B. Katz (2003) reminds us in his account of how the horrors of the holocaust were facilitated by the production of written texts that circumvented questions of the human and the humane – in other words, of the ethical.

The framework that I develop and use to guide my reflections on writing praxis is premised on a postmodern, situated notion of ethics. But it extends that view, so that judgements about the use of rhetoric, while provisional and contingent, always depend on writers' capacity to assume (and remember) the asymmetrical relation between themselves and their readers, and to imagine what it means to be in a different – often less powerful – position. In other words, an ethical position is imbricated in writers' capacity to imagine – to defer or refer their own place to the place(s) of others. Judgements about the use of rhetoric also depend on writers' sensitivity to the public nature of language – to its potential to mean things and to do things – in ways that either challenge and try to redress or reinscribe and intensify undemocratic relations and social and human injustices.

This approach to rhetoric and writing, briefly outlined above, partly explains my studied avoidance, in discussions about professional writing, of writing 'solutions' to be found in templates, protocols, prescriptions, checklists, generalised dos or don'ts of language use, structures and styles. My firm belief is that each of our writing activities, however apparently mundane, is an instance of unique material practice. As well, our agency and the limits of that agency as individual writers – the extent of our capacity to direct the course of our and others' knowledge and experience – are crucial determinants of whether we write, as well as what and how we write.

The responsibilities which I argue are attendant on the roles of professional writers are certainly not straightforward or easy to embrace. Nevertheless the potential impacts of writers' words on their intended and other readers cannot be underestimated. Chapter 2 aims to reflect on the situatedness of writing and reading positions and practices, and to consider the potential for as well as the challenges of reciprocal exchange between writers and readers. Each position is, of course, implicated in the other.

Chapter 2 opens by examining the contexts of corporate or institutional writers, and investigates the kinds of constraints – economic, legal, corporate – which inevitably delimit and compromise writing practices. Only by consistently reimagining the positions of readers and the possibilities for forging connections with them can we, as writers, try to develop an ethical rhetoric through the documents we write. The second part of the chapter offers a reading of a single political document to illustrate professional writing as a medium of public dialogue, and as an opportunity for involving writers and readers together in the journey towards a more equitable society. Disputing a common perception of professional writing as simply the achievement of objectives, I argue that writers' genuine attempts to imagine and acknowledge readers' knowledge, experience and values in the rhetoric of their texts are crucial if debates are to be inclusive and ongoing, and in order that writing may be practised as a form of reconciliation.

## Writing for us or writing for *all* of us?

As I've been preparing the manuscript for this book, the term 'sexing up', to describe the linguistic practice of embellishing or spicing up 'the truth' has, almost overnight, become a global media cliché.[8] Of course the practice of sexing up is closely related to that vividly evoked by the term 'spin'. Spin is what many public relations and marketing writers have traditionally done to give their stories a particular emphasis or bias, and is what has now become normative and certainly pervasive practice for all kinds of writing in the professional and public realms. So perhaps only a sexy new expression like sexing up will do today, because we're unfazed by and even accepting of the ubiquitous activity of spin and its overriding aim to serve the objectives and enhance the profile of its speaker or writer. Both spin and sexed-up language work to deny or significantly obscure their contestability, their potential for challenge by alternative voices, other perspectives: in short, they attempt to deny their intertextuality. While such aims are, arguably, perfectly appropriate to marketing and the promotions or publicity side of public relations, I would contend that they are misplaced in just about all other kinds of professional writing developed for communicating with others.[9] Chapters 3 and 4 are specifically concerned with challenging writing practices that, because largely self-oriented, have a diminished capacity to acknowledge and encourage the crucial role of readers' responses in attributing meaning and value to texts.

In Chapter 3, for example, I look at the production and availability of public information on the Internet and its potential for advancing the process and practice of democracy through debate and the sharing and extending of knowledge and experience. As many have argued, Internet technology provides exciting prospects for involving increasing numbers of the community in democratic exchange. However, my contention is that, operational and other constraints notwithstanding, the rhetoric of public, political and corporate sites may often work to obscure the possibility for the exercise of individual and collective agency. The predominance of a rhetoric of self-promotion and marketing can dissuade people from actively exploiting the Internet as a network of engagement: as a genuine experience of connecting with others to wrangle over and develop ideas and beliefs, and to encourage mutual awareness and understanding of others.

Chapter 4 is interested in public information of a more specific kind: narrative accounts of social responsibility, now regularly produced and disseminated by organisations and corporations. As a result of various pressures exerted by the community that they demonstrate accountability, many businesses today, particularly large, international companies, feel compelled to narrate to their various stakeholders written stories about their activities as moral agents. By their very nature, moral narratives, perhaps more than any other, are narratives that only writers and readers *together* can tell. This poses obvious difficulties (and significant ethical questions) for those companies who fail to distinguish social responsibility texts from those that are expressly designed to market and promote their products or services. The fact that a lengthy lawsuit, only recently settled in the US courts and which I consider in the course of the chapter, has been fought over this issue indicates the timeliness of reflecting on this mode of and approach to professional writing. The implications for the dynamic relation of rhetoric and writing to real world practice are also salutary.

## Writing and now-ness

One of my aims in this book is to convey my sense of professional writing as immediate and committed practice: it involves us with others; it activates our relations to others and makes our responsibilities tangible. Sometimes this sense of immediacy may be less apparent when we write standard letters or reports or when our readers are unknown or remote. When we write through email, however, this is rarely the case.

The proliferation of email exchange in public life has significantly expanded the field and the focus, as well as, of course, the practice of professional writing. It seems to me that the idea of what it means to be professional has also been visibly and usefully extended, as the boundaries conventionally separating the private and public 'sides' of email writers become fluid through their use of this medium. Chapter 5 examines these and related matters. With massively increasing numbers of people engaging in professional writing through email, we are offered a perfect opportunity to pay attention to how written language makes a dynamic contribution to the forces shaping our cultures and changing our lives. The ongoing (theoretical and practical) oscillation between understandings of language as a vehicle for carrying independently formed meanings, and as inseparable from writers and readers who are positioned by and who themselves constitute and interpret language as different meanings is also thrown into relief in email communication. This, then, is an opportune moment to reassert the ethical demands placed on us to make imaginative use of rhetoric, refusing to be held hostage to decontextualised notions of language that, in the end, can only serve to alienate us from others.

# 1
# Marking the Space: Writing as Ethical, Imaginative and Rhetorical Praxis

Is writing in the public domain inevitably about impersonality and detachment? Are writing subjects to be (always) absent as well as (sometimes) invisible when writing in a professional capacity? And if we aren't able to talk to ourselves when writing as professionals, how do we manage to write to others meaningfully? The above questions challenge a common assumption about the conventions of professional writing. They also raise a series of broad questions concerning the writer's agency and the roles of the text and of the reader(s) of documents in the public domain. I hope to address those questions in the course of the discussion below.

Professional discourses, now proliferating in the print and electronic media, regularly interweave a complex of languages – those of specialist and public or general knowledges, of information and persuasion, of public and community relations, of law and regulation, of citizenship and morality. It seems to me to be crucial that we provide a space for emerging and professional writers to develop as critical writers and readers of those cultural texts which to such a great extent govern, regulate and change our environments of government, industry, institution, community and home.

I first attempt to outline the parameters of professional writing as an intellectual discipline and as 'real world' practice; at the same time I am acutely aware that the problems attendant on naming and categorising are typical of our postmodern predicament, where 'the very idea of a discipline must be open to critique' (Blake 1997, p. 164). The discussion develops from the premise that writers of professional texts, often communicating from institutional or corporate positions of relative power, are responsible for negotiating meanings with their readers, and not simply with understanding their reading audiences primarily to facilitate the achievement of writing objectives. I also reaffirm professional writing's particular significance as a broad disciplinary field and as professional practice in the contemporary public, institutional, corporate and workplace environments. I then go on to argue that necessarily underpinning the suppleness of this area of theoretical and practical endeavour are three key interrelated notions: ethics, imagination and rhetoric, which can be harnessed to explore the activities of writing and production on the one hand and reading and interpretation on the other. The processes of pedagogy, practice and critique in the field become dynamic when these notions, which, I argue, are necessarily interdependent, are both theorised and explored as contextualised, localised features integral to professional writing practice. In contrast to current preoccupations with texts and readers, which often result in the elision or obscuring of the importance of writer agency and responsibility, I consider ethics, imagination and rhetoric as central to the processes involved in both the production and reception of professional writing: texts are written as well as read, motivated and intended as well as interpreted and responded to. There is no necessary or easy symmetry between the contexts of reading and writing, nor between the scope of intention and motivation on the one hand and that of interpretation and response on the other.

## Professional writing: marking the territory as discipline and practice

My working definition for professional writing is deliberately broad and flexible. I take my cue from Sullivan and Porter's (1993) mapping of the shifting terrain and interests of professional writing as an academic discipline, which has extended the boundaries of the field in important ways. Sullivan and Porter's paper marked a significant milestone, especially in its moves to reconfigure professional writing as praxis, and the role of the professional writer as 'not to better represent [a] company to the public, but, rather, to help the company better understand the needs and interests of the public' (1993, p. 414).

Professional writing and its orientation to the other and to the public good is precisely the focus of my definition of professional writing's (potential) purpose, function and value. The reflections on professional writing in this book also cover areas elsewhere individually categorised as technical writing or communication, composition studies, workplace (or mundane) writing, public writing, corporate communication, business communication, public relations writing, computer-mediated communication, computer writing and Internet writing.[1] And as the references at the end of this book demonstrate, my work owes a significant debt to research from and publications in all these areas. However, it seems to me that these distinctions, with their focus on writing in a particular environment, in the service of a specific function or through a particular medium, may inadvertently work to obscure or make subordinate what is pivotal to each and every professional writing field: the ethical obligations of writers to readers, as those are imagined, established and modified through written texts, and the rhetorical and material relations those texts set up or develop.

The field of professional writing embraces any written communication (other than that explicitly produced or circulated as art) disseminated or displayed in the organisational or public domain, and having as one of its functions the communication of a specific intention or objective in relation to specific or general reader(s). It comprises those texts designed to affect readers directly or indirectly: to elicit response, to encourage or circumscribe action, to instruct, to persuade, to modify or extend information, knowledge and perceptions, to affirm shared goals, and so on.[2] Examples of professional writing would include, but not be limited to, workplace, corporate, government, organisational, institutional and community-based writing, texts constituting public and political information and debate, and public relations writing. I explore only a small range of professional writing texts in this book: corporate project proposals, client letters and audit reports; government reports designed to contribute to the development of public policy; corporate responsibility documents developed as part of an organisation's public relations function; business, community-based and government websites; and workplace email. Professional writing can be developed and communicated or exchanged electronically or as hard copy; between individuals or groups of individuals representing themselves or writing on behalf of public or private organisations; or between organizations and their individual clients or their general publics. Because my interests lie primarily in the imaginative, ethical and rhetorical processes and effects of writing in particular social contexts, like Sullivan and Porter I concentrate on the writing 'both by specialists in writing itself and by specialists in other areas who write in the workplace' (1993, p. 415).

A primary focus on the communicative *objectives* of professional writing, still typically found in many how-to-write manuals, threatens to keep us stuck in the one-way model of communication (sender-message-text-receiver). This focus also serves to undermine professional writing's significance as a creative, critical and dialogic process, central to which is the imaginative negotiation of rhetorical and ethical issues and choices relating to language and to its forging of specific relations between writers and readers. Writing in a professional capacity involves negotiating meanings: it requires writers being self-conscious about intersubjectivity (even when the subjects/readers being communicated with are unknown). It is therefore about writers imagining the social, cultural and economic place of the reading others, since it involves a considered evaluation of the range of potential readers' interpretations and responses to a given text. In other words, professional writing involves writers negotiating a socially valid correspondence between their communicative objectives as represented by texts, and the readers' real scope for purposeful action or response in their interpretations of those texts.

But surely it's not art? Some might argue that the account of professional writing briefly outlined above depicts it as having pretensions to creative writing. There is no doubt that, in the Australian academy at least, professional writing has historically suffered from comparisons with its seemingly more glamorous and sophisticated cousin.[3] Certainly, in Australia, in the UK and in the USA, where the profile of creative writing programmes is now comparatively strong (see, for example, Krauth 2000; Harper 2003; Bizzaro 2004), the more recent emergence of professional writing as a discipline (in the last decade or so) has paralleled (though is not necessarily coterminous with) the increasingly vocational orientation of the university sector. As a result, professional writing has sometimes been regarded by the broader academic community as a field of dubious intellectual integrity (and see Woods and Skrebels 1997).[4] Unlike in the USA, where professional writing has developed out of well-established literature and composition and business and technical writing programmes and out of the classical discipline of rhetoric (see Sullivan and Porter 1993; Porter et al. 2000), and where a number of robust peak bodies represent the interests of those disciplines, professional writing in Australia is still establishing its own (inter)disciplinary ground.[5] It is also true in the Australian and British contexts that professional writing is frequently embedded in or interwoven with other fields (such as English or communication studies) and programmes (such as publishing, editing, creative non-fiction), so that its status as a coherent discipline is difficult to determine.

There is no doubt that the practice of categorising can have crudely reductionist effects for both creative and professional writing: generally speaking, creative writing is allotted to the exclusive, and sometimes abstract realms of art and culture, professional writing to that of business and the hard-nosed 'real' world. To compound the difficulties, the terms professional writing and creative writing suggest qualitative as well as disciplinary differences.[6] The adjective 'professional' when used to describe writing implies competence, skill and efficiency, public recognition and social as well as economic currency: that is, professional as opposed to unprofessional or non-professional. (Such description is, of course, also linked to the legitimation of professional writing as a vocational discipline, an issue I briefly consider below.) The adjective 'creative' when allied with the word 'writing' implies originality, imagination, inventiveness, resourcefulness (as opposed, presumably, to convention, predictability, to dullness or mundanity). Other issues are highlighted by the oppositional constructions of these different writing fields. For example, when is creative writing not work? When does professional writing not involve a process of fictionalising? Can creative writing not be professional? Is professional writing not creative?

Let me quickly point out that I am not attempting to conflate professional writing with the genre of creative writing or writing as art-text: each has a distinct focus and cultural function. However, there is clearly a danger in too emphatically distinguishing the two areas, and thus in producing them as necessarily oppositional. The development of emerging writers' awareness (as both writers and readers) of texts as both formative and transformative are aims shared by both creative and professional writing disciplines. We need to maintain the connections between the two in order to endorse their respective value as vital components of cultural communication, and to resist, as Raymond Williams (1965, p. 54) argues, 'set[ting] "art" on one side of a line and "work" on the other; we cannot submit to be divided into "Aesthetic Man" and "Economic Man" ' (sic).[7]

Andrew Taylor, writing from an Australian perspective, suggests that, in contrast to creative writing, the discipline of professional writing is more secure within the tertiary sector, given the latter's assimilation into 'the job-oriented ethos of so much current university thinking about education' (1999).[8] I suggest we need to be extremely wary about the apparent comforts afforded by such legitimacy. This wariness would not mean refusing professional writing as a field that *can* prepare emerging writers to communicate effectively in the workplace and in the public sphere, but rather refusing the discourse of the market place as authoritative or unproblematic, unchallenged by the complexity or value of competing discourses.

An important and productive association can and should be sustained between the fields of professional writing and the liberal arts, rather than with vocationally or professionally oriented university faculties, such as business and marketing schools. By locating professional writing as a subject within the liberal arts/humanities, we can more readily signal our intention to focus on its cultural breadth and on the myriad purposes, functions and effects of the production and reception of public texts. And importantly, while recognising the reliance of a range of disciplines – economics, business, marketing and law, for example – on professional writing, we can nevertheless resist or interrogate those powerful discourses as 'natural' or inevitable ways of communicating.[9] Moreover, Theodore Zorn discusses the difficulties inherent in situating professional communication in professional schools, where the aggressive pressure 'to meet our "customers'" wants for career preparation' threatens to distract attention from 'critical thinking, theory and broader social issues' (Zorn 1998, p. 40). The function of professional writing should not be reduced to the function of 'servicing' any single discipline.

The importance of theorising professional writing, and of imagining it as process and practice rather than as product, competes with pressure (from university coffers, from employers, and even from students) to focus on the development of writing skills or effective writing. In other words, there is a pressure to 'just do it': to prepare students for employment, or to exploit professional writers' ability to write expediently, rather than to enable them to think about the complex processes involved in the practice of professional writing.

What is wrong with 'simply' developing writing skills? Such an approach creates the misperception that writing skills are separable techniques that can be taught and then simply applied, in isolation from the various social contexts in which public texts circulate, are read and interpreted, and in which their rhetorical effects have significant and often real results. In other words, we can learn (and teach others) to write grammatical sentences, to use language to produce specific effects, to organise our writing through conventional frameworks: letters, essays, reports, emails, and the like. If this is all that we do, however, we are not learning (or enabling others) to write (or to read) between the lines. In other words, we are not developing an awareness of reading and writing as ideological, *social and constitutive* practices that can have real consequences on others as well as on ourselves. Skills are rather more meaningful and valuable, it seems to me, when they are understood as appropriate (useful, effective and socially productive) for, rather than correct in, a given situation. Appropriateness suggests a sensitivity to the demands of context and of writers and readers – what should be done; correctness implies an absolute standard irrespective of situation, writers or readers. In this view, then, when related to appropriateness, mechanical issues (for example, those of grammar, syntax, style, spelling and punctuation, or the formal properties of genre) are also ethical, imaginative and rhetorical issues (those of value, meanings and interpretive effects). I think it is through this orientation too that mechanical issues can be more readily impressed on emerging writers as meaningful. Understood in this way the choices to be made about the use of the passive rather than the active voice, or a complex rather than a simple sentence, or a specialist rather than a generalist discourse, for example, can be seen as choices affecting our capacity to relate to others (ethically, imaginatively and rhetorically) in specific writing contexts.

As professional writers and educators we need to be integrating – truly integrating – our and others' exploration of and familiarisation with conventions and practices of professional writing (through reading and writing). We also need to critique those conventions and practices as features of workplace, interorganisational and public communication, of power, status and authority, and of professional writing as a dynamic element of various and complex communication modes.

Part of the process of learning to write professionally involves us as writers developing a sense of how to position ourselves (and to understand how we are positioned) as professional writers. What does that mean? What is the process involved in the move from 'simply' writing to writing as a professional, or to producing professional writing?[10] I would argue that the process involves our learning to imagine ourselves as part of a highly elaborate nexus or communicative social and public network, where our roles are not only or necessarily those of specialist writers but of specialists in any field for whom writing nevertheless comprises a significant part of our work. For example, as engineers, lawyers, academics, editors, public relations consultants, social workers, researchers, and administrators, consultants and managers in public and private industry we may all spend large chunks of our days on writing or writing-related activities. This network incorporates a complex of writers and readers, each of us shifting our relative positions (as the inscribers and as the interpreters of meanings) according to our changing discursive roles, our sense of proximity or distance to our readers, and our concomitant responsibilities as writers and as readers in different writing and reading contexts (and see Phelps 1990). We learn to write in organisational and professional contexts in the process or as a consequence of learning to read (in) those contexts.[11] Thus, we learn, through reading, who writes and to whom, and what and how they write. Most often, of course, we are writers and readers simultaneously: when we edit others' work, when we write collaboratively, when we adapt standard or template documents to suit particular communicative needs, when we respond to the texts – including reports, emails, memos, letters, questionnaires and forms – of others, and when we reflect on or revise our own texts. And as writers (and readers) of documents in an organisation or institution, for example, we are also and otherwise speakers and listeners, bodies, subjects with diverse histories, however much certain professional writing practices may seek to obscure that fact.

We also have a range of relationships within and beyond our immediate writing environment. We may in some writing roles be colleagues, peers or fellow citizens, in others managers, in yet others subordinates, and in others corporate or institutional representatives, and sometimes we may be trying to be several of these at once. The detailed analyses of numerous communicative failures relating to organisational culture, specialist discourses, different subject positions and perspectives, personal, professional and collegial relations and hierarchies, which led to the Three Mile Island and Shuttle Challenger disasters (see Herndl et al. 1991), although obviously extreme cases, offer pertinent illustration of the intricate web of connections though which writers are identified and implicated.

In relation to the experience of constantly having to shift positions as a writing subject, Gregory Clark explores the writing of ethical public discourse. He makes an interesting case for abandoning notions of professional writing as securing territory (securing readers) in favour of 'rhetorical interaction' or writing as travel, 'by locating the kinds of collectivities that are formed by interacting writers and readers in a concept of expansive space through which, in their interactions, they travel' (1998, p. 12). This approach, while seductive, does nevertheless need to be balanced by an awareness of the ways in which our 'journeys' as writing subjects are not always self-directed; we are also positioned and defined by specific social and cultural constraints. Seyla Benhabib makes the point eloquently in her discussion of narrative as a means of constituting identity:

> We are born into webs of interlocution or into webs of narrative – from the familial and gender narratives to the linguistic one to the macronarrative of one's collective identity. We become who we are by learning to be a conversation partner in these narratives. Although

we do not choose the webs in whose nets we are initially caught or select those with whom we wish to converse, our agency consists in our capacity to weave out of those narratives and fragments of narratives a life story that makes sense for us, as unique individual selves.

(Benhabib 1999, p. 344)

Even though Benhabib is specifically concerned with the 'life stor[ies]' we make and of which we are made at a broad cultural level, her comments are pertinent to my concerns here. I am convinced that, as professional writers, we are more likely to be committed to and more able to make sense of (or attribute value to) our corporate, institutional, public or political selves when we can develop and sustain a sense of agency in our roles as writers, when we feel we have actively contributed to our written texts' potential for interpretation and use. By extension, if our readers find our texts alienating it is likely to be because we have not considered their significance as interpreters – their respective and different potential for agency, for becoming 'conversation partner[s]' through texts we have produced.

## Imagination, rhetoric, ethics

I have mentioned that professional writing is concerned with the activity of negotiating meanings. The verb 'to negotiate', originally from the Latin, *negotiari*, to do business, to trade, is apposite here, since professional writing inevitably involves (directly or indirectly) some kind of business transaction: it involves issues of the economy, of power, of social interaction and of interpersonal and public relations. The term 'negotiate' also, however, suggests some kind of reciprocal relation between, in this case, writer and reader(s), in its sense of *conferring* together or discussing a matter with others, often (though not always) with the aim of reaching (provisional) agreement. The agreement in this case is over the significance and implications of the written text and its actual and potential effects – pragmatic, personal, social – for readers, for writers.

Of course, the 'conference' a writer of professional documents has with her/his readers is often imagined rather than real, but this by no means reduces its significance. To be effectively imagined such an exchange must also be imaginative. That is to say, the writing process must (as far as it can) be a crafted, considered evaluation of the respective sites of writing and of reading, of the moral and practical impacts or effects of the communicated text, and of the (range of potential) readers' interpretations and responses (and see Hassett 1995). Such a process demands that writers try to put themselves in the place of the reading other(s). In other words, to do professional writing is to be self-conscious about our place of and purpose for writing. It is to be, as far as possible, deliberate about the rhetorical and ethical choices inform-ing the communication practice. And it is to anticipate, again as far as possible, the ramifications of our words, our texts on individual readers and their worlds. Thus, I would argue that professional writing praxis, by interweaving the activities of imagination, rhetoric and ethics can assist writers and emerging writers in developing their capabilities as individual citizens, as a collective of professionals, and as institutional representatives who read and write with care. I use the term 'care' in Carol Gilligan's sense, to denote 'the connection between people [which] gives rise to a responsibility for one another, a perception of the need for response' (Gilligan 1982, p. 30). This idea of care is particularly important because it highlights the activity of writing as one of relating to others, of forging and extending relationships with others, and of being accountable to others for our writing practices.

In light of these remarks, I turn now to consider in more detail how ethics, imagination and rhetoric each has a critical role to play in professional writing theory, pedagogy and practice. I hope it will be obvious, however, that by considering each separately, their inter-dependence is ultimately underscored.

## Ethics

In general terms, ethics involves issues of responsibility, justice, care and equity. When I write of ethics in this book, I distil the definition to refer to the postmodern moral contexts of responsibility that guide different writers' or organisations' behaviour or activities in relation to particular writing and reading contexts. I refer also to the choices to be made in a writer's or organisation's forging, extending or modifying of relations with others through written texts. And I refer particularly to the way in which writers articulate certain values or beliefs and the way we privilege certain knowledge or information. I also refer to the language choices that we (are able to) make (or are aware of making) when we write, and the extent to which different readers are free or constrained to interpret those codes of value, belief, knowledge or information in their reading of texts.

But the introductory comments above make it all sound far too straightforward. In reality, the many pressures facing writers in the public and professional realms can undoubtedly serve as compelling distractions which preclude us from asking questions about the ethics of specific writing acts, let alone grappling with possible approaches to working through such questions. Writing in the multi-media channelled space of an economy in which knowledge is typically represented as product, and in which communicating is widely understood as getting 'our message' across to 'them' loudly and clearly (and profitably) can be, and often is, a fast and ruthless game.

Questions of ethics disrupt the game. They can't create a blueprint for a new one, however, given that, as Bauman argues, moral ambivalence characterises the human. A condition of moral ambivalence means that there is no certainty for us concerning questions about (or answers to) moral issues. Morality is not definitive. By extension, our actions are not finite: they cannot be claimed as wholly ethical or wholly unethical; and their impact may have long-term or indirect effects that we cannot know or predict. Nevertheless, that is not to diminish our responsibility for making the effort to find out, making the effort to imagine (see Bauman 1993, pp. 219–22, 2001, pp. 57–70).

Bauman evokes the complexity of a technologised postmodern scene; he insists that no codes or rules can offer a guarantee that we will do 'good', and maintains that 'moral phenomena are inherently "non-rational" ' (1993, p. 11) – they cannot be predicted, repeated or controlled. This understanding forces morality back into the realm of the interpersonal (where it surely belongs), to relations between people as they obtain in specific social contexts. Conceiving this moral ambivalence as a challenge to be embraced in the postmodern age, Bauman claims that it is only in this way that we can own ourselves as moral beings. Importantly, he situates moral ambivalence in the social space, a complex interaction between three interwoven but distinct processes: cognitive, aesthetic and moral 'spacings' (those that variously distribute the dynamics of proximity and distance in human relationships) and their different products.

> And yet though all three spaces deploy the notions of proximity and distance, closeness and openness – the three space-producing mechanisms are different in their pragmatics and in their outcomes. If the cognitive space is constructed intellectually, by acquisition and distribution of knowledge, aesthetic space is plotted affectively, by the attention guided by curiosity and the search for experiential intensity, while moral space is 'constructed' through an uneven distribution of felt/assumed responsibility.
>
> (Bauman 1993, p. 146)

There is thus a tension between these three processes, and Bauman argues persuasively that both the cognitive and aesthetic spaces are resistant to moral spacing. Moral spacing disrupts with 'unwashable stains of affection' the impersonal and indifferent, rule-bound cognitive/social space, which is governed and justified by reason. And moral spacing, with its propensity for attachment and responsibility for the other, is 'anathema' to aesthetic/social spacing, which (unlike cognitive spacing) thrives on the new, the ever changing, the never still (1993, p. 180). Nevertheless, ethical acts can *only*, of course, be performed in the social space, 'continually buffeted by the criss-crossing pressures of cognitive, aesthetic and moral spacings' (1993, p. 185).

Through envisioning a hypothesised writing situation, let's very briefly here try to realise these perhaps rather abstract notions of cognitive, moral and aesthetic spacings. Writers in a university collaborating in the redesign of the institution's web portal have, together with their designer colleagues, been briefed by the university management to develop a home page that represents the university as a forward-looking, resourceful, and ground-breaking centre of research, learning and teaching excellence. Each of the writer collaborators (one of whom is also a student at the university, another a part-time tutor, and another part of the university's public relations team) can, in varying degrees, recognise elements of the desired representation in their experiences of the institution's (and their own) practices and activities. However, they cannot ignore the widespread sense across the campus that the university's motivation to excellence is undoubtedly under siege. Extremely squeezed economic conditions mean that research, teaching and learning programmes are all being heavily compromised by reduced budgets, a lack of resources, increased staff-student ratios and so on. As employees of the university, the writers feel constrained to develop the website based on the vision of university management. Management expects that the website development team will deliver a polished product, and as professionals, the writers undoubtedly take pride in exercising their specialist knowledge and expertise. However, although they variously perceive aspects of this website vision as authentic, they are also uneasy about the overly optimistic, robust and coherent image of the university it connotes. For example, the writer who is also a student worries about betraying her sense of responsibility to advocate for her fellow students and for prospective students and their educational needs; she is troubled by her sense that the educational experience being promoted leaves out important parts of the story. Similarly, the writer who is also a part-time tutor at the university, whose teaching workload has increased significantly, and who feels burdened by the pedagogical compromises he has been forced to make is torn between his loyalty to the university and its public profile and his sense that he cannot sustain his current work practices. And finally, the writer who is also the public relations practitioner understands but has difficulty resolving the tensions inherent in her boundary-spanning function: in both representing the views of her employer and in responding to her sense of obligation to her stakeholder publics. Despite all these reservations, as creative professionals all the writers are nevertheless individually excited by their ideas for contributing to the production of a state-of-the-art site that will appeal to the institution's diverse stakeholders. In their creative enthusiasm for the project, they also share a sense that somehow the website facelift may engender renewed energy and prosperity for the university.

So what are the broader implications in the above picture of the clash of cognitive, moral and aesthetic spacings for professional writing as ethical action in the corporate, organisational, public and virtual (social) domains? First of all, I think it helps us, as writers, to understand the enormous challenges we face in our attempts to write ethically. We are positioned by corporate, institutional, political, legal and economic demands (or cognitive spacings), and by conventional and normative as well as creative, innovative and changing practices (aesthetic spacings), to achieve various objectives in our writing activities. And it is therefore clearly not easy to remain ever alert to our concomitant responsibilities to others who may be, directly or indirectly, affected by our writing in the face of those demands and practices. (See Chapter 2 for an extended exploration of this theme.) It also helps us to see that our moral endeavours, conceived through writing, are often likely to be compromised or thwarted, but that this does not mean we should resign ourselves to a sense of powerlessness or apathy. As with the writers described above, there will be no ready solutions to the dilemmas that daily face us in our writing activities. All the same, we need to confront, question and evaluate those dilemmas individually and collectively. To do so is to remain committed to the significance of language use generally and of writing specifically as ethical activity, and to retain a sense of agency in and a belief in the value of our praxis.

The significance of that agency and value, circumscribed though they inevitably are in the postmodern view, is illustrated by Bauman's depiction of the impersonal contemporary social space, one that is hostile to the particularity and primacy of the self–other relation. If we forget that 'moral responsibility – being *for* the Other before one can be *with* the Other – is the first reality of the self, a starting point rather than a product of society' (Bauman 1993, p. 13), then we may well feel helpless to effect any change for the better through our writing. In my view, to remember that our primary obligation, our being *for* the other, also helps to identify *who* and *why* we are, is to justify the centrality of the writer–reader relation to professional writing as ethical social practice.

The broad contemporary scene in which ethical action takes place is usefully explored by Bauman, and this scene-setting helps us envisage the complexity of professional writing contexts. But as I have already suggested, the professional writing praxis I advocate is first and foremost a process of writers relating to readers. Therefore, feminist accounts of how ethics is realised in situated discursive practice and of how ethics comes to life through the relationships we forge and extend are particularly helpful here. Iris Marion Young (see next section) and Margaret Urban Walker, for example, highlight the impact on moral relations of gender, race and economic inequities.

By exploring how 'theoretical-juridical' approaches to morality have traditionally favoured the powerful, Walker's work enables us to think about professional writing specifically in terms of power and difference. As professional writers we often write from positions of institutional, organisational or corporate power relative to our readers, and are therefore vulnerable to overlooking (or ignoring) their difference and potential for dissent from the claims of our texts. Walker's proposal of an 'expressive-collaborative' model for ethics, which draws attention to the role of language[12] in defining moral interaction and attitudes, helps redirect our focus on writing as a practice of relating to others. This model 'looks at moral life as a continuing negotiation *among* people, a practice of mutually allotting, assuming or deflecting responsibilities of important kinds, and understanding the implications of doing so' (Walker 1998, p. 60). (This idea is further explored in Chapter 4 in relation to corporate social responsibility.) Also, and importantly, the expressive-collaborative view presents 'the picture of morality as social negotiation in real time, where members of a community of roughly or largely shared moral belief try to refine understanding, extend consensus, and eliminate conflict among themselves' (Walker 1998, p. 64).

Of course, the 'social negotiation' that takes place between writers and readers is often outside 'real time', and is represented by the processes of writing and reading texts. In other words, a written text in itself cannot *be* ethical or unethical. Rather, the contexts of its conceptualisation, production and medium(s) of dissemination are contexts within which ethical judgements and choices are made and then communicated by writers. By extension, the contexts of a written text's potential for access, reception, interpretation and use are contexts within which ethical judgements and choices are made and validated or reinterpreted, reworked and used by different readers.

## Imagination

I consider as imperative the self-conscious refusal to separate professional writing from the ideas and processes of imagination, here conceived of as writers' thoughtful reviewing, renewing and repatterning of business, social and cultural relations with others as those are constructed through written texts. Imagination is therefore linguistic in character (Kearney 1998)[13] and, in this account, professional writing is reconceived as constitutive of relations between self and other rather than as a process with exclusively instrumental ends.

Clearly then, in this conception, imagination has significance as a reflective, practical and political tool; it is certainly not the autonomous sensibility of the Romantic imagination. And thus my use of the terms imagination, imaginative and imagining is self-conscious, intending to signify the important role that imagination plays – or should play – in professional writing. The use of these terms also aims to collapse the conventional opposition between the so-called aesthetic-subjective-personal and the practical-objective-social (see Berlin 1996, pp. 6–7). To imagine when we write in a professional capacity is to *attempt to* make present (in the planning and formulating of our texts) the actually or apparently immaterial: on the one hand, the various readers and the contexts of their interpretation of and responsiveness to the texts; and on the other, the rhetorical and moral issues at stake in specific communication and reception processes.

To emphasise the imaginative dimension is, moreover, to differentiate this genre of writing, as an academic and professional discipline, from its traditional associations with conventions, formulae, templates and products. Rather, it is to look at the seminal issue of writing and reading processes as contingent, provisional and unstable, and therefore as the negotiable exchange of meanings and values within specific communities. Therefore, by implication, the act of imagining also has a future orientation and, as Kearney (1998) argues, a utopian one too. It suggests the possibilities for connection with others in diverse spaces and different times, possibilities that must nevertheless remain sketchy and open rather than definitive and assumed.

This endeavour is, of course, particularly pertinent, given the prevalence of electronic mediums of communication. As Derek Foster puts it, 'the context of [computer-mediated communication] necessarily emphasizes the act of imagination that is required to summon the image of communion with others who are often faceless, transient or anonymous' (1997, p. 25). And for Bauman too, the responsibility to imagine (or in his words 'visualise') the impacts of action (or inaction) in a technologised world rests with the actors – for our purposes here, writers– themselves. However, 'the duty to visualize the future impact of action (undertaken or not undertaken) means acting under the pressure of acute uncertainty. The moral stance consists precisely in seeing to it that this uncertainty is neither dismissed nor suppressed, but consciously embraced' (Bauman 1993, p. 221).

When writing is understood as an imaginative process, then, it is necessarily an activity that is other-oriented, one interested in forging or extending relations between the writing self and others or otherness. To bring to the fore the imaginative dimension of professional writing is to draw attention to the complex process of conceptualising an appropriate ethical and rhetorical relationship (text) between writers, subject and readers. This clearly also involves the exercise of judgement, an activity which, as Hannah Arendt convincingly argues, has a dynamic connection with the activity of imagining (or, in her words, an 'enlarged way of thinking'):

> The power of judgment rests on a potential agreement with others, and the thinking process which is active in judging something is not, like the thought process of pure reasoning, a dialogue between me and myself, but finds itself always and primarily, even if I am quite alone in making up my mind, in an anticipated communication with others with whom I know I must finally come to some agreement ... And this enlarged way of thinking, which as judgment knows how to transcend its individual limitations ... cannot function in strict isolation or solitude; it needs the presence of others 'in whose place' it must think, whose perspectives it must take into consideration, and without whom it never has the opportunity to operate at all.
>
> (Arendt 1968, pp. 220–1)

Thus, to treat the activity of imagining as pivotal is also to encourage writers to consider and value the place of readers as legitimate sites of particular actions or reactions in response to texts; actions or reactions that may *differ from those desired by the writer*. This account has something in common with Iris Marion Young's notion of 'asymmetrical reciprocity'. Young's discussion is motivated by the aim to reconceptualise Seyla Benhabib's (1992) concept of symmetrical reciprocity, in other words, 'moral respect as a relation of symmetry between self and other' and 'moral reciprocity as entailing that the perspectives of self and other are reversible' (Young 1997, p. 38). However, my use of the term 'imagining' is problematic in Young's account. For her, the activity of imagining misleadingly suggests that, as subjects, we are able to put ourselves in the place of others, to reverse our perspectives, to see things from their point of view, in order to reach understanding or agreement. However, my notion of the process of imagining aims to *retain* the sense of what Young calls our 'irreducible and irreversible' difference from others (see Young 1997, pp. 49–50).

Young argues that when making moral judgements, we need to take the perspectives of others into account through dialogue – premised on openness and questioning – and so recognise our relations of asymmetry, admit the fact that our (social, gender and economic) positions are not interchangeable. We can then learn to understand one another across difference. We can also, as a result, relativise our own perspectives, set as they are against those of others, and together with these others gain an enlarged understanding of our world (Young 1997, p. 59).[14] This democratising impulse is one I reflect on in more detail in Chapter 3 in relation to communicating via the Internet. And Clark cogently summarises that impulse: 'we need to imagine the discursive collectivities that are essential to individual and social life in a way that requires participants to acknowledge the distinctiveness and the differences of others, and to commit nonetheless to the transformative work of cooperation and connection' (1998, p. 22).

By extension, and as subsequent chapters will aim to illustrate, this approach challenges the notion of professional writing as the representation of image or self-image (language conceived as unproblematically reflecting the self-contained subject) rather than writing as an *imaginative* process (language conceived as constituting the subject in specific relation to an other). In the latter view, writing is an unfinished, necessarily open, reciprocal and ongoing activity. Given our cultural and commercial emphasis on the importance of image, with the concomitant pressure to present a coherent subject or seamless organisational identity, for example, professional writing is regularly concerned – some would argue, necessarily so – with effectively representing a desirable self-image. A well-rehearsed argument posits that a coherent corporate image enhances corporate credibility (see, for instance, Petelin 2002). I would counter that credibility should be an ethical at least as much as an economic imperative. We now need to concentrate more on corporate, institutional, political and public credibility as an ethical imperative, and this will also enable us to understand the primacy of – and experience the process of – writing as an imaginative and ethical activity.

## Rhetoric

'The primacy of signifying practices in the formation of subject and society means that language can no longer be seen as the transparent conduit of transcendental truths' (Berlin 1996, p. 68). The term 'rhetoric', in its popularly and most widely used sense, is often represented as opposing 'reality', as if an apparently objective reality could actually be expressed through 'good' language, truth-ful language. This all too familiar misconception does, nevertheless, alert us to an important characteristic of all rhetoric, of all discourse, as offering a *version* of knowledge, truth or reality. Kevin DeLuca puts the same idea slightly differently, when he remarks that 'within a discursive frame, rhetoric is no longer an instrument in the service of reality, but, rather, becomes constitutive of the meaning of the world' (1999, p. 342).

Rhetoric (as theory and practice) can be approached productively as *vitally* connected to the notion of imagination, and the activity of imagining effectively treated as integral to the processes of ethical writing and the interpretation of language effects.[15] Otherwise rhetoric cannot deal adequately with writing as a process of 'going to meet others', or of the written text as a site of the shifting and competing beliefs, values and interests of, for example, government, corporation, community or individuals.

Therefore, rhetoric, as I use the term in this book, is 'a primarily verbal, situationally contingent, epistemic art that is both philosophical and practical and gives rise to potentially active texts' (Covino and Jolliffe 1995, p. 5). It is thus social–epistemic rhetoric that, as Berlin, embracing a postmodern view, suggests, 'enables senders and receivers to arrive at a rich formulation of the rhetorical context in any given discourse situation through an analysis of the signifying practices operating within it' (Berlin 1996, p. 84). In other words, such rhetorical praxis is concerned with investigating the inscribed and interpretable effects (semiotic, practical, cultural, subjective and collective) of written communication, and with the related significance of power and of knowledge of those effects. As well, the focus on language *effects* (readings, significances, consequences) embraces the centrality of the (often imagined) relationship between writers and readers, and presupposes the functional and ethical dimensions of professional writing. Clearly such writing very often *does* something (whether intentionally or not); it can have real and material results (and see Porter 1998, pp. 150–1). It is clear, therefore, that professional writers harnessing this rhetorical approach will focus on how effects are produced, what those effects are likely to be (how far they are self-conscious or knowable, as far as the writers are concerned), and to what extent the effects intended by the writers can be supposed to match those desired, understood or interpretable by their potential readers.

As theory and practice, social-epistemic rhetoric can productively draw on the tenets of both postmodernism and feminism for its strengthened articulation.[16] As writers, then, we can harness rhetoric as a praxis sensitive to issues of social, economic, ethnic and sexual difference, and to issues of power that either sustain or challenge those differences. Such an approach to rhetoric also keeps us alert to the relative power positions from which writers write and readers read, and encourages us to pay attention to which texts get written at all and by whom they are read. It allows us to consider how far readers are at liberty to become or have an interest in becoming responding writers themselves, and how far writers are prepared or allowed to become readers – that is, to interpret their texts from the place of the other. This rhetorical praxis can also help make us, as writers, aware of the capacity of language to construct different modes of subjectivity and intersubjectivity. It also keeps us vigilant about the dangers of utterances that universalise, naturalise or standardise, and it helps us critique the conventions that set in opposition self and other, private and public, fact and fabrication.

Perhaps most importantly, when conjoined with ethical and imaginative praxis, assuming this rhetorical attitude helps us pay attention to otherness: to our reliance on, and yet ultimate lack of control over, what is brought to bear on our texts' interpretation by others. While the meanings generated by our language choices may be intended as certain, unambiguous and precise – and to be shared by writers and readers alike – those meanings are beyond singular interpretation. Instead, meanings are provisional; they may serve but they will also, inevitably, elude and exceed our intentions.

This idea can be usefully understood in the context of Derrida's use of the term 'iterability' (Derrida 1988; and see Benhabib 1999). Iterability, according to Derrida, conceives of language as repetition *and* as alterity: to be meaningful to another the language that we use must be repeatable. And yet in each of its repetitions, its meaning/significance alters: it becomes something (even if only slightly) different. This idea suggests how we need to grapple with the way in which the words we write to the other (our intended meanings) are necessarily open to the influences of other contexts for their reinterpretation (repetition and alterity), and for their extended significance. In this way we can appreciate, I think, the *rhetorical* and therefore *ethical* significance of writing as communication: as oriented towards (rather than at) others, imagining and acknowledging their positions and their rights to respond to our missives in a manner that may complicate or challenge or encourage us to re-evaluate our own aims, ideas and beliefs. Of course, when we *do* professional writing our aim is to achieve a close as possible correspondence between the meanings we intend through our texts and the interpretations others make of them. This aim demands that we put ourselves in the place of our potential readership: taking responsibility for imagining how they might respond to what we have to write. By extension, then, what does this all mean about the texts of others we interpret when we read them? Doesn't it also demand a process of imagining the different context of their production, attempting to evaluate the stakes invested in the writers' use of their words, and judging them accordingly?[17]

Because of language's iterability, our intentions can never be *fully* realised in the words we write: inevitably there will be some discrepancy between the activities or processes of intention on the one hand and those of interpretation on the other. Paradoxically, however, it is this discrepancy – this mismatch or discord in communication – that offers up the opportunity for dialogue (as a *continuing* negotiation of meaning) with others, and for the impulse towards (though not necessarily arrival at) mutual understanding. We can ignore this opportunity, of course, but if (and when) we do, the language we write is in danger of becoming a monotonous and repetitive drone – talking to ourselves, for ourselves, reasserting our own ground, with limited potential for sharing, extending, reassessing knowledge, ideas and beliefs in the light of others' language.

Thus, the texts we develop and critique involve our being self-conscious about how specific objectives are formulated as authoritative (professional) texts that address readers. They involve our analysing the (inevitable) partiality of written communication and the knowledges or ideas represented. And they also involve our evaluating the versions of culture, community, subjectivity and activity that readers may themselves subsequently imagine, realise and rearticulate in response to those texts.

## Conclusion

It may perhaps be a strange claim to make that imaginative, ethical and rhetorical praxis chiefly work to motivate our awareness that *all* our written texts – whether intended for a specialised or general audience, whether acting as forms of public relations, politics or workplace communications – are necessarily and always incomplete. Given the conventional and still widespread understanding of effective professional writing as constituting technically flawless, coherent and controlled, carefully reasoned and persuasive texts, that claim may also appear to be deliberately oppositional, and certainly one to be regarded sceptically by many working in writing-related fields in the public domain.

However, I don't see the two perspectives as mutually exclusive – not at all. For unless it is incomplete, even the flawless, coherent, controlled, reasoned and persuasive text will mean nothing at all, for there will be no opening, no point of intervention for readers to take it up and make some (other) sense of it: respond to it, act on it, argue with it, and so on. Surely it is our responsibility as writers to relate to others – to conceive and develop our writing projects as a process of imagined exchange. In such an exchange 'they' aren't reducible to 'us', our intentions, words and meanings aren't necessarily shared, and others (not only our primary readers) have the right to write too.

# 2
# The Struggle to Relate: Writers and Readers of Corporate and Public Documents

## Introduction

This chapter explores the complexities involved in the processes of writing public and professional texts, and also examines the material, political and even emotional effects of reading them. Through an overview of the issues that have a bearing on the preparation of client-oriented documents in the corporate sector on the one hand, and of the experience of reading public- and politically-oriented documents designed for circulation in the broader culture on the other, I argue for the importance of retaining the agency of the writing–reading subject.[1] I contend that this is the only reliable and viable position from which ethical relationships between writers and readers may be established and productively extended.

In the context of what he terms 'corporate composing', Porter argues that ethics is a social rather than individual matter, and that the implication of such understanding is particularly significant in the corporate context, where most writing processes are collaborative (Porter 1993). Given that central to ethics are the responsibilities, obligations and choices moderating the relationship between self and other(s), I couldn't possibly disagree with Porter's view. However, I do also want to retain the significance of the writer as a subject with ethical responsibility, so that a sense of agency – the possibility for individuals both independently and collectively to exercise some control over and to modify writing practices at the local or specific levels, even though that is *never* done in isolation from the social-professional network – is sustained. And I think it is equally critical that, at the same time, the potential agency of the reader is retained, so that the opportunity for the reader to forge an ethical relation and make a response to the writer's text is opened up.

As I suggested in the first chapter, however, and as I hope to demonstrate through example here, concentration on the writing–reading subject presupposes that subject as existing *always* in social relation with others. If, whatever its other functions or purposes, professional writing is a process of relating to others, then the process is initiated and enabled through the activity of imagining that relationship. This becomes especially important, as I shall try to show, when we consider writing from the workplace or from the public domain, where writers often represent a corporate, organisational, institutional or political entity in their writing practices.

My proposed shift of focus will not, of course, simply resolve the issues contingent on and pervading much writing activity. These include the sometimes disabling power inequities between writers and readers; the financial and legal constraints or demands compromising many corporate- and institution-based writing activities; and the institutional, political and cultural norms and traditions shaping the mode, content and style of document preparation and circulation. However, I do hope that my approach might help to reorient attention to the following concerns. Firstly, it aims to draw attention to the increasingly significant role of writers and of written language in public and political spheres in sustaining or changing (for the better) existing professional, public and political relations. Secondly, it focuses on the tensions, contradictions and limitations inherent in the position of the contemporary writing subject. And finally, my approach aims to identify the potential impacts, material and perhaps life-changing, of writers and their texts on their diverse and variously interested (and even uninterested) readers.

As Anthony Paré argues, 'no classroom-based simulation of non-academic writing can capture the complexity or intricacy of the original rhetorical context, nor can it make writing subservient to an institutional or community goal beyond the act of writing itself' (2002, p. 59). This is the case even when classroom discussions are contextualised and drawn from specific writing and reading practices: they still seem to leave out so much about the often messy, fraught, and complicated issues disrupting form and normative practice and affecting writing and reading in professional and public spaces.

As my examination below of the writing and reading of two kinds of reports produced for the professional and public–political domains aims to exemplify, even a genre approach that takes account of the situatedness of writing and reading practices, and that alerts us to the dynamic and changing properties of genre as social action (see Miller 1984, 1994) should not distract us from the numerous *additional* demands of and influences on writing and reading processes (see also Comprone 1993). We can remain focused on these often competing demands, I think, if we imagine writers and readers as subjects *in contact* and as thereby variously connected through genre. For writers this means imagining how we are configured by and how we reconfigure genre as we write and, most importantly, how that affects our relationships with and responsibilities towards our readers.

This insistence on the writer's imagining, as outlined in Chapter 1, is clearly an ethical imperative. The activity of imagining insists on writers reflecting on their (sometimes conflicting) subject positions as writers, and, by extension, on their relation or potential relation to readers; most importantly in ethical terms, but in addition often in economic or political terms. This may include, for example, writers considering the ways in which their relations with others will be modified or circumscribed by elements such as corporate or institutional identity, organisational and political culture, and standardised and conventionalised language forms and practices.

In the first part of this chapter I will look at the situation of the writing subject and at matters related to the process of writing in the corporate sector. I concentrate in particular on the issues involved in preparing documents, many of them reports, by consulting engineers for paying clients. Material for my investigation here is drawn from semi-structured interviews carried out with five engineers to discuss their writing practices, and from my review of a range of sample documents they have produced and allowed me to look over. While this research deals with writers in a specific writing context, I hope that it nevertheless raises concerns about and extends theoretical reflection on workplace writing and the production of professional documents more generally.

The second part of the chapter makes a very obvious (though I hope not jarring) gear change. I turn my attention to the function and impact of an Australian Federal Government report (Herron 2000), written in response to another report prepared by the Human Rights and Equal Opportunities Commission. This latter report – a milestone in the marking and publicising of Australia's colonial history and practices – documents hundreds of painful personal accounts of those Indigenous Australians forcibly removed from their families between 1910 and 1970 by authorities intent on 'assimilating' them into white, mainstream culture. I try to demonstrate how the government's subsequent report could therefore have functioned as a significant rhetorical step in the process towards reconciliation between Indigenous and non-Indigenous Australians, but how in fact it failed to do so.

One of the reasons for the chapter's gear change is precisely to high-light the way in which the notion of genre as an intricate and malleable medium for representing writer–reader relations – here the report format in particular – has to be developed very carefully when preparing writers to engage in effective, that is to say, responsible and imaginative communication with readers. Of course, genre is important, but using a genre approach rather than the relations between writers and readers as a focal point for developing effective writing practices too often generates the illusion of genre as a separable entity, meaningful apart from its contexts of production, circulation and interpretation. It can also result, despite our best intentions, in a focus on genre as a static 'container' into which ideas, arguments, information are inserted by the writer and removed by the reader (see Porter 1993, p. 131; Suchan 1998; Devitt et al. 2003), rather than on text as signifying the dynamic relation between writer, reader, context and culture, with all the responsibilities and complexities (and contradictions) attendant on those relations.

In other words, the situation of consultants writing a report in the corporate environment about technical issues concerning, say, the operability or health and safety provisions and standards of a given building for paying clients cannot be treated as equivalent to a government writing a report in the public domain in response to accounts of injustices committed against Indigenous peoples. That is not to deny that the writers in both realms are circumscribed by broadly similar limitations – financial, legal, corporate-institutional, rhetorical and so on. But those limitations are of a different order, and the specific ethical relations between the writers and readers in those different contexts are simply not reducible to generalised comparisons.

Another reason for the shift in the chapter is to allow for a greater emphasis on writing subjects and writing processes in the first part, and on reading subjects and reading effects in the second. Of course writing processes imply reading effects and vice versa. So while, as a researcher, I was particularly interested in the writing processes of the consulting engineers I spoke to, I was also a reader of their texts (though not one of their originally intended readers, of course). As an Australian citizen, I am positioned as an imagined reader of the Australian Government's report, though in that position I have inevitably drawn inferences from the text about the writing impulses and objectives of its writers. Thus, the examination of two very different kinds of orientation to writing in this chapter serves to highlight the concomitantly very different sets of relations between writers and readers motivated, inscribed and implied by different rhetorical contexts. It also puts into relief, I hope, the constraints that can distract or even preclude us, as writers, from imagining others when we write, and the ethically questionable value and even futility of professional writing when we don't engage in such imagining.

## 'Mundane' writing and the contemporary writer

The kind of corporate or institutional writing under discussion in this chapter is sometimes identified as 'mundane' (see, for example, Henry 2000). The term immediately sets up a problematic and qualitative opposition between the mundane and other kinds of (exciting?) writing. Mundane comes from the Latin, *mundus,* meaning world, and suggests the dull, the routine, the everyday – and from that the normative and practised forms of writing we associate with workplace, organisational or institutional settings. By implication, other writing (usually that produced outside the workplace context) thus becomes, in contrast, creative, unique, innovative and so on, and evokes an image of the author as an independent, self-contained originator and creator. The terms can be stacked up to develop what I'm hinting at here: the way in which so-called mundane writing can appear to lose its potential for our capacity, power or even desire as writers to intervene as significant communicators in public and professional exchanges.

But herein lies the danger. When we feel no investment in the writing, when we feel it doesn't matter, can't its very mundanity paradoxically become hazardous, as we forget language and text as sites of constructive activity and impact in which we implicate others (if only indirectly or inadvertently) as well as in which we are implicated? We may instead begin to treat language and texts as simply mechanistic, as important primarily for their more obviously formal (generic, grammatical, structural, syntactical) and procedural or instrumental properties. And we may begin to treat the language of mundane documents as remote from us in the ways it articulates (or fails to articulate) the value and importance of others. We may treat language and writing in this way, rather than as the process through which our relations with others are partly, or even wholly, in some cases, constituted.

At the conclusion of a seminal article focusing on the importance of recognising the complexity of rhetorical situations in which writers prepare and circulate documents, Linda Driskill makes a similar point:

> Creativity and personal involvement are essential for meeting the complex challenges of real organizational contexts. Too often, technical and business communication has been taught as a dry, mechanical

skill devoid of personal interest. When we recognize the importance of the context for writing in organizations, we see the significance of the issues resolved through communication processes. Writing well is not merely conforming to genre conventions, as some of the genre-based approaches have implied. Communicating in organizational contexts is essential to the vitality, and even to the survival, of organizations and society in a technical era.

(Driskill 2003, p. 119)

And, as Zygmunt Bauman remarks, in his discussion of the ways in which, in a technologised society, the moral self is in danger of being overlooked: 'out of the partial interests and focused obligations, no overwhelming responsibility for the Other, or the world, is likely to be patched up. The task-oriented action does not allow for an orientation point outside the union between the task at hand and the actor bent on that task' (1993, p. 198; see also Bauman 2001, pp. 175–200). Part of the problem with this view of mundane writing practices is the failure to reconceive writers as they exist in the contemporary space, where the originating of text, authorship and writing as forms of practice have taken on radically new meanings. Richard C. Freed, in his discussion of postmodern practice in professional communication, graphically defines these new senses of creativity and authorship:

> For in a world of copies, of simulations without origins, originality means assembling copies in a new way, like recombinant DNA, by taking existing bits and bytes of text and recombining them. Thus not only is the author already written, by the prescribed roles that the organization or group authorizes him to play, but his materials for discourse are already inscribed, in the intertextual system that allows him to speak. This so-called death of the author, however, doesn't mean his demise, only that the scribe is always already circumscribed [sic].
>
> (Freed 1993, p. 212)

It is in this different constitution as writers that professionals daily re-inscribe themselves and are inscribed *publicly* and *professionally* as subjects, negotiating a range of positions and discourses in communicating with others (see Henry 2000, pp. 33–4). I'm interested in how they might possibly retain their status as ethical subjects in that complex process of negotiation.

There is no question that, in the contemporary digitised environment, writing subjects are dispersed across many positions. And this also often means the pull of rhetorical responsibility – professional, corporate, individual, economic, legal – in several directions, often simultaneously. This makes our ability as writers to determine the focus of our ethical obligations to particular and general others difficult. We can only do that, I would argue, through imagining our relations with others as those are set up by our texts and their diverse rhetorics and discourses, and remembering how far, *with every key stroke*, we help to construct or modify (sometimes unwittingly) those relations through written language.

**Professionals. But professional writers?**

The writers I concentrate on in this part of the chapter are professionals, in disciplines outside writing, who nevertheless work in organisations, corporations or institutions, where the writing of various documents for a range of clients, whether emails, letters, memos, reports and so on, comprises a significant part of their working day and their overall professional responsibilities.

I am indebted to the involvement, in this part of my research, to a small group of consulting engineers. The engineers all work in Perth, Western Australia for Engex, an international, multidisciplinary engineering consultancy, which has offices throughout Australia and several more internationally.[2] The group specialises in the design and operation of building technology, offering a comprehensive range of services for the creation and ongoing ownership of a property. In addition to the core services design capability, the engineers' expertise covers a range of specialist areas, including environmental analysis, facilities optimisation and advanced engineering and building technologies. Each engineer works closely, sometimes independently, sometimes as part of a team, with a range of established and new clients on a diverse range of projects. The small West Australian office employs ten consulting engineers (all of them male), two drafting staff and three administrative support staff.

I have previously worked with around ten of the engineers, in writing workshops I conducted with some of them over several weeks in 2001 and the rest in 2002. Approximately eighteen months later, five of the workshop participants agreed for me to interview them about their professional writing activities, and for me to look over a range of documents (faxes, letters and reports) they have prepared for clients.

The engineers are, sometimes individually and sometimes collaboratively, involved in developing reports (building inspection, due diligence, proposals, audits and so on); writing letters, faxes and emails (for clearing up queries, presenting findings of relatively minor scale, quoting for smaller jobs and so on); writing specifications; and preparing power point presentations (usually for marketing purposes). They variously estimate that they spend between twenty and forty-five per cent of a day and up to seventy per cent of a week on writing and writing-related activities. For all the engineers I spoke to, however, the personal and, particularly, face-to-face interactions with their individual clients are indispensable to what they regard as effective working relationships. As Chris pointed out, for example, 'it's very, very important – and it's probably the most enjoyable part of [the job]'. Nevertheless, direct evidence of those relationships is, predictably, not represented in reports, nor in their letters or faxes; all the same, its significance cannot be underestimated. Because of the direct contact that the engineers have with their clients, as an alternative or in addition to their contact through written texts, the imaginative connections between writer and reader are, it seems to me, assumed or implied rather than expressly articulated in their written texts.

At the same time, and particularly in their roles as consultants, these engineers produce and also, literally, sell much of their knowledge in written form. And yet, as they are not specifically trained or formally qualified in the discipline of writing, they generally do not perceive themselves as writers per se. When I questioned them about whether they considered themselves as either professional writers or as professionals who happen to write as part of their job, each of the engineers responded unhesitatingly that they regarded themselves as the latter (compare Paré 2002, pp. 58–9). Nevertheless, most of them qualified this answer by adding comments such as, writing 'is an essential part of what we do' (Simon); and writing is the 'output; what the client sees is writing' (Michael); the 'outcome is written' (Peter). As Dorothy Winsor comments, 'writing is viewed as part of an engineer's job but not as part of engineering, which presumably happens in some separate, prior realm' (1990, p. 58; and see Sales 2002).[3] All the same, the engineers agreed with the suggestion that their ability to write is bound up with their status as competent engineers. Michael sees the relationship between writing and professional status as 'very significant'. Simon remarked that 'the two [writing and competence as an engineer] are intertwined'. And Troy sees the two as having 'an extremely important relationship', explaining that engineers have 'a duty of care'[4] to communicate information appropriately to clients, thus suggesting the ethical responsibilities attendant on writing practice. Peter remarked that the ability to write is bound up with 'gaining acceptance by the [engineering and related professional] authorities'.

A brief examination of an excerpt from a sample document can serve to demonstrate the significant interrelationship of imaginative and appropriate writing practices, professional status and engineering competence, and ethical responsibility. The excerpt comes from letter composed by Simon to one of his clients (a company representative, whom he addresses by her first name in the letter's greeting), in which he presents an analysis of his and his colleagues' findings of exit arrangements in a local department store:[5]

The exit travel distance and the dimensions of exits and paths of travel to exit are prescribed in the Building Code of Australia (BCA) in clauses D1.4(d)(i) & (i) and D1.6(d)(ii) respectively. The centre portion of the ground floor between the escalators is not adequately served by the escape stairs (travel distances to these doors exceed BCA limitations). To enable the prescriptive requirements to be met, at least two of the three sets of automatic doors are required as exit doors for use in emergency situations. The nominated doors would require illuminated signage complying with [Australian Standard] 2293 and we also recommend that signage be displayed adjacent to the door highlighting to occupants that the door is not available as an exit during after hours periods and one of the other doors should be used. We also recommend that such signage include a diagram showing the location of the other four exit doors available for use after hours.

Note: we have enclosed an architectural drawing with the exiting egress coverage and area of inadequate coverage highlighted.

Store Management would be best placed to choose those automatic doors to be used for emergency evacuation purposes. The remaining automatic door would then not be a required exit. The practice of bolting the automatic doors at the end of all business operations can continue.

During our investigation we also noted some other non-compliance issues, as our duty of care we bring these to your attention: the fire isolated stair does not adequately service the centre portion of each floor level between the escalators as the prescriptive distances are marginally exceeded.

The opening sentence of the excerpt introduces the regulatory frame-work (BCA) within which the engineers make their assessment. The rel-evant code clauses are cited, suggesting the writer's familiarity with them – and thus also his professional competence. However, it is their interpretation and application to the building in question, rather than their detail, that the writer rearticulates and summarises for the reader, in non-specialist language: 'The centre portion of the ground floor between the escalators is not adequately served by the escape stairs (travel distances to these doors exceed BCA limitations).' The use of the passive voice in these opening sentences establishes the apparent objec-tivity and hence the authoritativeness of the judgements made by the engineers. Required solutions are then proposed, together with refer-ence to the relevant Australian Standard,[6] which reaffirms the validity of the statements through reference to a nationally recognised body. The outlining of regulatory requirements then connects, within a single, compound sentence, to a recommendation by the engineers for the use of signage to highlight the doors' function ('the nominated doors would require illuminated signage complying with [Australian Standard] 2293 and we also recommend that ...'). In this instance, the close alliance between individual authority and more broadly profes-sionally and socially acknowledged standards is emphasised. Reference to the accompanying drawing indicates the writer's understanding of the reader's possible need for visual clarification of some of the text information communicated. The comment that 'Store Management would be best placed to choose those automatic doors to be used for emergency evacuation purposes' communicates clearly the writer's awareness of the limits to his capacity to provide advice to his client. And the belief (as suggested by Troy above) that the notion of duty of care lies in the rhetoric of presented information, is illustrated by the last paragraph in the excerpt. Interestingly, it seems that the areas of non-compliance noticed and brought to the reader's attention fell out-side the brief of the request for inspection. Perhaps this is why no solu-tions are recommended. It seems, then, that even duty of care has its (economic and rhetorical) limits.

In all the different ways highlighted above, in *my* reading of the text, the interdependence of language use, professional status and engi-neering knowledge and competence are set into relief. Nevertheless, as far as *the engineers* are concerned, rather than accepting technical knowl-edge as mediated (Winsor 1990), they regard themselves as 'translators' of or conduits for technical information for use by lay people. For example, Chris commented that 'we have to bridge the gap between the lay person and technical experts ... being in the middle [as a writer] is difficult'. Michael explained how important it is that information produced for a client 'makes logical sense to someone who doesn't know'. Troy explained that once you 'have the information', you have to 'relay it to various people'. As Paré reasons in his discussion of social workers' writing practices, writing from the engineers' perspective seems to be 'what they [do] in order to get something else accomplished' (Paré 2002, p. 59; see also Suchan 1995).

Nevertheless, the engineers did talk about the process of presenting or organising information according to client needs or demands. And Simon mentioned the 'struggle' that sometimes arises with a client over what should stay in or be taken out of a report. He used a striking image to explain that struggle by describing his inclination to include in a report the fact that 'the brass has been polished, rather than that [as the client would wish] it [had] never [been] tarnished'. Troy talked about how he adjusts his writing to suit his different clients, and while he said he couldn't explain what that adjustment involves, he was clear that his writing voice 'has an understanding of the person that's going to be reading it'. The engineers express here a sense of their responsibility towards clients born out of familiarity with them and those clients' particular commercial requirements, and also the economic ties that put pressure on the engineers as payees. Yet, as Simon's comment above suggests, this economic obligation is tempered by a sense of the engineers' duty of care as professionals to others than the client – to the prospective owners, occupants or tenants of a building, for example.

Despite, then, resisting identification as writers, the engineers do perceive sensitivity to not only primary, intended readers but to other potential readers as integral to their professional roles. In this vein, Michael stressed that 'politics is very, very important' in relation to the choices and decisions made in the preparation of a document. As a senior and highly experienced member of the consulting team at Engex, he has a sharp sense of the complexities involved in representing information to clients. For example, in one project, Engex has been employed to supply the design for the installation of geothermal energy for heating a community swimming pool as part of a larger refurbishment project. A letter to the project managers, written by Michael on Engex's behalf, demonstrates the tension between issues of environmental sustainability on the one hand (which geothermal energy facilitates and to which the company is committed), and equally pressing, immediate considerations of labour and finance on the other. In the letter, Michael attempts (via the project's managers, who are acting as client representatives and intermediaries) to alert the client, who has already opted for the environmentally responsible approach, to the benefits of adopting geothermal energy. At the same time, he seeks to emphasise the potential risks of adopting this approach without more considered investigation of this option. A selection of short excerpts from the document demonstrates the rhetorical balancing act required in this case:

> ... Geothermal energy offers the potential for considerable long term energy and greenhouse gas savings and its adoption is welcomed.
>
> The construction of the deep bores required for the geothermal system involves approaches and risks that are very different to those that prevail in the traditional building industry, and these must be understood by all involved if this decision is to be pursued ...
>
> The fees involved for the hydrogeology ... are a much higher percentage of the contract value than typically found in the building industry.
>
> The drilling contractors are not unionised. We are unsure if this may create problems if they are working on a construction site ...
>
> We congratulate [the client] for taking a long term view and adopting the use of geothermal energy ... The use of geothermal energy involves approaches that differ from those normally encountered in the building industry, and it is essential that [the client] be fully informed of the issues involved and put in place measures to minimise the risks to all involved ...

Here the text's attempts to commend the client on its choice of energy supply is juxtaposed with a cautioning against premature adoption of such an approach. The letter is carefully constructed and, through its use of the rhetoric of risk, demonstrates that the engineer's task is not merely to 'convey' or 'transmit' information but to *reinterpret* and *reorient* apparently 'neutral' facts, practices, techniques and situations, both in the light of their convergence in a specific social, political and industrial context and in relation to particular clients, project personnel, prospective users of the facility, and so on. What we glimpse here is Michael seeking to engage the project managers and the clients (through his urging of the need for reciprocal discussion and evaluation) in risk assessment processes (see Grabill and Simmons 2003).[7]

## What's at stake in the writing process?

Bauman points out that, in the social space, 'obedience to rules specifically excludes empathy; the crowd-style togetherness plays on emotional identification with the "supra-personal" intolerant of personal specificity' (Bauman 1993, p. 144). In other words, in organisational or corporate contexts, employees often act in an environment that encourages loyalty to the organisation or corporation qua organisation or corporation, rather than to specific individuals within or beyond those structures. Similarly, in the context of professional writing, genre, corporate identity, organisational systems, law, authority – and each of these invokes or assumes a set of pre-existing or established 'rules' or norms – can serve to remove or at least distance writers from readers.[8] At the same time, of course, they may well serve to make possible, to regulate and monitor, and make intersubjective relations more equitable.

I have mentioned above the pull of writers' various responsibilities, and in the engineers' context I have so far indicated the importance attributed by them to their personal relationships with clients. I now want to examine other significant, sometimes contradictory, positions that the engineers, and, by implication, professional writers in general, continually have to negotiate (see also Debs 1993). The tensions between those positions, and the writing frameworks they provide, may well circumscribe the options for those writers to engage in ethical writing practices. For example, a (probably not exhaustive) listing of the engineers' various positions deployed through many of the documents they prepare for clients includes their roles as company delegates (in their representation through corporate identity discourse); as expert/knowing specialists (through deployment of their knowledge in profession-specific rhetoric); and as uncertain or equivocal subjects (as configured by an explicitly legal discourse or its influences on their professional rhetoric).

Let's look at each of these in turn. Paradoxically, the positions of the subject as knower and as equivocator are intimately connected, and for this reason they will be explored in the same section below. My intention in what follows is that the kinds of concerns raised might be broadly relevant not only to other workplace contexts but also to matters related to the preparation of other document genres.

## Who writes? Corporate identity, templates, standard texts

In what ways might corporate identity be problematic in relation to questions of ethics and writing, and in terms of the limitations it might, in some instances, impose on an organisation's members to act as ethical agents? Given that the ethics of human relations are premised on uncertainty and relations of difference, in what ways are corporate writers perhaps compromised when the contingencies on which individual acts of writing depend are elided by the requirement to reproduce texts that endorse and reaffirm the corporate character? Or in what ways are writers' ethical responsibilities to imagine particular others either obscured or unaccounted for in their roles as corporate (representative) writers? None of these questions seeks to deny the point that corporate identity can act as brake, monitor or regulator of what and how the writer writes, particularly in terms of the legal constraints framing its practices. And this aspect of its function may certainly aim to promote responsible relations between writers and readers, ensuring that writers do not, for example, abuse their position of privilege and authority when communicating with others under the aegis of a company banner. (Undoubtedly, the length and detail of the 'limitations' statements that appear near the introduction to many of the engineers' reports, itemising those areas *not* covered by an inspection or an audit, for example, have grown exponentially in recent, more litigious times.) Nevertheless, the influence of corporate identity on writing practices will have other impacts too, and some of these may certainly challenge if not compromise ethical writing practices.

There is an assumption in much of the relevant literature that a strong corporate identity signifies, unproblematically, a successful (and thus a 'good') organisation.[9] Much research in the field (emanating from business communication, public relations and marketing and management disciplines) therefore explores how to develop or sustain strong corporate identity. Corporate identity suggests coherence and uniformity (or the suppression from public view of difference or inconsistency, except where this serves to bolster the power of the all-embracing corporate identity). Today, coherence and uniformity are perceived, from a business perspective, as important as far as corporate recognisability and reliability, reputation, consumer awareness and so on are concerned.

By contrast, it appears that, as Leitch and Motion (1999) argue, Cees van Riel's theory of 'common starting points' (CSPs) offers a postmodern critique of the traditional notion of corporate identity and its focus on consistency. Van Riel defines CSPs as the 'central values which function as the basis for undertaking any kinds of communication envisaged by an organization' (van Riel 1995, p. 19). Leitch and Motion see as useful, in the postmodern context, van Riel's claim that if it possesses these common starting points, a company can 'present multiple images to its various publics provided that these images are consistent, not with each other, but with the organisation's CSPs. The corporate identity task is to manage multiplicity rather than to suppress it' (Leitch and Motion 1999). This approach does appear to be potentially productive in the communicative flexibility it might allow. However, it only takes account of multiplicity in the context of the company and the employees, rather than in terms of the multiplicity of *relations* that will always obtain between employees and their different individual clients or sets of publics. Can corporate identity, even one based on a company's values – its CSPs (assuming those are shared by the company's employees) – manage *that* multiplicity? I'm not at all sure that it can – or, indeed, that it should.

Corporate identity is implied not only in the company logo appearing on documents, but also in the templates, the standard genres and texts, the conventionalised language practices and their deployment by members of an organisation or corporation as they do their work. This is by no means to suggest that writers will actively acknowledge, accept or embrace the meaning and value of their company's corporate identity even as they use it. They may well feel they have little power to express their unease with or choice about their own role in the reinforcement or extension of corporate identity. Whether they do or not is not really the point here. What is at issue is the undeniable relation between corporate identity and its reinscription of employees' identities and their relationships with their clients through its rhetorics. An extract from the introduction to an Engex proposal to carry out a hospital energy audit illustrates this point clearly. (Michael, as the signatory on the document cover page, is treated as the author here, and certainly he would have been responsible for writing the introduction.)

---

Engex is an industry leader in the design and operation of building services and technology. We are committed to finding the best possible solutions for our clients and we assist clients in gaining the most from their investment in engineering services in the buildings they own and operate.

Engex has considerable experience in the field of energy management and has established a specialist division, the Asset and Energy Division, to provide this specialist service to the owners of existing buildings.

Senior staff from this division would undertake the energy audit for [the hospital]. The team specialises in energy audits and asset management work and is led by Michael Smith, who has over 20 years experience in the energy management industry in Western Australia. The staff are familiar with the Australian Standards, Private Hospital guidelines and statutory regulations involved in the design and main-tenance of building services and recognise these in our assessments and recommendations.

The company's professional profile, promoted through the third-person voice of the opening sentence, 'Engex is an industry leader ...', very quickly becomes interchanged with the (first-person plural) engineers and their focus on client needs, 'We are committed to finding the best possible solutions for our clients ...'. Similarly, the significant experi-ence of the company, outlined in general terms in the second paragraph, moves, in the third, to a focus on the individuals – 'senior staff' – making up the team. The experience of Michael, the team leader proposed, reinforces the idea of the extensive corporate track record by reference to his two decades of work in the industry and, by implication, of the range and breadth of his involvement in relevant industry prac-tice around the state of Western Australia. The sentence describing the team members' familiarity with pertinent regulations and guide-lines slips from the third-person voice (the 'staff are familiar with ...') to the first person, 'and recognise these in our assessments and recommendations'.

In this way the rhetorical boundaries between employee and cor-porate identities are certainly blurred and, in this case at least, mutually enhanced – at least from the company's perspective. Let's assume that Michael, as the writer in the context of this promotional discourse, is happy to represent the interdependence of his own professional iden-tity and Engex's corporate identity. Given that the extract above comes from a proposal to offer a client professional services, we might also assume that the client reader would be heartened to read about the combined capability and expertise being offered by this tenderer – both Engex the company and its individual employees.

It is worth remembering, however, that there may well be occasions when this commonly practised conflation of the writer's professional identity with the corporate identity, an identity which the writer repre-sents (and which, in turn, represents the writer) in their exchanges with client readers may not always be so apparently uncomplicated. What about, for example, a claims assessor working in an insurance company who feels uncomfortable about having to prepare in writing and pres-ent under her name, as a company representative, what she believes is a poor decision made by the company in response to a client's claim? Or what about the lawyer who, in written correspondence to a client (who is not a legal specialist) to explain why a claim has been rejected, feels compromised by the requirement to use obscure, legalistic terms whose use is sanctioned by their signifying the corporate and professional identity, but whose interpretability by a layperson is widely recognised as almost impossible? These are just two of innumerable comparable situations.

Other significant practices that help shore up corporate identity practices in the technologised working environment include using templates, copying and pasting standard text into documents, and acting as the collator of already established (already used or sold) ideas, information and so on. In many business contexts, these practices have clearly saved time, money and effort. In Engex, for example, Troy will copy and paste material from previous documents into a new one he is developing if it saves time, 'but only from my own reports'. And of templates he says, 'some I'd use; some I wouldn't go near'. For Peter, templates are useful as 'a starting point' and being able to copy and paste from previous into current documents in his view simplifies the writing process. Simon is happy to use templates and standard text, because 'writing can be time-consuming'. He will also use copy and paste facilities, though he is conscious of the client recognising already used material and questioning what they are paying for. Consequently, 'you have to add value to [a document] rather than just recycle it'.

A comparison of two Engex documents, one prepared by Troy, the other by Michael – two-page proposals (sent as faxes) responding to requests to submit quotes for carrying out relatively small jobs – shows the way in which sections of standardised text serve as the framework and structure of individual exchanges with clients. Each proposal uses the same opening address: 'Thank you for your invitation to submit a fee for professional services associated with the above project [named in the subject line]', before moving into specific individual details of the submission. The proposals are then both structured by the use of the same section subheadings and statements introducing those sections:

EXTENT OF WORKS
We understand the extent of work required to complete the project includes ...

SCOPE OF PROFESSIONAL SERVICES
The professional services offered would be aimed at ...

APPOINTMENT AND FEES
This offer is made to ... whom we understand will be our Client for the project and therefore responsible for the payment of our fees ...

PROGRAMME
Our submission is based on the following indicative programme for the project ...

QUALITY ASSURANCE
Engex is a Quality Endorsed company operating in accordance with International Standard ISO9001.

The standardised text thus serves rhetorically to delimit the written exchange and, simultaneously, to reassert corporate identity (here defined as recognisability and consistency) and the company's (professionally requisite) association with abstract notions of systematisation and regulation. However, in this company, even when templates and standard text are used and the facilities of copy and paste between documents employed, the engineers are also, for each writing activity, *directly* intervening by drawing on, producing and organising technical knowledge or information specific to the needs of an individual client. This does seem to mean, as their comments above indicate, that they feel individually engaged in the meaning-production process of each new document (and that for them this activity generates professional and economic value), even when that engagement is centred on the elements of text that they produce, rather than on its other elements (the template itself, standard text, etc.). As Simon remarked, 'we all have to take ownership of the documents we write'.

But what about writing environments where the opportunities for the direct intervention of writers are minimised? The writers' sense of distance from most or all elements of a document could, quite conceivably (and understandably), result in their personal disengagement from (at least some parts of) their texts and, by extension, from their readers: 'It's not me, it's not mine. I'm not the writer; I'm simply the collator. I only have an abstract relation to the (standardised) text, and therefore only an abstract (immaterial, insignificant) relation to its readers, their response to the text and its impacts on them. That's the company writing, not me; it's mundane writing, not meaningful, valuable writing.'

For the individual consultant engineers in Engex, corporate identity and corporate culture[10] appear to have various but generally not undue influence on their professional practice – and in this respect they may well not be typical. Here, it is particularly interesting, however, given the company's recent (and ongoing) overhaul of its corporate image and identity in a bid to heighten its profile as a group committed to 'sustainability and engineering design values' (client newsletter 2003). The changes have included refurbishment of the group's offices, incorporating design and materials reflecting the focus on sustainability; and the development of a new logo, standard templates and fonts.

The engineers' responses to a question about how far they perceive corporate culture, style or identity influencing their working practices reflect their different ideas of their positions vis-à-vis the company. Troy commented that Engex adds 'name and presentation to what I do'. (On the other hand, however, he also pointed out that 'we're [management's] product'.) Michael, a long-term employee of the company, admitted he was 'a bit cynical really' about the new corporate image, as he sees the changes as 'superficial'. For Simon, the notion of corporate style influencing his approach to his own work is 'something foreign'. Peter said that the changes in corporate image would make no difference to his work practices unless a company directive were issued, instructing him to make any such changes. For all the participants in this study it seems that the focus is on fulfilling their responsibilities as technical experts and advisers, and on communicating their knowledge to clients; in their view, corporate identity is subordinate rather than integral to that process.

### Expertise and authority – let's qualify that

Reports, proposals, letters and faxes: despite being identifiable as genred texts, all such corporate, client-oriented documents are necessarily disjointed, since they serve several functions simultaneously. For example, and as we have seen, they reaffirm corporate identity; they also construct (or perform) expert knowledge and articulate professional authority and professional standards. They do all this, however, in a litigious commercial sphere, and in a knowledge economy premised on an awareness of its power and influence as well as on its instability and vulnerability. These documents may also be explicitly represented by an individual writing subject addressing specific others, at the same time as they serve as representative corporate texts functioning more generally as forms of promotion in the public and professional realms.

Expertise is communicated both explicitly and implicitly in Engex's corporate documents. For example, it is commonly declared openly in proposals responding to client projects. Very often here, the specialist knowledge and experience of the team proposed for work on the project is outlined in a specifically designated section. Thus, in a proposal to carry out an energy audit of one potential client's local council facilities, Chris's credentials, as one of the team members, are outlined: 'Chris is a Project Engineer in the Assets and Energy Division ... where he is responsible for the maintenance/energy management of [two local councils'] property portfolio. He has a strong working knowledge of chilled water systems, aquatic centre services and building management systems.' Chris's role and function in the company, together with a listing of his specific areas of expertise are, in this context, directly claimed and presented to the client for evaluation and judgement. Once such a description is accepted by the client (an acceptance typically signified by the awarding of the project to Engex), then expertise becomes differently articulated.

The paragraph below, taken from a short fax prepared by Simon to report to an existing client on an inspection of a public building that he undertook to determine the adequacy of existing fire services, illustrates the shift to an implicit but nonetheless effective representation of expertise:

> It would not be possible to adequately cover all the galleries and minor plant spaces in the building using the external fire hydrants. Fire hydrants are reserved for the use of trained fire fighters, not the building occupants. The installation of internal fire hydrants is not seen as substantial benefit to protect the building, as there is only one fire compartment.

The use of the impersonal active or passive declarative statements, for example, 'it would not be possible ...', 'fire hydrants are reserved for the use of trained firefighters ...', and 'the installation of internal fire hydrants is not seen as substantial benefit ...' assumes the authoritative tone of uncontestable, 'given' facts, and avoids any hint of Simon's findings as the subjective interpretation of a scenario. In this way, Simon's expertise becomes *embedded* in the rhetorical mode of the description of the building's fire services, and is powerfully, if only implicitly, realised through it. These performative and declarative functions of language are evident in many of the documents prepared by the Engex engineers for their clients. This is certainly the case in reports describing the findings of a building inspection or even in the more formal due diligence report. A comment in a report, for example, that a building is safe actually *creates* it as safe for clients. In their positions as experts, the consulting engineers have conferred power to use language performatively and to demonstrate their expertise. As Troy observed, 'people tend to look at you as the expert' and 'it's important for me to basically let you know that I do know what I'm talking about'. And Chris remarked that 'you need [the clients] to know why they're paying the money'.

So much for the rhetorical construction of the position of expert. However, experts, as writers, are routinely (even if not self-consciously) placed in particularly fraught ethical positions in the contemporary corporate environment.

As Bauman argues persuasively, the heteronomous nature of action in relation to experts and the advice they give (or usually sell) to clients removes moral responsibility from both expert and client. It removes responsibility from the expert because their action is justified by the 'law' of economic gain, and from the clients because their action is justified by what the experts have told them is 'right' to do. Bauman's claim is worth quoting at length, to clarify this idea:

> The heteronomous nature of action ... is less obvious or not visible at all when the command appears in disguise, in the form of 'advice' given by 'experts' – persons acting in the roles on which have been socially conferred the authority to pronounce binding (true, effective, trustworthy) sentences. Heteronomy is still more difficult to detect when such advice is 'purchased' by the 'customer' from *experts* who have no power to coerce: consumer freedom manifested in commercial transaction, and the subsequent freedom of the client to apply or disregard the purchased instruction, effectively hide the fact that the advice is the product of someone else's definition of the client's situation, someone else's vision of the client's weal, and someone else's criteria of distinguishing right from wrong, proper from improper ... It is true that an employee of an organization is paid money in exchange for his obedience to the bosses' command, while a market customer himself pays money in exchange for the expert's command to which he may then be obedient. Otherwise, however, the advice of experts does not differ much from the command of the bosses in its impact on emancipating the action from the moral responsibility of the actor and submitting it instead to the heteronomously controlled standards of gain and instrumental effectiveness.
>
> (Bauman 1993, pp. 128–9)

From this perspective it appears, then, that writers have a monumental task to make concerted and determined efforts to imagine readers *through* but also *around* the social mechanism that Bauman describes. They need to do this, difficult though such attempts may be, by looking beyond paying clients (or paying employers) to others who may be affected, directly or indirectly, by their expert or knowledge claims.

However, the story is even more complicated in the case of the engineers' (and many others') writing practices. The performative power they exercise through their writing also needs to be qualified (by the engineers and by the company) as protection against potential charges of producing the 'wrong' knowledge; for example, in case a building, having been represented as safe, is found to be (represented by someone else as) unsafe, after all. That power-knowledge also needs to be qualified because the expert doesn't, of course, necessarily *know* all. And this destabilising of the position of expert produces a further dilemma for the engineer cast in that role. Chris puts it succinctly: 'It's difficult if you're not sure about something to say you're not sure, because [clients] expect you to be experts. But you have to say you're not sure.'

What we find, then, in many client documents is a tension between performative statements, on the one hand, and tentative, cautious statements that qualify those, on the other. For example, in one due diligence report's executive summary we find the following remarks:

> The Mechanical Services *are* fit for purpose, *incorporate* high quality equipment and *appear* in fair condition for their age. Following the completion of the proposed equipment replacement, the system *should be* in good condition. (Italics added)

Notice the performative gesture articulated by the words 'are' and 'incorporate', and their tempering by the words 'appear' and 'should be'. This kind of vacillating is becoming increasingly typical of such reports in a contemporary business framework heavily influenced by risk management practices. It demonstrates writers' awareness of the tension between their role as experts and the limits or monitoring of that role by a legal rhetorical framework designed to protect citizens against experts' irresponsible practices.

The engineers' sensitivity to the increasing threat of litigation means that, as Simon commented, 'certainly there has to be a tone change [in the wording of reports]', and as far as Michael is concerned, 'you have to be careful what you say'.

Porter draws attention to the ways in which the threat of lawsuits may positively influence a company's attitude to its writing practices: 'Litigation makes a company conscious that it has corporate composing practices, that these practices are ideological and political, and that inadequate composing practices can cost them a lot of money and get them in a lot of trouble. Litigation can motivate companies to review and critique their standard composing practices.' Porter also points out how 'litigation makes a company aware of the importance of critique', given that 'litigation is itself a form of critique' (1993, p. 136). There is no question that for the Engex engineers the legal framework insists that they consider their texts and the possible repercussions of their writing on their companies and themselves. But it does also, if only secondarily, encourage them to think of impacts of texts on readers, and the ways in which texts can have material, real-life consequences. As well, the legal requirement to exercise 'duty of care' in relation to clients and others, as mentioned earlier in the chapter, also suggests the difficult balance that writers such as the consultant engineers must strive to maintain between written communication of expertise and an expressed awareness of the limits or fallibility of that expertise.

As far as language used in the body of a report is concerned, Peter explained that, 'I write in a certain language that tries to minimise [threats of litigation]', and several examples of the verbs used to preface his statements can be found in a letter to a client concerning the design of a fire system for a community facility: 'it is likely that ...', 'it appears that ...' and 'I have assumed that ...'. The effects of this equivocal use of language are often, of course, ambiguous reports that may well frustrate client readers who may be looking for clear direction or confirmation about a preferred course of action.[11] So, while the resulting rhetoric may suit the needs of Engex's legal representatives, it may not necessarily suit those of the clients themselves (and it may be meaningless to other interested lay readers). The engineers talked about how company lawyers have indeed become increasingly involved in reviewing documents and amending language in certain significant reports. Michael cited the example of one document, a maintenance contract he had recently prepared, which the company's legal representative had then modified, misunderstanding, in Michael's view, the term 'comprehensive'. Michael explained this point to me further in a follow-up email.

The lawyers did not understand what the term 'comprehensive' means in our industry. A comprehensive contract is one in which the maintenance contractor accepts the risk of breakdown and attends to all breakdowns within the fixed charge. 'Comprehensive' was taken to mean 'thorough' by the lawyer. The lawyer spent lots of time on the contract issues and practically ignored the scope of work, which is where most of the risk is in my humble opinion.

For Michael, the focus that he felt it was important to achieve for Engex and for his clients had been obscured in the process of the text's adjustment to suit the interpretation and requirements of the legal discourse community (both that of Engex and the client).[12]

The privileging of legal over other discourses is, of course, a very common phenomenon, and yet, as Britt et al. point out, it is also *not* inevitable. These authors argue that the law itself comprises 'two competing discourses that are essential to its existence: (a) the discourse that relaxes its constraints and admits interpretation and morality (without which it could not do its job) and (b) the discourse that denies this admission, a denial that is necessary if law is to maintain its authority over other interpretive discourses' (Britt et al. 1996, p. 226). When the interpretative capacity of one group of readers is elided in favour of another's, then a reviewing of the ethics of certain rhetorics must surely be timely.

**Pause for reflection**

It would be impracticable to suggest or even desire that, for every key stroke that implicates them in a company's identity or in questions of expertise and authority, corporate writers should individually and separately confront and try to resolve all the concerns covered in this part of the chapter. Nevertheless, I hope to have initiated a discussion of issues that are not yet adequately accounted for, either in research into ethical writing praxis, or when educators seek to develop emerging writers' capacity to write effectively and responsibly in professional domains. Quite deliberately, many questions have been asked and very few answers proffered. This is because I certainly do not want to prescribe the roles of writers in an organisation or to delimit the focus of their diverse communicative responsibilities towards the company and various other stakeholders. That is something that can only be deliberated on by writers themselves, in their own writing contexts, together with those (present or imagined) whom their writing affects either directly or indirectly. What I am advocating, however, is an increased and continuing self-consciousness about writing praxis. For professionals who do not consider themselves to be writers and yet who spend a significant part of their working day on writing activities, I suggest our task as writing educators is to stimulate and encourage in them the function and value of such self-consciousness. Moreover, by outlining the ways in which organisational writers' roles are variously circumscribed and thus considerably complicated, I am nonetheless keen to sustain a strong sense of writers owning some individual or collective agency, as well as responsibility, for ethical and rhetorical relations forged and extended with readers.

## Reading–writing in public

As I argued in the previous chapter, professional writing is a process of negotiating meanings, and involves a reciprocal relation or (imagined) conference between writers and potential readers. To be effectively imagined, professional writing as negotiation or conference must involve a careful evaluation of the respective sites of writing and reading, a self-consciousness about the rhetorical choices, and the concomitant possible ethical and practical impacts of and responses to the interpreted text. The first part of this chapter also considered the practical and discursive constraints impinging on professional writing praxis. Such constraints notwithstanding, professional writers, as I have been suggesting, very often write from positions of relative power.

Therefore, I aim to demonstrate in this part of the chapter that it is perhaps most particularly in such instances that professional writing requires us as writers to move towards the other (ideologically, emotionally, ethically and imaginatively) through our communication, and (to a greater or lesser extent) to encourage the other to come closer to us. This is an effort of approximating, which suggests both the notion of coming close and that of mutual concession – giving something (up) to the other – and requires an awareness that our exchanges will (as they should) be interrupted by competing texts, concerns and interests. The texts we write to/for others don't simply go from us; we are implicated in their transmission, even as we inevitably relinquish control over their interpretation and use. We must therefore bear some responsibility for the texts' potential destinations, their potential rewritings and their potential significances; and in this responsibility we can at least approach, and at best reach understanding with, our interlocutors, our readers.

As with the case explored here, political debates initiated and articulated through the discourse of written (print or electronic) texts today are a significant component of deliberation and the development of government and public policy. In a democracy, such debates should surely stimulate rather than discourage open and productive discussion or argument with readers-citizens in all their diversity. In other words such texts, particularly those written from positions of relative authority and influence (for example, by government, government agencies, public and private bodies, corporations and/or organisations), should aim to open up another (a subsequent) space for engagement. They should invite the participation of others, and particularly of 'outsiders': those hitherto under-represented by recognised or authoritative voices and bodies (institutions, organisations), those who need to make public their so-called private concerns. Writing, in this account, can be considered as a form of reconciliation, a coming to proximity with the other. Bauman, drawing on the work of Emmanuel Lévinas, uses the term 'proximity' in his discussion of the ethical relation that subsists between two people: 'proximity is the realm of intimacy and morality; distance is the realm of estrangement and the Law' (Bauman 1993, p. 83; see also pp. 85–8).

So my task here is to emphasise the crucial responsibility of writers to imagine the potential for reader agency in the interpretation and use of texts, *whatever* the medium or context of exchange. The kinds of changes I envisage and advocate for professional writing in the account below are undoubtedly ambitious. Nevertheless, I believe such changes are crucial if we are really serious about creating societies that both encourage and endorse the rhetorics of diversity and inclusiveness now pervading the public discourses of democratic cultures. And importantly, as Paré argues, 'writing in professional contexts serves particular ends, and unless those ends are changed, writing practices will remain the same' (Paré 2002, p. 59).[13]

## Background to the report

In Australia, during the late 1980s, the process of reconciliation was initiated and then formally established by the introduction of the Council for Aboriginal Reconciliation Act 1991. The process of reconciliation was chiefly intended to improve the relationship between Indigenous and non-Indigenous Australians (importantly through developing understandings of Indigenous cultures) and to overcome the social disadvantage of and achieve social justice for Indigenous peoples (see Sanders 2002). The Mabo land rights case (in 1992)[14] and the passing of the Native Title Act (in 1993),[15] by discrediting the concept of *terra nullius*, which had held since the arrival of white settlers in 1788, were also significant milestones; they served to heighten the sense of urgency about addressing issues related to Indigenous rights (see Augoustinos et al. 2002).[16]

Reconciliation involves remembering the past, recognising, acknowledging and reflecting on history as it is told from the point of view
of another, particularly someone less often heard or read. However,
as political theorist Paul Muldoon argues, reconciliation must not
be defined according to 'the national interest', and thus as 'a means of
burying the past once and for all', since implicit in that approach is 'a
kind of collective amnesia' (Muldoon 2003, p. 187). In other words, reconciliation does not mean the muting of quieter voices and less powerful texts by louder voices and more powerful texts, in order to present
an apparently unified text (qua nation) that has assimilated and dissolved all differences. Rather, reconciliation may act 'as a means of
realigning power relations between the coloniser and the colonised', by
a form of truth telling 'constituted through public discussion and
debate' (Muldoon 2003, pp. 187, 188).[17]

Since its publication in 1997, *Bringing them home: the national inquiry
into the separation of Aboriginal and Torres Strait Islander children from their
families* (*Bringing them home*), prepared by the Human Rights and Equal
Opportunities Commission (HREOC), has enjoyed a popular if contro-
versial status rare for a public report. The recording of hundreds of
painful personal accounts and the exposure of the often traumatic experiences of Aborigines removed from their families in Australia between
1910 and 1970 was a significant move towards making hitherto largely
silenced, personal and collective Indigenous histories public and highly
political. The nearly 700-page report traces the history of forcible separation of mixed-descent Aboriginal children from their families in
Australia's states and territories, carried out ultimately in order 'to control the reproduction of Indigenous people with a view to "merging" or
"absorbing" them into the non-Indigenous population' (HREOC 1997,
p. 31). The report goes on to describe the consequences of removal, the
effects of institutionalisation, of abuse, and of separation from family
and community. It outlines the grounds for reparation, arguing that 'the
policy of forcible removal of children from Indigenous Australians to
other groups for the purpose of raising them separately from and igno-
rant of their culture and people could properly be labelled "genocidal" '
(HREOC 1997, p. 275; see also pp. 270–5). The report also recommends
steps to be taken in order to make reparation. Further, it details the
range of services to be made available to those affected by separation,
and it critiques and advances the case for changes to contemporary
practices of separation relating to child protection and welfare and to
juvenile justice programmes. These areas of focus in the document

are interspersed with the evidence and submissions of individuals, organisations and governments. Also interwoven are transcripts, some a paragraph in length, others running to a few pages, which record the (oral and written) testimonies of individuals' experiences of removal policies. Here, the accounts from three witnesses whose stories are reproduced in *Bringing them home* can only hint at the widespread suffering and loss experienced by those individuals who have become known as the stolen generations:

> ... We had been playing all together, just a happy community and the air was filled with screams because the police came and mothers tried to hide their children and blacken their children's faces and tried to hide them in caves. We three, Essie, Brenda and me together with our three cousins ... the six of us were put on my old truck and taken to Oodnadatta which was hundreds of miles away and then we got there in the darkness ...
>
> When I finally met [my mother] through an interpreter she said that because my name had been changed she had heard about the other children but she'd never heard about me. And every sun, every morning as the sun came up the whole family would wail. They did that for 32 years until they saw me again. Who can imagine what a mother went through?
>
> > *Confidential evidence 305, South Australia*
> > (HREOC 1997, pp. 129–30)

> ... We were completely brainwashed to think only like a white person. When they went to mix in white society, they found they were not accepted [because] they were Aboriginal. When they went and mixed with Aborigines, some found they couldn't identify with them either, because they had too much white ways in them. So that they were neither black nor white. They were simply a lost generation of children. I know. I was one of them.
>
> > *Confidential submission 617, New South Wales: woman*
> > *removed at 8 years with her 3 sisters in the 1940s;*
> > *placed in Cootamundra Girls' Home*
> > (HREOC 1997, p. 152)

I had to relearn lots of things. I had to relearn humour, ways of sitting, ways of being which were another way totally to what I was actually brought up with. It was like having to re-do me, I suppose. The thing that people were denied in being removed from family was that they were denied being read as Aboriginal people, they were denied being educated in an Aboriginal way.

> *Confidential evidence 71, New South Wales: woman who*
> *lived from [the age of] 5 months to 16 years in*
> *Cootamundra Girls' Home in the 1950s and 1960s*
> (HREOC 1997, p. 203)

The brief selection of narratives above poignantly crystallises the immeasurable value of 'the social production of truth made possible by the creation of a public forum for "story-telling" ' (Muldoon 2003, p. 194).

Another key feature of *Bringing them home* is the outlining of a number of recommendations, which were specifically 'directed to healing and reconciliation for the benefit of all Australians' (HREOC 1997, p. 4). Key recommendations from the report include those relating to reparation, consisting of:

1. acknowledgment and apology,
2. guarantees against repetition,
3. measures of restitution,
4. measures of rehabilitation, and
5. monetary compensation.

(HREOC 1997, p. 651)

Just ahead of the tabling in parliament of the *Bringing them home* report in May 1997, Prime Minister John Howard, in his opening speech at the 1997 Reconciliation Convention, indicated that an apology to Aboriginal peoples would not be offered: 'Australians of this generation should not be required to accept guilt and blame for past actions and policies over which they had no control' (Howard 1997).

At the end of December 1997, the Federal Government responded to the *Bringing them home* report with the announcement of a $63m package 'in practical assistance' to the Indigenous community. The funding was directed to a range of initiatives, including facilitating family reunions, setting up counselling services, family support and parenting programmes, and establishing an oral history project (Commonwealth Government 1997). But yet again, the government refused to apologise for past atrocities committed against Indigenous peoples, explaining that it did not believe 'our generation should be asked to accept responsibility for the acts of earlier generations, sanctioned by the law of the times' (Commonwealth Government 1997, p. 1).

Two years after the publication of *Bringing them home*, in November 1999, the Australian Senate, the legislative upper chamber of the Australian Federal Parliament, called for an inquiry into the implementation of recommendations made in the report. (The inquiry itself was called in response to one of the recommendations of *Bringing them home*.) Referred to the Senate's Legal and Constitutional References Committee, the inquiry invited submissions from individuals, organisations and state, territory and federal governments. It not only involved the assessment and evaluation of written submissions and of the *Bringing them home* report, its recommendations and their implementation, but also public hearings at which individuals, including members of the stolen generation, appeared as witnesses.[18] On behalf of the Federal Government, the Minister for Aboriginal and Torres Strait Islander Affairs, Senator John Herron made a submission to the inquiry – the responding and, many would argue, highly contentious, report that I analyse briefly below. Because this written submission to the inquiry was thus anticipated and approached – by stakeholder groups, as well as the wider public and the media – as a significant contribution to the debate about reconciliation in Australia,[19] it serves as a specific consideration of professional writing as part of a democratic process (or text) of ongoing public and political debate, rather than as a finished product (the final word).[20]

It is not by coincidence that the political text I have chosen to critique is one written in the context of public and political debates about reconciliation between settler and Indigenous people in Australia. I concentrate on selected aspects of the text, in order to reflect on the ethical questions raised by and the material impacts of its rhetoric as a political text in Australian society.[21] This endeavour is important because, as Christian R. Weisser argues, we need to examine the significance of public writing in context, and so 'highlight the ways in which material forces shape what gets said, who gets heard, and how these forces have structured public discourse throughout history' (2002, p. 98). In this case, I argue that the writer, adept at the game of adversarial politics, pays insufficient attention to the uneven discursive field on which some particular writing and reading practices take place. As a result, the potential for forging productive and ethical relations (not to mention mutually agreed policy) between writers and readers is missed.

In addition, and to give this discussion broader applicability, I endeavour to open up the report (and those other texts to which it 'writes back') to the metaphoric significances of writing–reading practices as potential instances of reconciliation. This means that my reflections on reconciliation as an ideological political issue and as a set of approaches and activities are simultaneously reflections on professional writing praxis. So, for example, comments such as Muldoon's on 'truth-telling' about the past in relation to processes of national reconciliation (in Australia and South Africa) become doubly powerful: 'in the first instance the burden of responsibility for seeing differently rests with members of the dominant culture … [however], both participants to the conversation must be willing to undertake an imaginative entry into another worldview – both must accept the obligation of democratic reciprocity' (Muldoon 2003, p. 194). Such an attitude is precisely that which I advocate for professional writers, and for their responding readers.

## The report as a corrective

As I have mentioned, the Federal Government's report was submitted in response to an inquiry called by the Senate and referred to its Legal and Constitutional References Committee. Part of the Australian Senate's role is to provide a check on government, and one way in which it does this is through its committee system. Senate committees investigate and scrutinise specific government activities, legislation and policy (Parliament of Australia 1998). As with all such inquiries, this one worked within the framework provided by its terms of reference. When the committee invited submissions to its inquiry, it also advertised its terms of references in newspapers in all capital cities in Australia. In essence, the terms of reference called for the inquiry to investigate the adequacy, effectiveness and impact of the government's (1997) response to *Bringing them home*; to determine appropriate ways for the government to set up an alternative dispute resolution tribunal to settle claims for compensation; and to establish processes and mechanisms to provide a range of support services for members of the stolen generation, and education for Australians in Indigenous culture.[22]

The government's submission consists of a 56-page report, organised into two parts. Most notable in the report overall is the highly selective response to the inquiry's terms of reference. The first part (24 pages), entitled 'Introduction – the HREOC report' largely ignores the terms of reference of the Senate inquiry. Instead, it represents a refutation of the *raison d'être* of *Bringing them home*, in order, it claims, to investigate 'a number of key assumptions on which the report is based' (Herron 2000). Each of the (seven) key issues challenges not only the spirit but the integrity of *Bringing them home*:

Key issue 1: Who are the 'stolen generation'? (pp. 2–5)

Key issue 2: Why were indigenous children removed? Standards of the time? (pp. 5–12)

Key issue 3: Was there a 'stolen generation'? How many children were 'stolen'? (pp. 13–18)

Key issue 4: Why not compensation? (pp. 18–19)

Key issue 5: What has the Commonwealth Government done to help? (pp. 19–20)

Key issue 6: Responsibility for addressing the effects of indigenous child separation practices (pp. 20–21)

Key issue 7: The methodology of the HREOC Inquiry (pp. 21–24).

Only in part two (Herron 2000, pp. 25–55) does the report pay attention to the inquiry's terms of reference, although the writer also uses this section of the report to take strong issue with some of HREOC's key recommendations in *Bringing them home*. My analysis of the government's response focuses predominantly on part one, as it seems to me that it is here that the tenor of (dis)engagement with the rhetoric of *Bringing them home*, not to mention the terms of reference of the inquiry, is defined and heavily reinforced.

In contrast to the notion of writing as a form of reconciliation, the report writer develops an insistent *thematic* focus on the claim of 'benign intent' (the expression or its variants are used four times in the document)[23] as a defence of the forcible removal of Aboriginal children: 'It is not the intention of the Commonwealth in this submission to defend or to justify previous policies. It is the intention, however, to correct what appears to have been a misrepresentation of the nature and particularly the intent (e.g. alleged genocide) of those policies' (Herron 2000, Key issue 2, p. 6). This intent is paralleled by the *discursive* articulation of that focus in the repeated attention to the report's own objective (its own benign intent?) 'to correct' the rhetorical and methodological approach of *Bringing them home*. The writer of the government report expresses concern 'that the confused methodology and its consequential simplistic "stolen generation" terminology has distorted public understanding of the historical record' (Herron 2000, Key issue 1, p. 4). And a few pages later, 'the Commonwealth does not seek to defend such policies and practices; but it does wish to correct the HREOC report's misrepresentation of the historical record' (Herron 2000, Key issue 2, p. 12). Here, 'the historical record' is posited as a neutral object rather than as a rhetorical complexity and conflict of myriad perspectives, accounts and methods of articulation. Together all these necessarily *distort*, in the sense of reshaping and intertwining, *ongoing stories* constituting an ever-changing understanding of (in this case national) history. The historian Inga Clendinnen crystallises this point powerfully, when she remarks that

> stories are not only the preferred mode of human expression and communication. They are also insidiously powerful ones. History in the grand narrative sense will always belong to the victors. They will control the historical record and their point of view will be embedded in nationalist stories that can appear to be no more than innocent description. By controlling the past and the present, they will control the future, too – unless we can destabilise those self-congratulatory accounts of the past.
>
> (Clendinnen 2001, p. 12)

The report writer's objective to set the historical record 'straight' through the report not only undermines the value of a range of perspectives, approaches and voices in reconstructing and reviewing the past, but attempts to 'white out' or to muffle, with its own, louder, 'grander' narrative voice, the pain and suffering of Indigenous children caused by their forcible removal.

As with the reference to *Bringing them home*'s 'confused methodology', the report writer also bemoans the fact that the 'question of numbers' (of Indigenous children removed from their families) is dealt with 'in a mere one page of [HREOC's] 600-page report' (Herron 2000, Key issue 3, p. 13). As well, the anthropologist Ron Brunton, cited by the government as an authoritative voice, is quoted as saying that the HREOC report was not a 'rigorous, sober and factual assessment' (in Herron 2000, Key issue 7, p. 23). Brunton also expresses his concern that 'the Government and the public have been given an official report which is highly unprofessional and misleading' (in Herron 2000, Key issue 7, p. 24). Adopting a quasi-Cartesian logic to evaluate the quality and accuracy of *Bringing them home*, Brunton's rhetoric rehearses colonial practices that undermine the value of non-rational experience. Such rhetoric also ignores the point that history is haphazard and always in excess of facts or numbers. Should the question of how many people suffered matter more than or obscure the knowledge that people did indeed suffer? Authentic personal histories are always *structured* by emotion and passion: love, joy, suffering, pain, loss. Our understanding of 'professional' and its association with notions of the complete, the assured, the precise and the competent need re-evaluating whenever these overwhelmingly connote a pseudo-science of self-containment and self-sufficiency, a quantifiability of knowledge and experience.[24] By extension, the tendency of the term 'professionalism' to connote this simplistic hierarchical structuring of discourses and to exclude those rhetorics that disrupt the conventional (rational) pattern also need interrogating. Or, as Barbara Couture argues:

> If in speaking and listening to [and, by extension, writing to and reading] others we choose to value *only* rhetoric that adheres to the constraints of demonstrating intellectual coherence and of support-ing a single, preferred epistemology within a single knowledge domain, we will ultimately face a wholly untenable result: denigra-tion of human value, paucity of spirit, and wholesale dismissal of the complexity of the very world we live in.
>
> (Couture 1998, p. 59)

Despite expressing confidence in the possibility and desirability of harnessing an objective methodology for the writing of history, the report writer, paradoxically, does understand the doubtful status of objectivity when it comes to the matter of monetary compensation for members of the stolen generation. 'There is no existing objective methodology for attaching a monetary value to the loss suffered by vic-tims of alleged government failures of the type evident in relation to separated children' (Herron 2000, p. 48). However, as Regina Graycar, commenting a couple of years earlier on what she describes as the gov-ernment's 'disingenuous' remarks relating to the question of monetary compensation for Indigenous peoples, has explained: 'what is, or is not, compensable at law is more a matter of political judgment and govern-ment policy than it is a matter of any inherent legal understanding of compensability' (Graycar 1998).

In addition to 'correcting' *Bringing them home* on methodological and factual grounds, the report seeks to fix the former's improper use of language: 'The phrase "stolen generation" is rhetorical' (Herron 2000, Key issue 3, p. 18) proclaims the government's text. Of course it is. The term 'stolen generation' (not actually used in *Bringing them home*, but now in broad, if contentious, currency in Australia, referring to those directly and indirectly affected by the policies of removal) is, as all lang-uage is, rhetorical: it creates effects – evocative, emotional – and it offers a perspective. According to the report, however:

there are two basic flaws in the 'stolen generation' concept:

- the first is that, as the BTH report acknowledges, between at least 70 and 90 percent of Aboriginal children were **not** subject to separation; and
- secondly, the evidence that a proportion of those removed fitted within the stereotype of 'forcible removal' is only anecdotal and has not been subjected to proper scrutiny.

(Herron 2000, Key issue 1, p. 2; bold and italics in original)

The choice of the word 'concept' underscores the continuing struggle to make of 'stolen generation' a semantic abstraction. However, rhetorical ethics reminds us that 'stolen generation', as used in this context, is a metaphor delineating the felt experiences of thousands of Indigenous Australians, not to mention the impacts of those experiences on their immediate and extended families and communities.[25] Philip Eubanks argues that metaphor is not only rhetorically charged but rhetorically constituted: 'no metaphor is spoken or written except in the context of a sociohistorically bound communicative situation' (Eubanks 1999, p. 95). Clearly the term resonates for vast numbers of non-Indigenous Australians too; despite the government's efforts, it resists assimilation.

Moreover, the description of the personal Indigenous narratives related in *Bringing them home* as 'anecdotal', and the lament that their veracity has not been tested, 'subjected to proper scrutiny' (Herron 2000, Key issue 1, p. 2), again implies the writer's desire to contain and limit histories within a paternalistic package.

One of the recommendations made in *Bringing them home* was that the government make funding available to Indigenous agencies 'to record, preserve and administer access to the testimonies of Indigenous people affected by the forcible removal policies' (HREOC 1997, p. 651). In its response to that recommendation, the government declares (in tabular, note form) its allocation of:

$1.6m over 4 years [to the National Library] to undertake an oral history project. Project fulfils a need in the indigenous community to tell their [sic] stories. Stories of missionaries, police and officials will also be collected providing a *balanced historical record* of this period. At the completion of the project, the Library will publish a book based on the stories collected.

(Herron 2000, p. 33; italics added)

While this initiative is to be applauded,[26] is it necessarily a more legitimate endeavour than that contained in *Bringing them home*, or than that which Indigenous agencies themselves might independently administer? And can the 'public' language of Indigenous Australians only acquire authenticity when mediated by a state-recognised authority? (Incidentally, the text here also represents an assumed ignorance of the *massive im*balance between the government and Indigenous people in terms of relative power, volume of voice, and political and social clout.)

As the above examples of the corrective approach indicate, the report responds to the traumas of the stolen generation in a depersonalised, cool and detached rhetoric, as if deliberately to distinguish itself as epitomising the dispassionate and the 'objective' (and thus, conventionally speaking, professional, authoritative). There is a steady and marked avoidance of any sympathetic, let alone empathetic, engagement with individuals' experiences. Instead, we are presented with depersonalised remarks in highly abstract language: 'The validity of the subject of the [*Bringing them home*] report has been accepted in the government's \$63m response to its recommendations' (Herron 2000, Key issue 7, p. 21).

Other concessions to the truth of the accounts presented in *Bringing them home* are generally made through careful, negative constructions and convoluted syntax, so that their sense is actually obscured. For example, and as we saw above: 'between at least 70 and 90 percent of Aboriginal children were **not** subject to separation' (Herron 2000, Key issue 1, p. 2). And: 'This is not to say that children separated in circumstances other than the archetypal "stolen child" scenario have not suffered trauma as a result of having spent a proportion of their childhood away from their families and communities' (Herron 2000, Key issue 1, p. 4).

The comments of Senator John Herron during a televised media interview, in response to questions about the tone of the government's document therefore remain unconvincing: 'It's hard to get passion across in a submission. You've got to put it in words. You can't portray emotions in words. It's very difficult to do' (Australian Broadcasting Corporation 2000). Nevertheless, as we have seen, Herron, signatory to the government's document, evidently recognises – and criticises – the emotive use of language in *Bringing them home*.

As the points above seek to demonstrate, what emerges from a brief consideration of the government's report, in terms of its participation in the dialogue about reconciliation, is its concerted and self-conscious attempt to *distance* itself from rather than engage with the text to which it responds. In other words, the writer attempts to avoid approaching or approximating the interests of readers and forestalls reciprocity through an attitude of distancing and correction. As long as this attitude is maintained, writing cannot be a form of reconciliation, an activity that involves reciprocity and mutual conference. For, as Lévinas reminds us, 'language is fraternity, and thus a responsibility for the other, and hence a responsibility for what I have not committed, for the pain and the fault of others' (Lévinas 1987, p. 123). In light of this observation, it is worth noting too that it is 'regret' (see Herron 2000, ii and p. 55, for example) rather than apology that the report writer expresses for past atrocities such as those are described in *Bringing them home*. But what kind of accountability or responsibility could 'regret' ever suggest? Saying sorry demands an addressee – *someone* to say sorry *to*. Not so regret. Regret is self- or situation-oriented rather than person- or other-oriented.

## Another pause for reflection

To write its submission as a rhetorical *response* rather than *corrective* would have facilitated an ethical exchange, an ongoing dialogue between the government and Australia's Indigenous peoples, and would have dispelled the misconception that there is a monological truth about the past to be established. Rather than such insistence on the achievement of its (one-way) objectives, then, the government's text might have imagined the place of the reading others and the various ways in which they might respond to what was written.

According to this view, if our professional writing is truly to engage with others, then it necessarily involves our learning to write, and to read and understand, the language of others, a language we may not have encountered, let alone acknowledged, at least publicly, before. The texts we write, if we value their being read, will have to admit, to articulate, the possibility of the valuable difference of others' positions, history and language.

One of the prime minister's contributions to the wrangle over the meaning of the term 'stolen generation' harnessed a significant and telling metaphor. John Howard, speaking on Melbourne radio, urged

Australians to 'stop this navel gazing about the past' and to get on with the future (*Weekend Australian* 2001, p. 1; see also p. 4). The remark highlights a refusal to gaze: to write or speak imaginatively about citizens' moral connections with each other, and therefore with the living past, and its difference. Howard's demand that the process of reflection should 'stop' is symptomatic of the corrective, straitjacketing impulse to close down the negotiations – articulated through (here government-sponsored) public texts – for reconciliation. But the drive for reconciliation in Australia and elsewhere, articulated in part through a democratic rhetoric of professional writing that acknowledges the complex truths constituting our history, won't stop here – or there. Barbara Couture's remarks in this context are again pertinent: she argues that we need to reconceive truth as

> living in *continued human interaction*; thus, truth finds no victory in declaring a single argument wrong or its author in error. Nor does it deem it necessary that we seek the final word, for such finality only forecloses the possibility of truth by dismissing someone who may yet speak. And further, such silencing of others threatens the essential direction of all our activity, which is toward more perfect interaction with an other, that is, with all we perceive to be outside of ourselves, in order to know all that is other as well as we presumably know ourselves.
>
> (Couture 1998, pp. 26–7; italics added)

Similarly, public texts, if we do acknowledge the value of their iterability, can offer to readers and to writers a forum for discussion about the differences of truth and history from diverse human perspectives. The range of voices that such texts will then admit and embrace can foreground their human-ness and the moral dynamic of their appeal.[27]

### Pulling the threads together: concluding questions

Law, economics, professionalism, expertise, authority, corporate and political identity: as depersonalised concepts and structures, each of these – often effectively and productively – defines and organises human relations in the corporate, institutional and public spheres. Nevertheless, they are inadequate as standards of moral arbitration, although they may often be misperceived as relieving writers from taking ethical responsibility for their writing practices. Therefore, I suggest we pose the following questions as we prepare to write, in order to reorient our focus to an awareness that every act of writing bears both individual and collective ethical responsibility, even in the face of apparently overwhelming limitations.

Who is writing and who is the writing for? The question may, at first, seem an easy one to answer when we write as professional experts on behalf of a company or organisation and when we receive direct payment for producing our knowledge in written form for our clients. But how far might our positions as experts, and as corporate representatives involved in the production of knowledge for financial return obscure some important ethical implications of our writing practices and their impacts not only on our clients and their specific interests or investments, but also on others? Alternatively, when our writing is not directly conceived of as a product to be 'bought' by another, but as making a contribution to ongoing democratic, public debate, are we then justified in writing primarily to further our own agendas? And, if so, can we defend that approach in ethical terms, that is to say, in the face of the other? When we write from positions of relative power, how might we ensure that the power our writing represents or the knowledge it privileges does not stifle the potential for readers' responses, responses that may not accord with those our agenda has either anticipated or allowed for?

In what ways does the rhetoric we use as writers help to sustain or to modify the relations of power that obtain between us and our readers? And how far do the different discourses we employ (technical, political, economic, legal and so on) constrain our capacity to relate to our readers as moral, human beings, and to imagine the ways they may be affected by our texts? How might these constraints be overcome? How might we use rhetoric to help reshape, if necessary, those texts, or elements of those texts, which define or reaffirm corporate or institutional identity, or abstract notions of the law or economics or technology, or conventional notions of professionalism, for example? And how might we revise those texts that might at first seem to require little in the way of our direct intervention as active writer-producers, but which, for that reason precisely, repeatedly hinder or distract us from engaging with our readers and their responsive or alternative texts?

# 3
# Public Information: Up for Debate or Up for Sale? Writing via the Internet

In the developed world's age of 'communicative abundance' (Keane 1997, 2002), where technologies are increasingly sophisticated and their spatial and temporal reach through multiple channels extensive, the opportunity to communicate with others is certainly made easier.[1] What communicative abundance can enable, as a result, is for diverse, sometimes harmonising, but also frequently discordant texts and voices to be represented and to engage in discussion. These texts collectively challenge the idea of a singular or universal text of truth, reason and propriety. As a result, argues John Keane, communicative abundance has the potential to enhance the democratic project, given that it encourages us to acknowledge the world's complexity, to accept diversity, and to develop the capacity to make informed public judgements (Keane 1997, p. 7).

I argue in this chapter that professional writing, through the medium of the Internet, has the potential to play a significant role in facilitating the democratising processes (or texts) of exchange and debate in developing and presenting public information. I explore how technologies of written language and the Internet *together* may be able to facilitate reflection, debate, discussion, decisions and further enquiry about the issues, needs, values and dreams of writers and readers in the public and political domains. In this view, one of the professional writer's key responsibilities is to ensure that the agency of individuals directly or indirectly addressed in this form of writing is not obscured, suppressed or ignored, but that that agency is, as far as possible, acknowledged and engaged. This is, of course, a huge ambition today, in a discursive global media space (within and beyond the Internet), where the overwhelming volume of information flows threaten to silence less powerful individual subjects, minority groups or communities, particularly when they are more than consumers – when they are alternatively or, in addition, citizens, participants and interlocutors. As Andrew Feenberg observes, 'the fundamental problem of democracy today is quite simply the survival of agency in this increasingly technocratic universe' (Feenberg 1999, p. 101).

The kind of professional writing I'm exploring in this chapter, then, is that which generates and makes available a particular category of public information: texts in which the views, practices and judgements of readers as well as writers,[2] all citizens in a democracy, are implicated. In other words, citizens at large – or sectors of those citizens – have (whether voluntarily or not, whether acted on or not) an interest in this type of public information, precisely because it has the potential to affect or influence their daily lives, work and education, rural and urban environments, family and community activities, lifestyle and health choices, political decisions and so on. Such information is made available by public and private bodies alike, often those with considerable power: central and local governments and their agencies, business and industry, educational and cultural institutions and news media, to name a few.

In cultures of the developed world, political, bureaucratic, economic and social activities and decision-making processes can increasingly appear detached from individual human concerns and desires. This is despite the fact that technologies such as the Internet have enabled governments, corporations and organisations, in accordance with the requirements of democratic states, to make their activities and processes publicly available, ostensibly for promoting a range and diversity of comment, debate and dispute about them. It seems to me, however, that the rhetoric of much of this public information – and my understanding of rhetoric embraces the ideological relation of textual form and content to specific writers and readers – offers little incentive to readers to treat the information as public. In other words, writers all too rarely represent such information as a shared text of mutual and general concern, which readers are encouraged to reflect on, explore and take specific action on (and perhaps independently of or even contrary to the desires of the writer).

Public information is contingent insofar as it depends on *reciprocal contact between writers, texts and readers* for its meaning to be realised and for its relevance to people's lives to be recognised. Without this contact, public information floats free, a pretty package maybe, but lifeless and irrelevant.[3] Thus, it is the point or process of contact between writers and readers that enables the orientation of public information as real and meaningful. This understanding, of course, removes from information the status of an object 'out there', and questions the adequacy of such definitions as 'information is data that have been organised and communicated' (Marc Porat via Manuel Castells in Dutton 1999, p. 31). Such definitions take no account of writing and reading contexts, without which, I will argue, information is impossible to define.

It is important, therefore, to stimulate a discussion about the kinds of responsibilities that writers of public information bear and the kinds of challenges they face in terms of opening their written texts to potential readers via the Internet. While much clearly also needs to be done in terms of developing the infrastructure of the Internet, and while there are many challenges to face in relation to regulatory and legislative restrictions of its flexibility, reach and use, this chapter suggests that as professional writers we might make a specific contribution to the process of democratisation *now*, by reimagining our use of rhetoric in the context of writing public information for the virtual public domain. It suggests too that as producers of this kind of information, we have an ethical responsibility to try and connect meaningfully with a volume, range and diversity of publics previously unavailable to us.

The notion of 'e-democracy', particularly in its broadest, as well as in its more strictly political, sense is clearly relevant to the discussion. In the case of the latter in particular, much has already been written and many significant initiatives have been and continue to be developed and implemented in many parts of the world, including the USA and Australia and the UK. Here, e-democracy (or its variants – digital democracy, cyberdemocracy, virtual democracy) involves the practice of using technologies unrestricted by temporal or spatial limits to enhance and expand democratic government practices at national, state and local levels.[4] In their current manifestations such practices include using the Internet as a forum for public consultation in relation to government policy, setting up Usenet discussion groups for public debates, running deliberative polls and so on.

I am, however, keen to extend the base of the notion of e-democracy, by exploring the ways it is expressly constituted and articulated in the rhetorical processes of electronic writing and hypertext[5] practices related to public information, rather than merely in the ways it is facilitated or restricted by Internet technology itself or by government and corporate policy, regulation or restriction of that technology.[6] We are so absorbed in exploring the Internet as a technology that we often take absolutely for granted the other technology on which it also largely and crucially depends – writing.

As I see it, an active commitment to writing and organising public information for sharing with rather than selling to others is a vital precursor to the successful implementation of e-democracy. It is the texts of public information that can help to generate the context (the virtual public sphere) in which the democratic process might thrive.[7] Indeed, those texts symbolise, in one sense, the architecture and the attitude from which public engagement and debate can take their cue. Thus, before we can hope for whole groups or communities to become involved in the democratic process online, I think we need to look at public information texts available on the Internet to determine the degree to which readers, as concerned participants and as citizens, are motivated to become active in those texts' mobilisation as part of the democratising process.

## E-democracy and democratising texts

'The great promise of the Internet has long resided in its capacity to invigorate democracy by opening up the political communication process to the voices of the many rather than the few' (Coleman 2001). Stephen Coleman and others (for example, Blumler and Coleman 2001; Coleman in OECD 2003a, pp. 143–60; Griffiths 2002; Kamarck and Nye 2002) point to the Internet as the medium through which, in the twenty-first century, citizens' flagging optimism for meaningful engagement in, not to mention cynicism about, politics and political processes in liberal democracies has the potential for renewal.

As Mary Griffiths points out, however, just because 'vast numbers of people are online and because the momentum of e-government is accelerating', e-democracy will not necessarily emerge as a result (Griffiths 2002). Nevertheless, as I briefly outline below, many governments are taking e-democracy seriously indeed, by commissioning research projects, investigating the development of Internet infrastructure, and implementing online government–citizen schemes.[8] Democratic debate and discussion is happening beyond government too. As deference to those in authority wanes, so the expectation grows that political and industry leaders should consult with people on matters that affect them as consumers and as citizens (Blumler and Coleman 2001, p. 10). Organisations and corporations are therefore using Internet technologies to expand their roles as corporate citizens, and to demonstrate their accountability to and engagement with social as well as commercial capital. It seems in some instances, however, that these government and non-government initiatives are technologically rather than values driven. What is also evident in many instances is that insufficient attention is being paid to the use of written language as integral to the democratising process.

As I have suggested above, it is through electronic writing that we might exploit an opportunity to motivate interaction with citizens on matters that have an impact on all our lives and experiences. I use the term interaction loosely here: not only to indicate the facility for one-to-one, one-to-many or many-to-many communications that the Internet enables, but also for the potential for Internet users to employ the medium as an aid to individual or collective reflection and education: to access a diversity of texts and writers in relation to a given issue, to reproduce or modify texts and text genres, and to produce new, alternative texts to share with others and continue debate. This is naturally very exciting for the field of professional writing, given the possibilities it offers to extend and encourage communication as a complex network of productive, ongoing exchanges and transformations. Hundreds of thousands of individuals may be addressed through one text, but each of those individuals can, should they choose, separately and differently respond, from a range of subject positions.

So what does writing as a democratising process entail, where writing is first and foremost imagined as a process and not a product?[9] If we remember the significant democratic ideals of inclusiveness, shared power and recognition of diversity, we can make a start. This writing will surely have as one of its objectives the aim to encourage debate about the ideas, claims, or proposals it articulates, rather than simply to persuade readers to accept the writers' point of view. It therefore resists dogmatism or closure. In order to be sensitive to the responses of others, the writers of a democratising text will also be self-conscious about identifying the partiality of their own position, the context of their writing and its aims in relation to readers. In all of this, the writers thus also respect the agency of their readers – their different subject positions, their different contexts and their specific interests in the text. In this way, the text is developed as a shared one – not a commodity up for sale, but an ongoing process of representation and interpretation.

There are also particular ways in which the democratic impulse of writing can be specifically drawn out through the Internet medium, ways in which the writing of the public information we are concerned with in this chapter can be enhanced. As many commentators have pointed out, the Internet does have the potential to flatten power hierarchies, the potential to challenge power inequities between individuals or between groups, or between institutions and individuals. (As we shall see, however, it also has the potential to entrench them.) Mark Poster implies that the process of individuals reading, interpreting and then writing responses to electronic writing involves a 'construct[ing] of their identities in relation to ongoing dialogues'. He is at pains to point out that this construction of identity does not refer to a foundational subject, but rather 'connote[s] a "democratization" of subject constitution because the acts of discourse are not limited to one-way address and not constrained by the gender and ethnic traces inscribed in face-to-face communications' (Poster 2001, p. 184). Poster goes on to qualify his claim, by commenting that gender and ethnicity do not become immaterial in Internet writing exchange, and that imbalances of power are not inevitably redressed by the medium. He does, nevertheless, importantly draw attention to the Internet's potential for modifying power relations and enabling dialogue or conversation between parties. Implied in this potential for the Internet is for readers to become writers too: to review texts, to revise them to suit different contexts, different writing–reading relations, different purposes.

The Internet, as a medium of access to a mind-boggling network of information, also offers the writers of democratising texts the easy opportunity to locate and to point readers through hypertext links to related texts: texts that develop, texts that interrogate, texts that balance, texts that complicate the one in question. Such an excess of alternative texts is also, of course, a salutary reminder to both writers and to readers not to be too precious about their own texts: to recognise that their value is importantly related to and needs to be judged in light of many others.

By harnessing email, audio and video technologies, writers can also, through their electronic writing, make a concerted gesture towards involving responsive texts, different voices, other bodies and diverse activities beyond their own writing contexts, so that the democratising text may open out onto a cultural, temporal and spatial expanse outside its frame. In this way too, the writing can move outwards, establishing its place and its context in the mesh and clash that is the Internet, and exceed the restrictions imposed by the closed circuit of a singular text and a narrow perspective.

It is clear that the democratic use of language alone is not going to engender citizens' engagement. And it is also clear that the claims, attitudes and writer–reader relations established through written texts need to be reinforced and extended by other social and political practices in order that they are not dismissed as hollow rhetoric. All the same, because the use of language represents and may either reinforce or modify existing power relations, and because language itself gains increasing significance in a knowledge or information economy (see Fairclough 2001), then how the authors of texts articulate public information and how they address and relate to their prospective readers is crucial.

## Information and reciprocity

When is public information not 'simply' information?[10] When it has the potential to affect or influence our lives as citizens, service users, students, parents, workers, voters, patients, employers, taxpayers, unemployed ... in other words, very often.[11] Information is therefore a form of rhetoric – of writing – that sets up, reasserts or modifies a specific power relation between writers and readers. Porter argues the importance of our remembering this fact, when he discusses the increased corporate effort to redefine the concepts of text and writing in the Internet context, 'not as "expression" or "free speech" but as *information* – and a consequent move to define information as a product to be bought and sold' (Porter 1999). It is therefore crucial that we remember that public information is something to be shared not owned, and that, as writers, we have an ethical responsibility to make it more than simply 'available'; we have to suggest or invoke its potential for shared ownership through our writing practices.

These days, most discussions about information in the contemporary context inevitably turn to the Internet as the medium in which it is most concentrated and prolific. For example, Tim Jordan remarks that

> cyberspace represents the most extreme example of [the] general acceleration of the production and circulation of information because it is constituted out of information. Further, cyberspace is not only subject to this acceleration but one of the factors creating it ... Information moves faster, in greater quantities and in different forms in cyberspace. Most powerfully, cyberspace increases information by releasing it from material manifestations that restrict its flow and increase its price.
>
> (Jordan 1999, pp. 115–16)

However, the sheer range of material available to the public on the Internet covered by the very baggy term 'public information' is daunting: from recipes, film reviews, sex counselling contacts, news stories and advertisements, to welfare benefit schemes, medical condition diagnoses, holiday destinations, environmental impact issues, corporate mission statements and university degree programmes, to dictionary definitions, political campaign agendas and virtual museums. All the items in that list may be represented on the Internet as public information, and therefore as instances of professional writing, but clearly they are not of the same order and we need to distinguish between them. How might we usefully do that in terms of professional and public writing praxis? I think the key lies in exploring the context of writer–reader relations implied by the specific rhetorical practices in question, the kinds of actions or responses that may be motivated by the texts, and the stakes involved in particular writing–reading exchanges.

For example, if I go to the Internet to find a recipe for a quick and easy chocolate cake, I'll tap the key words into a search engine facility and then select from the list that's presented. If the site I then pull up 'looks' reputable and professional at first glance (judging by a quick overview of the visual design and text layout), I'll probably print out the recipe recommended. On the basis of the text's use of the conventional rhetorical discourses of food preparation, I'll also assume that the recipe's writer is to be trusted as far as the recipe is concerned – in other words that the ingredients, measurements and directions provided are reliable, and that I can use them to bake that cake quickly and easily. In this instance, the text has an instrumental function, and its writer is probably only of interest to me insofar as he is able to direct me to bake a passable cake quickly and easily. I depend on his status as an authoritative and experienced 'cook' to make sense of his text. Having made such judgements, I don't feel I'm taking any great risks in following the recipe (I may adapt it slightly but am unlikely to radically alter the ingredients, or weights or measures recommended). Nor do I believe that using the recipe is going to result in any significant changes to my experience, values or understandings. (I may subsequently become known to my friends and family as a great baker of chocolate cakes, but that would probably not dramatically change my life.) For my part as a reader, then, the stakes involved in this exchange with the writer of the recipe are relatively low. The same can be said from the writer's perspective. Let's take the site www.Cooks.com as the source of the chocolate cake recipe in question. First of all, the author of the site/recipe is unlikely to know that I, an individual who is hopeless at baking cakes and who is in a hurry, have accessed the site or the cake recipe, and it doesn't really matter.[12] The site www.Cooks.com is a member of an industry network which offers advertisers the opportunity to post their advertisements on the site. So the author's interest in the readers in this case is principally a commercial one: the author wants readers like me to access (though not necessarily use) the recipes on the site so that we will also (and more importantly) pay attention, as consumers, to the advertisements displayed. (In other words, the writer will also hope that someone keen on investigating chocolate cake recipes is also interested in buying a mobile phone or security for their personal computer.) The writer's responsibilities are to develop or present a range of attractive, reliable recipes so that readers will visit and revisit the site, and follow up by purchasing products advertised there. (The developer of the site also has responsibilities in relation to the integrity of products advertised, but that need not concern us here.)

A quite different order of public information, and one with which I'm primarily concerned in this chapter, is illustrated in the following scenario. The case of a corporation that presents information on its website about the impacts of its industry on the health of its current and former employees will involve far higher stakes in the writing and reading processes than the case described above. Let's take the example of Alcoa, the global corporation producing primary aluminium, fabricated aluminium, and alumina, and its Kwinana refinery in Western Australia (www.alcoa.com). Recently, the company made available a text (a media release) on the Internet, introducing an independent report, which shows that cancer risks of current and former employees are no different when compared to the overall rate of cancer in the WA population (Alcoa 2003). As (hypothetically) a former employee of the refinery who, with others, has for a long time been very worried about the impacts of emissions from the refinery on my health, I make a particular point of accessing that information, hearing that it has been made available. From my experience as a former employee I already have my opinion about the writer's (my employer's, the text's) trustworthiness and integrity, and I will make judgements about the rhetoric through which this information is produced to either confirm or modify that opinion. Still retaining some sense of my identity as a former employee of Alcoa and having friends who still work there, I am also looking to see how my colleagues and I are interpellated by the text: are we acknowledged as valued participants in its potential for meaning-making? Are our concerns taken seriously? What opportunities does the text give us to transform the information: to interpret it in ways that will allow us to reflect on and perhaps revise or clarify or confirm our understandings, or to seek further related information, or to respond to the text's producers directly or indirectly? The writer too has considerable investments in the information. Presumably she is relieved to have a report confirm that the risks of cancer are not heightened by working for Alcoa and is keen to communicate that message. However, having knowledge of the employees' and the community's long-held beliefs and fears about the health issues, and aware of having to sustain goodwill and cooperation with employees and community for the longer term, she is also aware of her responsibility to produce this 'news' sensitively and not to suggest that it necessarily signals the end of the story (or the various participants' individual stories).

In the second example above, just one of an infinite number of public information writing and reading exchanges that may take place via the Internet, the significance of the process of imagining emerges. Of course, in the context of writing of public information for the Internet, we are often having to imagine generalised rather than particularised readers. Also, we are often not able to engage our readers in immediate dialogue in order to know more about their individual perspectives, their histories or the contexts of their relationships. Nevertheless, if we accept the value of the concept of asymmetrical reciprocity, and the differential relations of power, experience, and the individual and social contexts it assumes, we can more readily imagine the diversity of our potential readers, not to mention the challenges to democratise our texts that face us as writers.

In English grammar, the word 'information' is described as an abstract noun, one that has no referent in the concrete world. And indeed, it is through the context of its relation between writers and readers that information acquires its tangibility. It is the readers' process of accessing, interpreting and somehow responding to written language produced as information that makes the writers' textual production meaningful. In other words, information only becomes 'material' – that is, it comes to matter – through some level of *reciprocal contact* between writer[13] (and the institutions, groups, industries or interests they may represent) and reader.[14] The level and kind of that contact obviously depends, as the above examples show, on the particular motivations of writers and readers, and on what kind of information is in question or how it's going to be used. Of course, in many instances of developing and presenting public information, writers might need to establish only minimal reciprocal contact with readers, as in the case of the cake recipe. In such cases the writers may be principally concerned with issues of visual and linguistic appeal and appropriateness – with issues of clarity, style and presentation – so that readers may access and use or buy the information for their own purposes. By contrast, increased potential for reciprocal contact will presumably be required, and a sense of the writer's perspectives on the information and on its particular relation to and impact on its readers, when a proposal for amending equal opportunity policies in public service employment are outlined by a government minister, or environmental pollution levels in a specific location are explained by a CEO, or when community adult education initiatives are proposed by a local council and so on.

It is the contexts in which all the above kinds of information are situated and the ways particular information is intended to be or is actually accessed, interpreted and used by various readers that will obviously be what makes it matter, what makes it meaningful, beyond the merely statistical, factual or instructional, for example. For the Internet, this issue of context becomes particularly important, as the medium incorporates, juxtaposes and combines so many and such divergent topical genres: science, entertainment, art, history, politics, education, health, sport, pornography, real estate, finance, literature. It also has the potential to harness elements from a range of media genres – text, film, sound and image – into its own interactive representations. However, this multiply-genred Internet (see Green 2000) doesn't have the history or the formal boundaries that conventionally help guide producers or writers in the process and practice of relating to others, to publics. As a result, the digital space creates new ethical pressures or demands on those who produce electronic texts as public information designed for forging reciprocal contact with others.

In Castells's definition of information quoted earlier in the chapter, the significance of the writer–reader relation, a relation that is central to the writing and reading of public information, is elided. What is also elided, and what the paragraphs above have suggested as crucial, is the writer's responsibility to imagine connections with readers in the process of writing public information. If information is represented as a given product or commodity 'out there', then where is the potential for the reader's reciprocal engagement with its text?

## Readers as participants rather than consumers

Information represented essentially as a commodity is presumably intended only to be considered in terms of whether readers want to buy or consume it, or not, rather than, for example, to reflect on or interrogate its meaning and relevance to themselves, their families or their communities, or to consider how they might adapt or modify it for their own purposes. When the exchange of information is reduced to a commercial transaction, with a focus on commodity, the effects and impacts of information on readers is obscured and the responsibility of writers to readers as citizens is overlooked.

As writers of public information for posting in the digital space, we are bound to ask ourselves who we are writing to and what the purpose and aims of our writing are. And as the Internet is increasingly used as a space for doing business, for buying and selling commodities, it becomes more difficult, but consequently even more important, to remember that readers are not only or always consumers. Lelia Green (2000) raises the provocative question about whether we should see the Internet audience as genred. In the context of the writing and reading of public information on the Internet, I would suggest that the best we can do as writers is to construct our imagined readers as participants.

As I see it, the subject position of a participant has three especially important implications for the writer's ethical responsibilities, for writing as a democratising process, and for power relations and identity. Firstly, a participant implies a subject whose identity is explicitly relational, and who takes a part or shares in an activity with others – so the dynamic and reciprocal relation between writer and reader is highlighted. Much writing theory and practice in recent years has seen a shift towards focusing on the needs of the readers rather than those of the writers. Generally, though, this concentration on understanding readers has served mostly to allow writers to more effectively achieve their own objectives, and ignores the ethical implications of such an approach. In the Internet environment, where conventional relations of power and hierarchy are disrupted this tactic is ripe for reconsideration. When, as writers, we acknowledge, through the form and content of our texts, the active part the readers have to play in making those texts meaningful and productive, then we can more readily acknowledge our texts as public texts, and our writing as part of the democratic process of power sharing. It seems that this was at least part of the motive for Australian journalist, Margo Kingston, to begin her now hugely popular Webdiary (Kingston 2004) as part of the newspaper, the *Sydney Morning Herald*'s online presence. In the Webdiary Charter, devised in 2001, Kingston explains that 'that there is a vacuum of original, genuine, passionate and accessible debate on the great political, economic and social issues of our time in the mainstream media, despite the desire of thinking Australians in all age groups to read and participate in such debates'. The Webdiary has enabled newspaper readers to become writers as well.

Secondly, to conceive of readers as participants is not to preclude the possibility for them to be simultaneously *other* than, or *additional* to, their identities as participants – workers, teenagers, activists, women,

men and so on. Porter argues that in a postmodern rhetorical ethics 'distinct identities must be recognised', and readers not universalised or homogenised (Porter 1998, p. 152). However, the writer of public information for the Internet is not necessarily always able to predict those distinct identities, and focusing on one may mean that others are marginalised or excluded. This might well result in writing–reading relations perpetuating already existing imbalances of power, for example, in terms of social and professional, ethnic or religious status. So, if instead writers focus on the readers' participatory role as primary, then writers can also focus on the promise for those readers to share power, and for the possibility of the unpredictable manner of their engagement and response. Beverly Bickel (2003), for example, offers a fascinating account of the way in which the Revolutionary Association of the Women of Afghanistan, through its Internet presence (www.RAWA.org), established in 1997 (twenty years after the organisation itself was founded by a group of Afghan women intellectuals), has promoted the roles of its users as participants in their struggles for democracy and women's rights. The website, which has become RAWA's 'office', is now a global forum for debate and engagement through a range of genres and functions (archives, petitions, reports, statements, discussions, videos, narratives, poetry, email exchange, an unedited guest book).[15] Bickel summarises beautifully, I think, the way participation works here through and alongside difference:

> With Afghan women designing and broadcasting their oppositional message in the face of nearly complete lack of public access, brutal physical and intellectual repression, and a powerful contending wartime discourse, their Net-amplified voices have played a significant role in teaching, mentoring and inspiring visitors from around the globe and in building an international network capable of supporting the creation of an alternative reality for Afghan women and people we may never completely know.

> (Bickel 2003)

Finally, the notion of participants also imposes no restrictions on the potential for difference of the participating subject from the writer. The participant's ambiguity or even anonymity – in terms of freedom from the constraints imposed by association with particular social, economic, sexual, professional, generational, ethnic or religious identities – also means that the writer needs to be acutely sympathetic to the potential range and diversity of readers. In contrast to the liberating possibilities envisaged by this view, David Holmes, considering the notion of interactivity in relation to the Internet space, sees the lack of mutual recognition between writer and reader as a potential threat. Without the 'socially shared meanings' that mutual recognition makes possible, writers and readers cannot, according to Holmes, acknowledge the contexts of production (that is, the writer cannot be sensitive to the reader's context of interpretation of the information and the reader cannot imagine the writer's context of preparing and writing the information). As a result, argues Holmes, 'a worldly connection can be made with unknown others, while no responsibility has to be taken for its consequences' (Holmes 1997, p. 37). While I acknowledge Holmes's concerns, I think the lack of recognition between writers and readers presents exciting, if daunting, opportunities for electronic writing. We are going to have to learn to write differently, aware of our added ethical responsibilities for imagining the engagement of (often) unknown and (always) diverse readers.

The section below begins this process by examining a few sample texts of public information available on the Internet, to highlight the ways in which we might reconfigure our role as writers genuinely committed to the democratic project I have outlined.

## E-democracy, government and public information

In this section I look at some examples of the representation of selected information from a range of sources. The particular examples have been chosen because they are likely to be readily identifiable by many of this book's readers as having some relevance to their own lives as public information. Nevertheless, the specific points I make in my readings of the sample texts are also intended to have a bearing on the electronic writing and reading practices relating to e-democracy and information more broadly: beyond the political sphere and context to non-government, corporate, academic and cultural arenas.

My starting point, therefore, is the home pages of heads of national government from the USA and Australia,[16] and I also draw on selected information from other government, industry and community sites as a means of comparison. In so doing, I hope to show that the selection, organisation, and articulation of certain kinds of information as public can serve rhetorically either to extend or inhibit the processes of e-democracy.

In Australia and the USA, as in other countries around the world, the Internet is becoming the one-stop shop for the public to access government services and commerce.[17] These are significant points of contact with government, and have been developed to a fairly sophisticated extent. Nevertheless, they do not serve, nor are they intended to serve, the purpose of extending e-democracy.

E-democracy government initiatives are a more recent phenomenon. In several countries many e-democracy schemes – involving citizens in online policy consultation or setting up interactive forums for public debate on an issue, for example – are still at the level of the discussion paper, trial or the testing out of new technologies and their usability or viability as facilitators of the democratic process.[18] However, if they are genuine commitments, and presumably they are since they involve ambitious and significant commitments of intellectual, ideological and technological energy, as well as taxpayers' great expense, then surely those in power have an obligation to ensure that a democratic rhetoric constructs government communication of related public information at *all* levels, and not simply in those areas where these approaches are being developed. However, for the moment at least, ethical and rhetorical approaches to developing e-democracy through the use of text seem to be underdeveloped at the highest level: the home pages of the political leaders of the USA and Australia. It is through an analysis of key features of the websites of US President George W. Bush and of Australian Prime Minister John Howard that I hope to support that claim.

The (subtext of) consumerist and marketing discourses that, many would argue, properly belong in the representation of information on government services and government business activities to readers also pervade those areas where they are, I contend, misplaced. Given that they are the figureheads of national liberal democratic institutions, the representative Internet texts of George W. Bush and John Howard might reasonably be expected to articulate a democratising rhetoric. I certainly recognise that part of the function of these sites must be to promote the capabilities and strengths of the leaders of the representative democracies they describe. At the same time, I also believe that this needs to be finely balanced by an awareness of the responsibilities to motivate participation and to share debate with potential readers– citizens. In other words, the information presented on these leadership pages could effectively serve as an educative contribution to the democratising process itself.

However, some readers would still claim that these websites *legitimately* constitute a form of political advertising. In that case, even if it is understood that both sites indeed properly function to 'sell' their political leaders, then those leaders are presumably being promoted to the citizenry as models: as symbolic and practical exemplars of democratic government. I would argue that they fail in this political advertising function too, as the self-referentiality and exclusive self-aggrandisement they perform strike me as contradicting the very spirit and drive of democracy (even if of the representative rather than participatory kind).

Writing from a marketing management perspective, Lars Thøger Christensen (1997) argues that, despite the fact that much discussion about the ways in which new media technologies have opened up the possibility for organisations to engage in two-way communication with their markets, 'the dialogue organized by marketing often closes in on itself'. He thus suggests that the dialogues that many organisations establish with their markets can be described as 'auto-communication, that is, self-referential communication through which the organization recognizes and confirms its own images, values and assumptions; in short, its own culture' (Christensen 1997, p. 199). Following Yuri Lotman, Christensen also points out that 'auto-communication takes place *whenever* the selfperception of a sender ... is being enhanced or transformed (as opposed to informed) by the sender's own message' (Christensen 1997, p. 207). In my view, it is a form of auto-communication that (inappropriately here) constitutes the Bush and Howard home pages.

This consumerist approach to representing democratic leadership is, I think usefully related to Thomas Meyer's (2002) highly persuasive exposition of the 'colonization' of contemporary democratic politics by media. Meyer argues that the powerful and pervasive logic of the mass media in the West is 'densely interwoven with its economic structure' (2002, p. 35) and, concentrated on the dissemination of stage-managed, newsworthy media events, politics are governed by an 'uncompromising presentism inherent in the media's production time' (2002, p. 46). This overbearing logic has reduced democratic politics and its processes (which operate through a quite different logic and on incompatible, far more extensive timeframes) to 'mediacracy'.

> On democracy's behalf, mediacracy thus invokes the democratic principles that information should be widely available and participation as extensive as possible. As an unintended side-effect of its democratic bias, it intensifies pressures for a politics of image-making even in the political system. But that is what makes it increasingly difficult for the vast majority, in whose name all this is done, to monitor and influence political events in an informed, competent way.
>
> (Meyer 2002, pp. 55–6)

Influenced to the extent that they have their own website representations designed, written and managed according to the logic of the
commercial mass media and its consumerist orientation, the political
leaders of the USA and Australia miss the opportunity to engage their
citizens in informed democratic exchange. Each of the sites appears to
draw on and combine a range of genres and discourse 'fragments'
(see McGee 1990): journalism – current affairs, documentary and feature
or lifestyle magazine writing; (education in) politics, government and
political history; and biography. The American site in particular also
makes extensive use of a range of media: audio, photography and video.
Karen Stanworth's claim for the significance of a visual rhetoric to 'presidential rituals' from George Washington to George W. Bush is certainly
reflected here: 'to be effective President Bush has to be seen and not just
heard' (Stanworth 2002, pp. 111–12).

Given that the visual component of both sites analysed is significant,
my critique therefore also draws loosely on Sonja K. Foss's approach to
studying visual imagery from a rhetorical perspective. This approach is
concerned with the influence and impacts of images on readers and how
these can result in interpretations and evaluations extending beyond
those based on specifically aesthetic or semiotic considerations (see Foss
1994). Foss's expressed focus on the *function* of visual imagery rather
than on its producers' *intentions* (and their designed purpose) is also
important (1994, pp. 215–16). In the same way that my insistence on
the writer's practice of imagining the other aims to do, Foss's emphasis
on interpretive and evaluative processes properly, I think, shifts attention to the responding readers and, potentially, to ethical considerations
of rhetorical practice.[19]

On a superficial level both the sites offer a cornucopia of genred and
discursively various information from which the readers can select
and with which they can engage. The written and visual rhetoric provided on the sites might at first glance be seen as functioning to offer
readers (in part constructed in the role of quasi-students of democracy)
a range of pathways into variously mediated insights into the history,
structure, operations and current interests of government, together with
a sense of their relationship to that space as citizens and space for deliberation within it. However, it seems to me that the various written texts
presented work emphatically to limit the potential for reciprocal
contact. Because of their positioning of readers as consumers, their naturalising of the process of communicating information to others, and
their largely self-referential functions, both the visual and written
texts restrict the educative promise or the possibility for participant

engagement or interaction. Keith V. Erickson argues along similar lines, in his discussion of photo-opportunity performances by US presidents in recent decades. He suggests that US presidential rhetoric's 'visual turn', represents 'performance fragments', which 'practice exclusionary politics inasmuch as they relegate citizens to the status of spectator, and thereby blunt the dialectical process upon which democratic discourse depends' (Erickson 2000, p. 141). As well, and as my critique aims to show, the various genres, discourses and the range of media harnessed by the government websites to variously represent their information demonstrably work to control and confine rather than extend the scope (conceptual, experiential, temporal and spatial) of options for participants' engagement and interpretation.

Just before embarking on my analysis of the American site, I should remind readers that, as a non-US citizen, I am interpreting Bush's text as an outsider, a virtual, non-invited guest. (This is a little ironic, of course, given popular notions of the Internet as borderless space.) Quite clearly, it is American citizens who are rhetorically addressed by the site; its texts are oriented towards them, or rather to an apparently assumed sense of what it means to be American. As a consequence, my reading of the site's consumerist exclusivity is heightened, positioned as I am by its rhetoric as excessively other!

The US Federal Government's presidential portal, 'The White House' (www.whitehouse.gov) is the gateway to George W. Bush's home page (http://www.whitehouse.gov/president/) (see Figure 3.1).[20] The site is, superficially at least, quite different from its Australian counterpart. It is clearly more sophisticated and certainly far more a visual postmodern collage in its harnessing of Internet technology and its potential for incorporating a range of media – photography, video and audio as well as text – in addition to making greater use (technically, that is) of its interactive facilities. However, it seems to me that the potential for exploiting the capacity of this diversity of media to encourage and enhance democratic engagement and citizens' active involvement in the democratic process is thrown off balance and thus compromised by the intensively self-referential impulse of the site.

The layout of the page is clean (if busy) and symmetrical: a large central column, whose focal point, a photo image,[21] is framed by two narrower columns carrying text and photo images. The colours of the national flag, blue, red and white, dominate text and image. The website banner, 'The White House', tops the page and to the left of it is an image of the president's seal. The page is headed 'President George W. Bush' and below it, slightly to its right, in a different font and larger

*Figure 3.1* President George W. Bush's home page (www.whitehouse.gov/president/)

point size is centred 'Oval Office'. It is the imposing visual and symbolic authority of this government space together with its juxtaposition with (and apparent containment of) the figure and role of the president[22] that dominate the page. The text headers also serve to highlight the large central photo: the president seated behind his desk in the Oval Office in conversation with three of his speechwriters.[23] The scene is set up as though *not* set up: the president and his aides are apparently unaware that readers are glimpsing a moment of their day. The president is face on; his advisers are seated, in relatively casual poses, to the sides of his desk. Their attention appears to be focused on the president, who is talking with them. All the men are dressed in suits. The sunlight flooding through the window behind the president also serves to highlight his central position in the photo, and to put in relief the American and presidential flags to either side of his seat. The shot exposes the space as both home or haven and business office: the heavy drapes at the windows, the antique furniture, the sculptures and paintings, the deep carpet (whose lines radiate towards the president's desk) together represent a comfortable and privileged, if imposing, setting for serious work in progress. The sense of tradition and history, of calm, reason, security and order that the image also exudes is borne out and re-echoed by the other textual features that make up the page. As Erickson explains, 'political need typically motivates presidents to signal visually: (1) consubstantiality with the mythic presidency; (2) ideological authority, power and control; and (3) active leadership' (Erickson 2000, p. 142).

This fly-on-the-wall viewpoint on the Oval Office accorded to the reader of this image may be interpreted initially as reflecting the widespread cultural turn to public disclosure, to making accessible to citizens and transparent for them the processes of democratic government. Paradoxically, however, readers (Americans and non-Americans alike) do not occupy an empowered position of surveillance; our roles are clearly set up as respectfully distant observers rather than as participants; we are excluded from the privileged clique of intense and seemingly high-level discussion. And the positions of the photographic subjects certainly allows no 'reciprocity of perspectives', so that, as we will see with the textual features of the page, the relation between writers and readers cannot (even visually) be evoked as 'dialogically enriching' (Gardiner 1999, p. 61).[24]

Underneath the central image, the text headed 'President Bush's Policies in Focus' summarises the key themes of the 2004 State of the Union Address. (This text reappears daily.)

---

President Bush's Policies in Focus
In his 2004 State of the Union Address, President Bush discussed the serious challenges facing our Nation and the steps we must take to make America a more secure, more prosperous, and more hopeful country. The President laid out ambitious goals for the future, behind which all Americans can unite, and urged the Nation to move forward with the work that still needs to be done this year:

- Making America Safer with Decisive Action to Win the War on Terror
- Keeping America on Track for a More Prosperous Future
- Strengthening Health Care for Millions of Americans
- Building a Better and More Compassionate America for All

---

The text presents the president as proactive and forward-looking. In addition, as the grammatical subject of each sentence, his centrality is foregrounded and re-echoes his position in the image above. Although 'we' do feature in the paragraph as integral to the process of facing the country's challenges, that first-person plural pronoun is subsequently morphed into the third person ('the Nation', 'all Americans'), implored to follow the president's lead in implementing initiatives. The pragmatic, rational discourses of a 'just' war and security, of wealth and the economy comprise the bullet-pointed list of work that lies ahead. In each of the first three points 'America' and 'Americans' are depicted and insistently repeated as unified and coherent representations of a stable national identity. Interestingly, and by contrast, the final point employs a less direct, relatively more daunting task – 'Building a Better and More Compassionate America for All'. This last statement (to me, at least) suggests America as difference or difference in the making, and it also suggests the pluralism and diversity celebrated by democracy. It is the one statement on the page that does so.

Below this text is the box for 'Latest headlines', in which, each day, newsworthy (president-centred) items feature. The left-hand column of the page (which duplicates that on the White House home page) is made up of hypertext links relating to matters of current national interest and presidential office organisation and activity (under the headings 'Issues', 'News', 'Appointments', 'Offices', 'Major Speeches', 'Photo Essays').

It is the right-hand column of hypertext links, with its focus on matters relating to American presidential politics past and present that has the potential to encourage readers to take up their participatory roles as student-citizens. The column resembles the features section of a newspaper or magazine, though it consists of largely expository language – consistent with the function of disclosure. The first link is to the 'Presidential Biography', previewed as follows: 'George W. Bush is the 43rd President of the United States and was formerly the 46th Governor of the State of Texas'. This text is set alongside an image of Bush – side view, speaking on the phone. The rhetoric thus both offers readers information on the president's political genealogy and reconfirms his position of established authority connoted by the page's central image.

The next link is to the 'Oval Office Video Tour', where readers are individually invited to 'join George W. Bush as he takes you on a personal tour of the Oval Office'. Here the notion of citizens' opportunity to scrutinise (metaphorically) the architecture of government through a virtual exploration of one of its key architectural symbols is extended. As well, the rhetoric of pseudo-intimacy ('as he takes you on a personal tour') is promised by the invitation to view the video. The image accompanying this text is of the president at his Oval Office desk, reading glasses on and pen in hand, his gaze fixed off to the left of the frame.[25]

The pressures of the presidential office thus represented imply the privilege afforded readers granted the chance to 'enter' (vicariously) the busy workspace of government.

'President Bush's Cabinet' introduces the following link: 'One of the principal purposes of the Cabinet is to advise the President on any subject he may require relating to the duties of their respective offices.' Information on senior government positions and on their function in terms of their support of the key presidential role is presented in conjunction with an image of the president making a public address, flanked by two of his staff apparently applauding his words.

The next two links return to the twin themes of tradition and history, with the 'President's Hall' link (to a page detailing the biographies of former US presidents) accompanied by a portrait of Abraham Lincoln. A piece of infotainment trivia lightens the mood: 'President John Adams and President Thomas Jefferson died on the same day, July 4, 1826 – exactly 50 years after the signing of the Declaration of Independence.' The 'Oval Office History' link is supported by an image of the president pointing out a feature of the Oval Office to a visitor. The text reasserts the office as the hub of presidential process: 'the Oval Office is the president's formal workspace, where he confers with heads of state, diplomats, his staff, and other dignitaries'.

Next is the 'Military Office', described as 'over the years, [having] adapted to the evolving role of the President in American society, providing the highest quality service to meet the requirements of the Commander-in-Chief'. The language describing this office, another represented as oriented to the needs of the president, remains rather abstract (as 'service' provider), perhaps as a strategy to sustain some of the page's key discourses of order, control and stability. The role of the president as supreme authority, here of the military, is nevertheless underscored. An image of the president's helicopter, Marine One, hovering before the White House concentrates and visually frames notions of power and protection (even if this photo is captioned as depicting 'President George W. Bush arriv[ing] aboard Marine One for a tee-ball game on the South Lawn'!).

In the last item in this column, readers are invited to 'go to "Ask the White House" – an online interactive forum where you can submit questions to White House officials or read previous discussions'. Every couple of days a different White House official responds to questions submitted by members of the public. The forum is not truly interactive, but does follow a question-and-answer format. Readers can also suggest officials they would like to be involved in the forum.

So, what are the implications of Bush's site: what are its potential impacts and are they legitimate or ethical? As mentioned above, the site appears to have the trappings of the postmodern collage – the juxta-posing of different media, the merging of the highbrow with the popu-lar, the fragmentary, snapshot approach to presenting stories, histories and news. Nevertheless, this multiplicity of media and genre is not complemented by a comparable range of rhetorical positions. Rather, the site has the effect of underscoring the author function, which, as Nancy Kaplan points out, Michel Foucault (1984) would regard as a restriction on readers' possibilities for rewriting texts, and what she her-self defines as obstructing politics from becoming politexts (Kaplan 1995). As a consequence, the role of readers as participants whose involvement as citizens is depended upon for democratic processes to develop and thrive is also evaded. All this, despite one of Bush's com-mitments (according to his biography, available through a hypertext link) since taking up office being described as 'ushering in a responsi-bility era in America' and as calling on all Americans to be *'citizens, not spectators; citizens, not subjects'* (my italics). In light of the reading above, these comments appear disingenuous.

We see, in the American example, that information about government is not explicitly introduced to the readers by the president (as we shall see that it is in the case of John Howard). Instead, the material stands for, *is* government. So what is government in these representations? In its rhetorical style it surely resembles the (nightmarish) aspect of the post-modern hall of mirrors, where images are relentlessly thrown back and forth on themselves. Rather than using language and other media tech-nologies in an attempt to extend the zone of information's contact with and potential for transformation by others, the writers appear to turn the texts inwards, so that they echo and re-echo themselves, in a move that serves to exclude readers as participants and positions them instead as voyeuristic consumers. This self-referentiality is also ethically problem-atic, particularly when we remember the responsibilities of the writer to imagine ways in which public information is a shared process of mutual enrichment, revision and enlarged understanding. With such an over-bearing multimedia bombardment of writer-centred texts rather than ones seeking to establish reciprocal contact (multimedia does not mean multi-faceted or multi-perspectival here), the opportunities for readers to engage as interlocutors, to position themselves as other than consumers of government self-promotion are certainly squeezed.

As an Australian citizen, my position vis-à-vis the Australian prime ministerial site (www.pm.gov.au) is necessarily different, although it

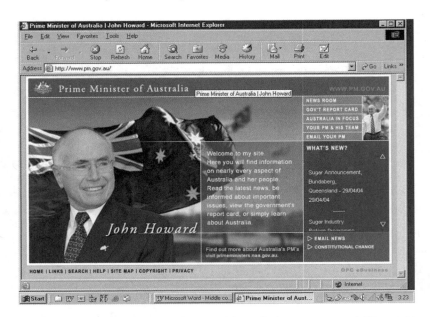

*Figure 3.2*   John Howard, Prime Minister of Australia (www.pm.gov.au) (Copyright Commonwealth of Australia reproduced by permission)

seems to me that the Australian site has its own distinctive rhetorical orientation, one surely connected to its relatively smaller role on the world stage (see Figure 3.2). John Howard's site, indeed it is John Howard himself, appears to be directly addressing, simultaneously, virtual visitors or tourists (non-Australians) and novice Australian citizens, all of whom, by using the site, might usefully learn something about Australia and Australian government.[26] (Howard's site is as much his Liberal government's view of Australia as it is a site depicting the prime minister's role and function.)[27] The site's individualised rhetoric is also, compared with its American counterpart, relatively colloquial.

The page's banner consists of the national coat of arms and the heading 'The Prime Minister of Australia'; to the far right is the website address. The focal point of the page is a colour, head-and-shoulders near frontal shot of the prime minister, positioned to the left of the screen, superimposed on a background of a breeze-filled national flag. The image is sufficiently sharp to allow the texture and fold of the Australian flag to be clearly depicted against a bright blue sky. Various other shades of blue combine with small chunks of text to make up a generally simple, open and uncluttered page. (Howard's head is centred on the Union Jack section of the flag, symbolising his sense of Australia's significant historical and constitutional ties with Britain.) The flag as iconic national symbol is thus suggested as coterminous with the head of government in a similarly iconic role. John Howard is formally dressed in jacket and tie, though this formality is tempered by his broad smile as he looks off to the right. In italicised font, 'John Howard' appears over the lower right side of the portrait. This central image of Howard is countered by the much smaller one that sits at the right-hand corner of the page: a snapshot of a spontaneously smiling prime minister, in shirt sleeves and tie, his left arm raised as in an enthusiastic wave to onlookers. The prime minister thus here functions as the more casual, sociable and interpersonal face of government.

Thus the visual images, focusing on Howard as individual personality, and devoid of the trappings of prime ministerial office, suggest a broadly up-front, direct, and among-the-people face of government. However, the page's central, introductory text, sitting alongside the prime minister's main image, while its tone is courteous and restrained, suggests a different, almost contradictory relationship between writers and readers:

> Welcome to my site. Here you will find information on nearly every aspect of Australia and her people. Read the latest news, be informed about important issues, view the government's report card, or simply learn about Australia.

Readers are very briefly, if genially, addressed in the second person as service users or consumers entering the virtual space. Interestingly, these 'you' are also implicitly positioned either as visitors-cum-foreigners (non-Australians) or as Australian novices in national and government affairs. The distinct (power) positions of writer and readers are thus firmly established. The site – which is explicitly stated as belonging to Howard ('my site') – is explained as a source of national information, current affairs and details on government achievements, which readers are encouraged to draw from freely. (The hypertext links to the right and at the bottom of the screen are broadly signalled through this introduction.) However, despite the use of mostly active verbs to suggest the range of activities available to readers ('you will find', 'read', view', 'learn about'), the information offered is presented as a *fait accompli*, available for scrutiny rather than for debate. For example, the offer to 'view' (rather than 'evaluate', for example) the government's report card (a catalogue of its achievements in office) suggests the writer's desired orientation of the readers to the material (though of course not an orientation obliged by such word use). Similarly, reference to 'the latest news' evokes a sense of the immediacy and contemporaneity of events represented on the site. However, the now-ness of the news is a more accurate reference to its disintermediation than to its temporality: on closer inspection, much of the 'news', as on Bush's site, apart from links to transcripts of various media interviews, consists of government-generated information of the government's perspective on the government's activities. Thus, readers are apparently interpellated as visitors-foreigners and as consumers trained to read from a singular perspective, rather than as agents who are also participants, motivated to use the available material in order to educate and develop their capacities as citizens in a shared democracy.

The text box at the upper right of the screen, carries the hypertext links 'News Room', 'Gov't Report Card', 'Australia in Focus', 'Your PM and his Team' and 'Email your PM'. The news room links to transcripts and audios of speeches, media releases, media interviews and conferences, photos and so on. The government report card, in a discursive inversion of conventionally understood power positions, hints at the accountability of government to citizens. (However, the report card itself presents the government's achievements as, rhetorically speaking, all grade As, and makes no gesture to encourage the readers' responsive evaluations.) 'Australia in Focus' offers facts and statistics about Australia, about its national symbols, its constitution and government and a section 'for kids'. The hypertexts 'Your PM and his Team' and 'Email your PM' pick up again the personalised rhetoric of direct address. The invitation to email John Howard, with its connotation of interactive dialogue, is a little misleading. 'After your message is read, an electronic acknowledgment will be sent to you. There will be no further electronic response from the Prime Minister' (though writers are informed that they may receive correspondence from the relevant office by post). The instructional, impersonal tone here (the question of who will read and who will respond to an email is evaded by the use of the passive voice) jars with the direct call to readers to correspond.

As a brief aside, it is worth mentioning that this representation of Howard's engagement with readers on the prime ministerial site makes an interesting contrast with that on his local constituency site – where he is John Howard, Member of Parliament (www.johnhowardmp.com). As his role shifts, so predictably does his sense of his readership, who now become 'residents', families', 'small businesses', the local 'community'. The tone of the text on this site, a generic blend of letter and personal speech, is markedly warmer, more intimate:

> Welcome to my site and thank you for visiting.
> As the Federal Minister for Bennelong it is important for me to keep in touch with local residents in many ways.
> This website provides a valuable opportunity for me to listen to local residents so that I can deliver for Bennelong families and small businesses.
> Please take the time to complete my Bennelong Community Survey or send me a message with your views.
> I hope you find your visit to my site interesting and informative.
> Regards
>
> John Howard
> PS: I can otherwise be contacted at my electorate office: [contact details supplied].

Howard is now emphatically positioned as a subject for whom keeping in contact with others is described as 'important', a subject who is a responsive listener, and whose constituents' views are explicitly invited (via email correspondence, by completion of a community survey, or through contact with the electorate office).[28] In this text, the role of the readers as consumers of information or as service users is played down, and their roles as citizens, who have a part to play in Howard's decisions about and role in shaping their community, is highlighted. Notably, however, his role as provider of services to customers remains, as the rhetoric suggests: 'This website provides a valuable opportunity for me to listen to local residents *so that I can deliver* for Bennelong families and small businesses' (italics added). In this articulation, the role of citizens as participants is obviated, while the intransitive use of the verb 'deliver' leaves the focus of Howard's commitment ambiguous.

The form and content of both Bush and Howard's sites takes the important contextualising process for granted, with the apparent intention of naturalising the visual and written texts, naturalising the information as true or given, and thereby naturalising the distance between writer and readers.[29] As a result, readers are bound to infer their assumed relation to and potential use of the site's material from the rhetorical style in which they are interpellated as readers, and from the way in which the material is presented. For readers who accept their designated positions and proposed orientation towards the material (usually because it conforms to their own sense of those), further investigation of the information presented may well pose no obstacles. However, for readers who feel their agency and potential as participants is compromised or elided by the site's form and content, there may well be a sense of disaffection with or distrust of the textual material and the institutions it represents. As professional writers involved in the development of potentially democratising texts, we need to take account of all these alternative readers and not focus our attention only on those willing to subscribe to our point of view.

## Public information: up for debate

Having looked at two of the less inspiring examples of democratising rhetoric available on the Internet, I'd now like to turn to more promising instances of electronic writing practices. Each suggests just a few of the many possibilities for developing texts that may resonate valuably and productively with reader participants in the sharing of public information.

Many commentators have noted the advances made internationally in e-democracy by local government entities (particularly when compared with those by national governments). The advances explored have generally been in terms of their using of Internet technology to facilitate debate, consultation and discussion with citizens as participants. As well, comment has been passed on the community-oriented and responsive approaches of local government initiatives. In addition, however, much can also be learned from the ways in which these sites imagine their rhetorical relation to their readers.[30]

For example, Camden Council, at http://www.camden.gov.uk/ccm/portal/ – a British local government site – like many local government sites around the world, has made significant inroads into developing its e-democracy potential. Interestingly, while it does not have the appearance on first glance of advanced technical interactivity, as the North American Federal Government leader's site certainly does, its interactive potential, in the sense of the term outlined earlier, is far greater. The Camden Council home page, which essentially serves as a portal to a range of council services, activities and information – for example, main sections consist of 'Council and democracy', 'Social care and health', 'News', 'Complaints and suggestions', 'Camden talks – get involved', and so on – balances the rhetoric of consumerism and service provision with that of democracy and citizen engagement and involvement.[31] There is a sense, then, in which the portal itself, the gateway to services, events, activities and information, composes the rhetorical face or identity of Camden Council; an identity dependent on its orientation to others for its meaning. And that orientation means that readers can access the information and move outwards, beyond the site: by finding out how to get involved in scrutinising council activities, or how to have a say in order to become involved in local decision-making processes. By contrast, as the discussion about the prime ministerial and presidential sites has shown, the identities of the Australian and US governments are overpoweringly self-referential, focusing on self-image rather than imagining their relations to readers as potential participants.

A couple of hypertext links from the Camden Council home page are worth remarking on briefly. First of all, the invitation to make 'Complaints and suggestions' struck me almost as a joke, so rare is it to come across (in either government or non-government spheres) an invitation to readers to identify cracks in organisational armour, to intervene and comment on areas for improvement.[32] Next, the hypertext link for 'Council and democracy' is another rare sighting.[33] I have not seen 'democracy' mentioned on either the US or the Australian government sites. (In fact, on one occasion I keyed 'democracy' into the search facility on John Howard's site. The Netscape notice appeared, informing me that 'an illegal operation' had been performed and the site was promptly shut down.) On the Camden site 'Council and democracy' leads to several other links, including descriptions of councillors' roles and responsibilities, council meeting agendas, live webcasts of council meetings, and detailed descriptions of the different channels readers might access to put forward their views. A sense of the council's potential vitality and vibrancy as dependent on participation in a wide range of possible activities implies not only the central importance of participants' agency but recognises the value of and their responsibility for contribution to the democratic process.

I suggested above that a significant failure of the Howard and Bush sites was the naturalising of their identities (and those of the institution or organisation they represent) and of the process of communicating with would-be citizen-participants. An alternative to that approach is demonstrated by the US-based Community Arts Network (http://www.communityarts.net/). Of course, the function of this site cannot be compared to that of the government sites nor does it have the same range of competing interests, activities, responsibilities or citizens to address. Nevertheless, I do think that the national government leadership sites could usefully reconsider their role as writers of public information and as role models for democratic engagement in light of Community Arts Network's ethical and imaginative rhetoric. The site uses part of its 'Welcome' page to explain what it is: 'an international resource focusing on the work of artists and their community partners – projects and programs that actively promote the arts as part of education, political life, health recovery, prisoner rehabilitation, environmental protection, community regeneration, electronic communication, and more'. It also lays out its rationale for providing hyperlinks to particular resources, and the statement is worth quoting in full:

> We see [the community arts] field as the cutting edge of art today. This work is complex, sophisticated, informed by intense research in multiple disciplines. We believe that it should be viewed through a variety of lenses. Therefore, much of the material in our database is cross-filed under several categories, and will appear in different searches, in different contexts. We see this construction as a living archaeology. It is our hope that users of this Web site will be able to find not only the information they seek, but the context in which that information is framed.
>
> Why have we gone to all this trouble? Because we want not only to present this information, but to see it go to work. We hope that users of this Web site will be able not only to create better community arts projects, but to integrate this work into community development, into education at all levels and into the public conversation. In short, we want to change the world.
>
> (Community Arts Network 2004)

In this account there is a self-conscious attempt to articulate the contextual framework for the information presented, an attempt to represent it as constructed rather than as natural or given (or finished, or dead). By depicting the database of information available as 'a living archaeology', the writers also suggest the sense in which information has a history but is not past, and in which its 'living' hints at its prospective future through readers' 'go[ing] to work' with it and reshaping it for use in different spaces and other times.

It may be claimed that while these comments on the creative possibilities might be expected and appropriate for an arts organisation, their applicability to public information in other domains is doubtful.

I'd question that. The rhetoric used on the site seems to have gained energy through its departure from a consumerist discourse. And even consumer-oriented sites might benefit from this example, if only in an attempt to balance their auto-communicative, self-referential impulse and make imaginative contact with both sceptical consumers and disaffected would-be participants.

It seems that Shell, the global energy company, had taken such a step,[34] in one section at least, of its highly impressive, slick and largely consumer-oriented website (www.shell.com). Although by 2004 the style and orientation, if not the broad focus, of the pages had changed considerably,[35] in 2003, a number of pages on the site were devoted to what the company called 'Issues': climate change, human rights, new energy, globalisation, biodiversity, business integrity. In the introduction to these, the writer remarks that, given its 'responsibility to be a good corporate citizen',[36] the aim is to explain 'our approach to issues that matter [to] you, and also the dilemmas we face as a multinational. Many people around the world have different points of view. You may not always agree with us, but we always promise to listen.' For each of the issues listed the company devoted considerable space, within a number of subsections, to exploring the particular issue. For example, under 'Globalization' was a hyperlink to 'Global brands: symbols of trust or exploitation?' Here the writer described the history of branding, illustrated brands' contemporary ubiquitousness (quoting Naomi Klein, author of *No logo*, and her evocation of brands free 'to soar' through cyberspace 'like collective hallucinations'), and briefly debated the morality of branding (including mention of its own dubious corporate activities in Nigeria and its involvement with Brent Spar). The piece concluded with questions about who has more power: global corporations or consumers. The answer proffered in the final sentence was that 'only time (as sponsored by Accurist) will tell'.

This Shell text could quite easily be interpreted as the ultimate in postmodern irony or as an accomplished, glib performance of auto-communication. However, unlike the national government sites explored, this text does openly acknowledge the contingency of its position and it does open a space for readers' potentially oppositional views. The rhetorical questions, the acknowledgment of other perspectives and contradictory arguments, the admission of the complexity of ideas, beliefs and values about globalisation and about corporate vis-à-vis consumer power can only introduce the debate. But at least they do so, in what may be read as a spirit of democratic openness and the willingness to challenge and be challenged. Naomi Klein clearly reads the text otherwise, however. She perceives the 'new Shell goes Zen' image overhaul (following its experiences with Brent Spar and in Nigeria) as dubiously motivated and interprets its 'aggressive Internet strategy' as a defensive response to Internet activism (Klein 2001, pp. 421–30, 438). As far as her reading of motivation goes, Klein may well be right. Nevertheless, in the case of massively powerful corporations and institutions, we can still be optimistic about the impacts (if not yet confident about the motivations) of such texts – stimulating readers to imagine their own interventions into and uses for public information.

## Conclusion

The effect of writers' concerted attempts to control public information, of retaining the now long-discredited notion of the linearity of writing–reading relations may be that writers lose control altogether. The texts of public information presented on the Internet sites of both those responsible for modelling democratic practices and those self-consciously asserting their engagement in its development need to appeal to readers' crucial roles as agents. They also need to imagine participants in a shared process of democratisation. Otherwise those texts and those sites are unlikely to be used as an intertextual resource, educative tool, or means of reflecting on individual beliefs and values and modifying them in light of mutual awareness of the beliefs and values of others, of their fellow citizens.

While Kaplan celebrates the possibilities for transformation and evolution opened up by digital texts, she points to the threats they are also perceived to pose: she argues that the terms 'instability, promiscuity, corruption', which are often used to describe what readers (becoming writers themselves) can do with texts, 'reveal our fears' (Kaplan 1995). In the context of this discussion, it is therefore understandable that writers of public information, particularly those who currently wield significant power, might be anxious about presenting digital texts in a way that actually invites readers to intervene and use them as they will. However, as I have aimed to show, unless this invitation is openly made through the articulation of public information as a shared process of interpretation and exchange, then an exciting opportunity for engaging citizens with competing interests and different understandings in the networked journey to an expanded democracy will be missed.

# 4
# Challenging Unreliable Narrators: Writing and Public Relations

## Introduction

In this chapter I focus on public relations (print or online) texts, which an organisation or corporation circulates specifically to articulate directly or indirectly its understandings of its social responsibilities, and I discuss the ways in which its writing of narratives is used as a specific rhetorical device to define itself to its stakeholders as a socially responsible moral agent. I argue for public relations writing as a potentially valuable social activity involving the construction, circulation, contestation and development of narratives. Such narrative texts specifically include social responsibility reports, documents that are becoming increasingly significant in a corporation's demonstration of its understanding and implementation of ethical, business-related practices. Many other public relations texts, such as employee newsletters, community relations brochures, client magazines, sections of annual reports, Internet sites and so on, which devote space to describing issues related to social responsibility, are also implicated in this chapter's discussion.[1]

Through a critique of Nike's *Corporate responsibility report 2001*, I will go on to suggest why the public relations rhetoric of organisations and corporations may regularly be perceived by various stakeholders as hollow rather than meaningful, self-serving rather than other-oriented.[2] I will contend that for corporations, such as Nike, who engage in public relations practices of articulating their moral identity through constitutive narratives, and who are concerned to have that identity acknowledged and responded to as genuine and socially engaged, the activity of imagining others (interested readers) requires (literally) giving agency to stakeholders whose voices would complicate those narratives and their meanings. Nike, and similar business organisations, require the dynamic involvement, in their texts, of those stakeholders with whom the business is significantly connected, and particularly with those who are either less powerful, those who may not fall into the categories of investors or satisfied consumers, and those who actively challenge or question the ethics of Nike's practices. I suggest too that the imperative of such involvement is highlighted by the recent lawsuit in which Nike's claims to be a good corporate citizen were disputed. In considering what might constitute meaningful and ethical approaches to public relations as a socially conspicuous instance of professional writing, the chapter concludes with some ideas for engaging in and enabling such approaches.

### Corporate social responsibility in the twenty-first century

The growth of the concept of corporate social responsibility can be traced back to the activist, civil rights and feminist movements (Clark 2000) and the growth of consumer awareness in the 1960s, and of environmentalism in more recent years (Meech 1996, p. 66). The developing understanding of the relationship between private and public spheres, the growing support for the struggle to overcome social, racial and economic inequities and forms of exploitation, and the increasing focus on various forms of sustainability have come out of those earlier movements, and have influenced much contemporary thought about the place and role of business in culture. As a participating member of society – one that owes its position to and draws considerable benefits from that membership – private business, as a consequence, is widely believed to have social responsibilities. As Birch and Glazebrook argue, 'corporate practices and policies can no longer ignore the social, ethical, moral and, above all, cultural consequences of their partnership with society' (2000, p. 51). They also contend that business is pivotal in the process of shaping, influencing and 'doing culture' (2000, p. 51), thus highlighting business's involvement with rather than distinction from society and social values. The term social responsibility, therefore, has now come to be generally understood to define 'the attitudes and practices which distinguish those organizations which take heed of the wider consequences of their activities rather than being motivated by considerations of profit alone' (Meech 1996, p. 66).

### Postmodern – ethical, imaginative and rhetorical – approaches to public relations praxis

In contemporary Western culture, the practice of public relations is popularly regarded as primarily, and in some cases exclusively, a function of promotion and publicity. This view can work to public relations' detriment in terms of its perception and credibility as a form of authentic relationship building.[3] Alternatively, public relations is understood as a facet of marketing and advertising – even while its practitioners claim to be doing *public relations*: that is, forging and extending meaningful relationships with stakeholders. However, with corporate public relations increasingly insistent in its communication practices on relationships with its publics and stakeholders through social responsibility programmes, corporate governance activities, community relations programmes, philanthropic investments,[4] and so on, the ethical, rhetorical and imaginative dimensions of public relations are consequently foregrounded. It is this dimension of public relations writing praxis that I am interested in and propose to examine further below.

Of course, some readers may wonder why I even *consider* attempting a chapter that argues for the potential for productive narrative exchange between writers and readers through the medium of the public relations texts developed by large corporations. Given that the very mention of the term public relations is likely to raise eyebrows or, even more likely, the hackles, of many people, the attempt is a bold one, I admit. 'It's just PR' is an expression many of us use dismissively or pejoratively, indicating that whatever the message being communicated or activity being executed by a (generally large and powerful) corporation, the motives must ultimately be self-serving rather than stakeholder- or publics-oriented. There is also a sense in which attempting to tackle a topic evaluating the social and ethical functions and effects of corporate public relations narratives is too overwhelming, beset as any such attempt is by several significant *other* narratives in this context: of late industrial capitalism; of governmental and corporate powers and their global ideological and practical reach, influence and control (however indirect those are); and of widespread social and economic inequities. If we agree that capitalism dominates all other ideologies and that all political and philosophical beliefs and practices are subsumed by it, we may feel understandably reluctant to put up any resistance against this grandest of stories.[5] In addition, it can't be denied that conventional public relations practice (and even, until quite recently, most related theory) is largely driven by the imperative to maintain or extend the stronghold of capitalist regimes (Holtzhausen 2000, p. 97).

Why, then, bother to argue for the (some would say naive) vision of public relations as enabling a meaningful narrative exchange between organisations and publics, where public relations functions to facilitate democratic processes of ethical communication: negotiation, debate and dispute, between an organisation and its various publics, with the aim of effecting social change? And how can public relations be *enacted* through the written medium anyway, since the expletive, 'it's just PR' mentioned above is readily interchangeable with those other expletives 'it's all rhetoric' or 'it's just words'. We resort to using such criticisms when we feel that language – and the form and content it shapes and represents – is remote from or fails to adequately represent or approximate, for us, the realities of our experience of a corporation and its practices. But my claim that relationships with publics can be meaningfully forged is *not* a claim that written accounts are a *substitute* for interpersonal activity, exchange and the immediacy of face-to-face human relationships. Of course they are not.

Nevertheless, a significant proportion of the relating with the public that organisations (and particularly large national and multinational ones) do today is necessarily activated and mediated through written print or online texts. Businesses and corporations spend vast amounts of money on producing public relations texts, so presumably they have a very strong interest in those texts offering meaning and value to stakeholders.

From this perspective, I contend that language as rhetorical form and content should be a representation and self-conscious extension of and complement to the activities, attitudes and values it describes, the materiality of intersubjective experience.[6] As we saw in Chapter 1, the constituting of a text itself – its very writing – is an ethical activity and carries ethical implications: 'writing is an action involving an ethical choice about what one is to be and what one is to do. At the point when you begin to write, you begin to define yourself ethically' (Porter 1998, p. 150). And how far that identity and that action create an imaginative space or allow the responses, the articulations, the development of the story by others (by readers) constitutes an ethical gesture.

It will become clear that the approach taken in this chapter highlights the fact that fundamental shifts in much conventional corporate public relations theory and practice – in the very idea of what relating to stakeholders involves and what its functions and objectives are – are absolutely vital as well. It would, of course, be absurd to suggest the potential for or possibility of total overhaul of power within our capitalist systems in which public relations thrives. However, Foucault's description of power relations presents a scenario that makes the task of proposing and effecting such shifts a little less daunting:

> Power relations are not something that is bad in itself, that we have to break free of. I do not think that a society can exist without power

relations, if by that one means the strategies by which individuals try to direct and control the conduct of others. The problem, then, is not to try to dissolve them in the utopia of completely transparent communication but to acquire the rules of law, the management techniques, and also the morality, the *ēthos*, the practice of the self, that will allow us to play these games of power with as little domination as possible.

(Foucault 2000, p. 298)

To conceive of a notion of public relations writing praxis that proceeds 'with as little domination as possible' underscores the suggestions made through this chapter.[7]

Relatively recent moves by some public relations theorists in the United States, Great Britain and Europe to reassess and re-evaluate the theory and practice of public relations insist on a shift in both theoretical and practitioner perspective – from an organisation-centred approach to public relations to one that attempts to balance the needs of all players: the organisation, its diverse stakeholders and the broader community (for example, see Holtzhausen 2000; Daymon 2000; Vercic et al. 2001). This shift is, of course, related to the belief that organisations are members of society and bear community responsibilities that go with that position. Also, with the development of public relations as an academic discipline, there has been a concomitant shift in the view of public relations as professional practice (the just-do-it approach) to public relations as 'a conscious uncoupling of the intellectual agenda from the day-to-day thoughts, actions and preoccupations of practitioners' (Dozier and Lauzen 2000, p. 4). It seems to me that both these shifts have served to highlight the significance of public relations as having the potential to enact ethical, rhetorical and imaginative praxis.

First, with the move to acknowledge the needs (the claims, the voices, the texts, the values and the identities) of diverse publics as being as important as those of an organisation, public relations can begin to reflect on and work towards its (potential for) ethical and reciprocal engagements or exchanges with those publics. The ethical dimension of public relations defines the relationships between individuals, groups and communities and corporations in terms of their relative power, and how this power, in practice, influences their mutual obligations, accountability and responsibility, as well as their respective degrees of interdependence with each other. Many organisations and corporations self-consciously declare their interest and investment in these relationships. For example, Jim Cantalupo, Chairman and CEO of McDonald's, the fast-food corporation, writes in the introduction to the 2002 *McDonald's social responsibility report*: 'McDonald's has the honor of serving more customers around the world than anyone else. With this privilege comes a responsibility to be a good neighbor, employer, and steward of the environment, and a unique opportunity to be a leader and a catalyst for positive change. We recognize the challenges and the obstacles, but believe strongly in the importance of social responsibility' (McDonald's 2002, p. 4). And energy and petrochemical business, ExxonMobil's Chairman and CEO, Lee R. Raymond, announces in ExxonMobil's *2003 Corporate citizenship report: summary* that 'our directors, management and employees understand that exemplary citizenship, including high standards of business conduct, effective corporate governance, sound financial controls, operational integrity and community engagement, is fundamental to sustained business success – and sustained business success is fundamental to good corporate citizenship. You cannot have one without the other' (ExxonMobil 2004, p. 3). Similarly, sports footwear, clothing and accessories corporation, adidas-Salomon's *Staying focused: social and environmental report 2003* declares that 'while we have outsourced most of our production, we have not outsourced moral responsibility for the way in which our products are manufactured and distributed' (adidas-Salomon 2004, p. 6). As we have established, ethics is an activity, and its writing one form of social practice. So there is a reasonable expectation on the part of readers and stakeholders that corporations writing about their ethical activity will bear out their claims in their written texts as well as in other forms of practice. Thus, the fact that Shell, the global group of energy and petrochemical companies, provides an email facility on its website for people to post uncensored, publicly accessible feedback on Shell's activities[8] suggests that the corporation is interested in engaging with stakeholders, at least at the level of acknowledging and making available to others their views. How far those views might be debated and perhaps responded to or acted on by the corporation, is another matter, however. This point indicates the crucial role of written communication not only as a form of ethical practice but also as one necessarily coterminous with and contingent on other forms of social practice.

Second, the role of rhetoric in public relations – as *interactive* processes of communication and interpretation, involving the construction or inscription of knowledges, meanings and values by one party and their various understandings or reinscriptions by other (supportive, antagonistic, indifferent and so on) parties – also becomes crucial, and its dynamic links with ethical practice salient. In the domain of public relations, this relation between ethics and rhetoric is particularly important.

Traditionally, discussions of rhetoric in relation to public relations have been limited to examining the legitimacy of rhetoric as persuasion. By contrast and more recently, some public relations theorists have countered this tendency and broadened the discussion considerably by engaging in debate that is sensitive to the ethical implications of rhetoric (see L'Etang 1996, 1997; Heath 2000). As Heath points out, 'The rhetorical perspective assumes that ideas are not eternally dictated, mandated, or taken for granted. They are subject to dispute' (Heath 2000, p. 72). For example, rhetorical discourses in the community that foreground the significance of economic rationalism and profitability very often compete and conflict with those that emphasise the primacy of human rights or environmental sustainability.[9] The various interpretations of these discourses by different people in different contexts, and the subsequent impacts of those people's transformation of the discourses into particular actions or attitudes, will inevitably influence the relationship between one person and another, an organisation and its stakeholders, private business and the community. Rhetoric as a sense- and truth-making technology clearly has dynamic ethical, material and intersubjective effects.

It is important to notice in these accounts of rhetorical and ethical public relations communications that *consensus* and *mutual satisfaction* of all parties are not necessarily the desirable closures to be striven for. On the contrary, and as Lyotard points out in his discussion of the differend, such goals are misguided and may serve to disguise inequities and the difference in priority or interest that will still subsist at the end of any dispute: 'A case of differend between two parties takes place when the "regulation" of the conflict that opposes them is done in the idiom of one of the parties while the wrong suffered by the other is not signified in that idiom' (Lyotard 1988, p. 9).[10] An ethical rhetoric in public relations texts is sensitive to that conflict and the power that might obscure its opportunities for exposure. Such sensitivity appears to be demonstrated by the skin and body care retailer, The Body Shop, for example, whose website carries both (management) statements about its approach to employee relations, as well as comments (positive and negative) of Body Shop employees recorded in a survey (externally designed and administered) in 2000, on various aspects of their employment experience with and perceptions of the corporation (Kingston University 2002). For example, one (corporate) employee comment from the survey, responding to a question about the company's effectiveness in facilitating communication and related issues, reads: 'The Body Shop doesn't "walk the talk", and is as bureaucratic, hierarchical, secretive as many other companies that don't attempt to make a public show of values' (Kingston University 2002, p. 60).[11] Compare this with the HR Director, Mark Barrett's, comment in a more recent, company-authored report: 'The role of HR has been to help employees feel engaged in the business through improved and frequent communications, as well as direct consultation and the provision of wellbeing and other support programmes' (The Body Shop 2003, p. 4). Interestingly, the juxtaposition of conflicting voices could here be seen to demonstrate the strategies implemented by The Body Shop in direct response to earlier articulations of employee dissatisfaction. It remains to be seen, however, in future reports and in its other business practices, whether the differences between The Body Shop management and staff (in perception and experience as represented through their various rhetorics) will be used to help transform employer–employee relations into a more productive and equitable association.

Subsequently and finally, the activity of imagining becomes important in exploring and evaluating public relations praxis – that process of putting oneself in the place of the other, thinking oneself outside the space of self-security and self-gratification – both in the activity of public relations as communicative and interactive process and as theoretical distancing. I see the significance of imagining in Holtzhausen's reflection on the future role of the public relations practitioner operating in a context of 'dissensus' (rather than consensus): 'This state of dissensus will inevitably place the public relations practitioner ... in a position of choosing sides and speaking out in the case of what he or she views as an injustice ... In [this] boundary-spanning function, a position of dissensus will force the public relations practitioner to recognize and respect differences on the side of both the organization and its publics' (Holtzhausen 2000, p. 108). The postmodern act of imagining entails an acknowledgement of diversity and dispute, and highlights the fact that situations can be promoted and created in which 'new meaning' is produced 'through difference and opposition' (Holtzhausen 2000, p. 107). Public relations writing's capacity to genuinely imagine the place of the other in order for organisations and corporations to meet their various social obligations is still, as I will show, severely limited. And if we assume as genuine one of Nike's (explicitly) stated (and other corporations' implied) goals as being 'to see things through the eyes of the worker' (Nike 2001, p. 27), then the ideas raised through this chapter may assist in extending that capacity.

## Public relations, narrative, and stories about morality

Public relations writing organises and represents an organisation and its people, their situations, experiences, actions and their effects over time through verbal patterns that give them order and coherence as a narrative. Such writing thus seeks to identify itself to its stakeholders.[12] The narratives may take the form of official public relations documents, such as reports, newsletters or website material, for example, produced by the organisation, as well as those constructed by marketing, advertising, the news media, activist groups, employees, subcontracted workers, consumers and, even by hearsay, through public and private conversation, rumour, speculation and so on. The understandings and perceptions of an organisation circulating at any one time are largely developed through readers and writers' interactions with such narratives: the stories encountered, responded to and modified by diverse stakeholders. Inevitably then, there will be multiple narrative versions that help define the organisation's identity at a given moment, and these versions will vary depending on who is constructing, who is making sense of them. For example, for many Western consumers today, Nestlé the world's largest food company, is commonly perceived through its marketing, advertising and ubiquitous retail presence as a company producing a wide range of quality convenience foodstuffs: coffee, chocolate, yoghurt, infant formula and so on. For consumers in developing countries and for an activist organisation such as Oxfam Community Aid Abroad, however, Nestlé is a disturbingly powerful corporation that has a monopoly on the milk production industry in countries such as Sri Lanka, and charges exorbitant and, for many potential customers, unaffordable prices for its product.[13] And yet for shareholders, Nestlé is a corporation whose healthy annual growth and profitable returns make it a very attractive company to invest in.

Increasingly, and given the significant public expectation that they perform as responsible social actors (particularly following the recent and recurrent exposure of various and widespread malpractices), corporations tend to be regarded as unitary bodies, whose attributes and values resemble those of moral human agents. (Think, for instance, of how often a corporation is referred to as 'deceptive' or 'greedy' or 'caring' or 'fair'.) Moral agency can usefully be understood 'as an effect of sociohistorical interactions that reflect *processes* through which the boundaries of an actor are drawn and justified' (De Winter 2001, p. 100). We can therefore regard the corporation as a collective moral agent, 'located within a specific set of historical relations with state and societal actors, and bearing the larger responsibility of contributing to social justice within the communities in which it produces' (De Winter 2001, p. 101). While the representation of a corporation as a unitary actor can hide the complex network of relationships that together constitute the organisation, and while it might tend to obscure the agency and responsibility of individuals within it (see Chapter 2), it is this interactional process that results in the attribution of corporate moral agency (De Winter 2001). Nevertheless, however powerful the organisation, and however influential it might be in constructing dominant, widely heard narratives about itself as a moral agent, the roles of readers and publics, in interpreting those narratives into significant understandings of the organisation, is crucial.[14]

This is not to ignore the fact that not all interpreters and meaning-makers are likely to have the same degree of influence in representing their stories and their understandings of stories to others. In other words, the stories exchanged are not equally forcefully told, mediated or understood: the capacity to disseminate preferred stories, the exposure of those stories to publics with different degrees of power, and the cultural credibility accorded to certain discourses harnessed to articulate stories, all help account for *how* or even *whether* stories are communicated in the first place, and, if they are, whether they take hold in the social imagination. The so-called McLibel case is an interesting, if quirky, example of the ways in which various stories and understandings of the fast-food corporation were transformed or modified by various stakeholders during the course of its protracted (two-and-a-half-year) libel case against two individuals, Helen Steel and Dave Morris, in England in the 1990s. Steel and Morris had been part of a group responsible for the publication and distribution of a leaflet called 'What's Wrong With McDonald's – Everything they don't want you to know'. The leaflet claimed that McDonald's exploited children through its advertising campaigns, and its staff through its work practices. It claimed the company's production processes were responsible for causing environmental damage and cruelty to animals. While the judge ruled against the fast-food company on some points, he did find that the defendants were guilty of libel on others. They were ordered to pay £60,000, but refused. McDonald's did not pursue the case. The case also demonstrates the ways in which, in certain instances, the stories of relatively powerless underdogs can be harnessed as effective tools to challenge conventional bases of control and influence.[15]

Postmodern accounts of narrative also alert us to the idea that the stories that public relations constructs about an organisation are not definitive – in fact they are only meaningful when endorsed, accepted, responded to, challenged, disrupted, contested and so on by public readings of those narratives. All of this suggests the interpersonal process of telling and interpreting narratives, that it necessarily involves an engagement and an exchange between tellers and listeners, writers and readers and, moreover, public relations narratives – like all narratives – have gaps in them: public relations can never hope to tell the 'whole' story, despite the fact that all kinds of narrative do, it seem, have that totalising impulse: 'the formal project of narrative syntagmation [is] to encapsulate completely its descriptive object, i.e., to achieve a state of plenitude in relation to the narrating subject's appeal to the Other' (McQuillan 2000, p. 20).

Stories about an organisation are likely to be appropriated by different publics within the context of cultural narratives that make those publics' own lives meaningful. Stories are only valuable in the moment(s) of their contact between writers and readers, and that contact generates variable degrees of tension, since narrative is re-interpretable and re-presentable by diverse readers as alternative narratives or 'counternarratives'. 'The condition of the counternarrative arises because the form of the narrative syntagm cannot express a totality of experience, although it attempts to disguise this necessary "failing" in the imaginary figure of closure. Counternarratives are a necessary part of the communal narrative-matrix and are therefore necessary to the prolongation of inter-subjective experience' (McQuillan 2000, p. 23). It is this concept of the counternarrative that further emphasises the pivotal – ethical – dimension of storytelling. These days, the most frequent and publicly visible or publicly accessible counters to corporate public relations narratives are those produced by activist organisations, such as Greenpeace and Amnesty International,[16] for example, who campaign on what they regard as the most critical gaps in corporations' narratives, in relation to environmental and human rights issues respectively. Other activist groups, such as McSpotlight or the NikeWatch arm of Oxfam Community Aid Abroad, target or scrutinise the specific activities and draw attention to the absences or glosses in the narratives circulated by an individual corporation.[17] There is also the Center for Media and Democracy's site, PR Watch, a non-profit, online organisation that reports on what it perceives as malpractices perpetrated by the public relations industry internationally.[18] And, of course, there are a host of other, more informal, counternarratives that will be generated – from private conversations in coffee shops to public debates published in the news media, for example – that will each develop alternative understandings of what constitutes a meaningful story about a corporation.

The impulse of the counternarrative might otherwise be compared with the notion of dialogism, as Bakhtin uses the term. Bakhtin's reflections on language, and on novelistic discourse in particular, help to clarify the view sketched above of an essentially postmodern view of narrative and the meanings it generates in different contexts and by different writers and readers. The dialogic property of narrative, that is, its (internal or external) encounters with contradictory or competing meanings, ensures that

> the living utterance, having taken meaning and shape at a particular historical moment in a socially specific environment, cannot fail to brush up against thousands of living dialogic threads, woven by socio-ideological consciousness around the given object of an utterance; it cannot fail to become an active participant in social dialogue. After all, the utterance arises out of this dialogue as a continuation of it and as a rejoinder to it – it does not approach the object from the sidelines.
>
> (Bakhtin 1981, p. 276)

If we focus on the public relations narratives circulated by organisations (through various mediums) about themselves – and particularly in relation to their self-description on issues of social responsibility – what seems to be missing? Why are so many publics' responses to stories of 'good works' by a self-described ethically sound corporation often those of disbelief, cynicism or distrust? Bakhtin's notion of dialogism, also a significant feature of his understanding of the relation between self and other, as manifested through narrative may help us again here:

> I am conscious of myself and become myself only while revealing myself for another, through another, and with the help of another … To be means to be for another, and through the other, for oneself. A person has no internal sovereign territory, he is wholly and always on the boundary; looking inside himself, he [sic] looks *into the eyes of another* or *with the eyes of another*.
>
> (Bakhtin 1984, p. 287; italics in original)

The feminist philosopher, Margaret Urban Walker, throws further light on this idea of narrative as a responsibility to the other: 'In all of its expressions, morality is fundamentally *interpersonal*; it arises out of and is reproduced or modified in what goes on between or among people. In this way, morality is collaborative; we construct and sustain it together' (Walker 1998, p. 10). In her 'expressive-collaborative' view of morality, in which she argues that 'a *story* is the basic form of representation for moral problems' (1998, p. 110), her comments have an important bearing on the social responsibility narratives of corporations.

Walker suggests that three types of narratives subsist and intertwine in our making of coherent moral stories of our lives: narratives of relationship, narratives of identity, and narratives of value. Briefly, in Walker's account, narratives of relationship are those of a 'relationship's acquired content and developed expectations, its basis and type of trust, and its possibilities for continuation' (Walker 1998, p. 111). Such narratives develop – are constructed from our experiences – out of our encounters with others, whether those are brief, episodic or ongoing. Our investments, responsibilities, obligations and needs – practical and ethical – both in individual relationships and between different relationships will necessarily vary and change over time. Through our relationship-centred narratives, our integrity is often put under pressure, since our decisions on how to move on with our stories are inevitably bound up with others' needs and situations. However, our narratives of moral identity, derived from the decisions and choices we make and the actions we take (or don't take) in our relationships with others, are concerned with defining how our specific moral attachments (our moral relationships) help define for ourselves and for others *who* we are: 'where we stand and what we stand for' (Walker 1998, p. 112). Spanning and supporting both these kinds of narrative is the narrative of moral values: the stories that articulate what holds meaning and significance for us, and what we come to deem important or less important through our history of relationships with others and through our (changing) understandings of who we are. 'We learn progressively from our moral resolutions and their intelligibility and acceptability to ourselves and others who and how we are and what our moral concepts and standards mean' (Walker 1998, p. 113). This summary, although it cannot do justice to the richness of Walker's own account, nevertheless emphasises the centrality of the process of interaction between self and other for the development of moral narratives. The applicability of Walker's framework for such narratives constituted as written texts – representing rhetorically intersubjective experience – can be demonstrated by turning our attention to the case of a written document by Nike – its *Corporate responsibility report 2001*.

## Corporate social responsibility texts and the case of Nike

Many corporations, having now assumed their roles as collective moral actors (by taking on the activities and the rhetoric of corporate social responsibility) have also, as we have seen, assumed 'an identity that cannot be delimited to their role as economic institutions maximizing the profit of stockholders' (De Winter 2001, p. 110). This complex identity, and the tensions and contradictions it articulates, is represented in the social responsibility texts of large corporations.

Typically, in such texts, an organisation, through its self-representations as a moral actor engaged in significant relationships and attached to specific moral values, gives a narrative account of its history, current activities and future plans in relation to social or community endeavours. These might include descriptions of work practices, environmental sustainability initiatives, community consultation programmes and so on. There is one sense in which such accounts are necessarily self-sufficient and coherent: the documents stand as sense-making testaments to an organisation's efforts to 'do the right thing' in its practices. However, while it is to be expected that the narrative discourses of marketing and advertising and even of publicity and promotion, will be presented as self-assured, complete and coherent (their functions and objectives most often support this approach, after all), corporate responsibility narratives describing the (first and foremost) ethical relationships between particular people in particular social, economic and environmental contexts presented similarly have quite different rhetorical effects. In the latter case, I would argue, the attempt to create the illusion of completeness, integrity, flawlessness, smoothness (with moral goodness implicit in those qualities) is highly problematic, and certainly one possible cause of public disbelief or cynicism. The 'complete' story implies self-enclosure and immunity from interpersonal contact/contamination. It contradicts the notion of a moral narrative, because it entails leaving out of the storyline those who would necessarily disrupt its flow or coherence. By extension, this approach produces distrust because the implication is that the story needs no readers to render it meaningful (to carry on, to develop, to disrupt or to change the course of the story through their involvement in it), and/or to judge or evaluate it.

Precisely because such narratives as social responsibility documents *call out to the other for their legitimacy*, and because such texts represent (or stand in the place of) material or physical connection with others, they are bound – if they are authentic – to be tentative, incomplete and incoherent, in the sense of not 'worked out', not finalised, not stitched up. Nike's report goes much, much further than many other corporations' reports in terms of its detailed (if selective) reflection on its activities and self-criticism of many of its past practices as well as the limitations of some of its present ones. Nevertheless, the report is imaginatively limited and its rhetoric therefore ethically questionable.

The *Corporate responsibility report 2001* is a slick publication (available in hard copy and online)[19] carefully designed, in true postmodern style, to simulate a well-used, crudely assembled, interdepartmental document. (The hard copy of the report, which is obtainable on request from Nike, is contained in a faux interdepartmental envelope.) 'Admittedly it is incomplete, a bit of a mishmash' writes Phil Knight, Nike's CEO, in the 'cover letter' attached to the inside cover of the hard-copy document. As with its website, Nike in this document 'consciously configure[s] images as part of [its] public discourse' (Salinas 2000, ch. 2, p. 6).[20]

The report's visual impact is powerful and appealing: photos, maps, graphs, illustrations and text are collated in a highly organised mock-up of chaos. As the introductory text (in a font recalling manual typewriter type and forming a palimpsest over a whole-page photo of boxes and shelves containing Nike office bric-a-brac) remarks: 'Throughout this report you will see snapshots of Nike people working on corporate responsibility projects and programs, old files, e-mails, ticket stubs and the like. We thought it important for you to get the texture of this work as well as its substance' (Nike 2001, p. 3). This suggests the self-conscious 'play' of form with content, where the 'substance' of corporate social responsibility is in part evoked by the 'texture' of work in progress, and of its innumerable, complex and contradictory elements: people, places, statistics, technologies, products, ideas, values, issues.

The fifty-five-page document covers five areas of corporate social responsibility: 'Environment', 'Labor Practices', 'Nike People', 'Community Affairs' and 'Stakeholders'. As well as presenting the mission or goals and giving an account of the company's (personnel, operational, administrative and financial) activities in each of these areas, the document presents a narrative of its progressive ethical development and evolution. 'The document you hold is our first step in systematically communicating the things we've done to evolve ... We are, after all, just beginning to understand what a sustainable business means ... For now, *it offers an honest self-assessment of our progress'* (Knight's cover letter, in Nike 2001; italics added). This sets the tone for the reflections articulated in the document that follows: a tone that is both confessional and visionary, though largely self-oriented.

Also in his introductory letter, Knight quotes from the corporation's so-called 'Maxims': 'Nike exists to pursue opportunity and enhance human potential' (in Nike 2001). We can see here how the language of branding (see Klein 2001, pp. 3–28) – evoking lifestyle, values, cultural beliefs, emotions – draws on the discourses of ethics and morality, and of personal and social relationships. So there is an immediate connection between branding language, if you like, and that of public relations; assuming we understand public relations as described above: as developing and negotiating ethical relationships between an organisation and its publics. Knight goes on: 'As a citizen of the world, Nike must Do the Right Thing – try to be transparent about what we are doing right, and about what we are doing wrong; embrace diversity; drive sustainability' (Knight's cover letter in Nike 2001). It is interesting to witness here the shift from Nike's 'Just Do It' culture to a 'Do the Right Thing' culture, from the abstractly amoral to the explicitly moral speech act. Through the conflation of marketing or branding and corporate social responsibility discourses, Knight's letter attempts to sell the idea of his company's ethics – its moral goodness.

Repeatedly through the document, Nike confesses to and evaluates its responsibility for the negative impacts of past and present corporate social responsibility activities, and acknowledges that problems have not been eradicated. 'How well do we do monitoring [of labour practices]? Not well enough' (Nike 2001, p. 28). Here the rhetorical question-and-answer technique offers a clear instance of the company's impulse to self-assessment, and even to self-recrimination: 'By far our worst experience and biggest mistake [in relation to labour practices] was in Pakistan, where we blew it' (Nike 2001, p. 30). However, these confessions do remain relatively comfortable and unthreatening, as the direct responses and judgements of others (for example, Nike's subcontracted workers, their families, communities, auditing and monitoring bodies) on these activities and their repercussions are excluded. That said, the Nike report certainly sets itself apart from reports such as McDonald's and ExxonMobil's, for example. Those companies use their reports very much as instruments of self-promotion and as expressions of corporate vision. The McDonald's report, as a case in point, makes no mention, with one exception (see McDonald's 2002, p. 38), of any former or current practices that have been challenged by various stakeholders, although it does repeatedly stress that its corporate responsibility processes are part of its ongoing education and development. For example, the chairman of the company's corporate responsibility committee, Walter E. Massey, describes the report as 'a valuable roadmap that will enable McDonald's to measure its progress and enhance its standards of performance' (McDonald's 2002, p. 5). And in relation to sustainability initiatives, the writer of the report comments that 'we are embarking on a journey in which the answers are not obvious' (McDonald's 2002, p. 18) and that 'we are dedicated to learning' (McDonald's 2002, p. 19). These kinds of visionary statements, by their self-conscious disconnection from those that are reflective, self-scrutinising or dialogic tend to lack credibility.

In the Nike report's 'Stakeholders' section, we have a clear illustration of the way in which a narrative of morality, such as Walker describes (see above), is significant in making coherent ideas about corporate relationships, identity and value. The narrative opens with an admission that, in the past, Nike's relationships were largely financial- and stakeholder-focused. However, 'we've learned the hard way that our view of the world was not as informed as it should have been. In the last few years we have had dialogue with the vast range of stakeholders in civil society' (Nike 2001, p. 54). However, a comment suggesting Nike's discomfort with this claim of engagement in 'dialogue' follows: 'If anything *the pendulum has swung too much the other way*, connecting with over 100 external non-profit stakeholder groups, including environmental organizations, human rights groups, students, colleges, trades unions, socially responsible investor groups, government, academia and consumers. Engagement ranges from information and dialogue to collaborative projects and multi-year programs' (Nike 2001, p. 54; italics added). A pie chart summarising the range of Nike's relationships is also depicted (Nike 2001, p. 55). Values are enumerated systematically: belief in principle of engagement, seeking of common ground, importance of relationship yielding 'real value' (Nike 2001, p. 54). Identity through these pages emerges as the corporation's maturing moral identity – progressive, even pioneering, in its efforts to forge links with a range of stakeholder groups and to establish a global system of accepted social accounting principles. However, it seems to me that the narrative lacks authenticity as a result of its singularity of voice and the absence of an acknowledgement of the centrality of the interpersonal, or 'moral life as a continuing negotiation *among* people' (Walker 1998, p. 60). We cannot claim to be authoritative judges of our own narratives or our own identities; self-description isn't enough, given that it exposes a lack or even an absence of moral engagement with others. 'Moral justification ... is from the first and at the last interpersonal. It is with and from others we learn to do it, and learn that we must. It is to others we must bring it back to do the work it is intended for: to allow and require people to account to one another for the value and impact of what they do in matters of importance' (Walker 1998, p. 114).

However, only certain 'people' are allowed into the pages of the Nike report as subjects: Nike management and staff. The texts of those with whom Nike's relationship has been and continues to be notoriously fraught are absent, except in the abstract, that is. For example, the section entitled 'Labor practices' is introduced by the Director of Corporate Responsibility Compliance, who intersperses his discussion about the challenges of achieving approved working practices and conditions with reference to the typical (female) 'Nike worker': '*You are 22 and single. You are in the third year of your first job. You were raised on a farm. Your supervisor is a woman, four years your senior. Your section leader is a foreigner. He doesn't speak your language very well.'* By maintaining the Nike worker as a necessary or inevitable stereotype 'always one constant: a young woman, who is 22 and single. She is in the third year of her first job' (Nike 2001, p. 26; italics in original), the rhetoric minimises the potential for readers to engage with the worker as a human agent; rather, she remains at a safe, immaterial distance, despite the illusory effect, created by use of the second person, of her being directly addressed by the writer (and see Walker 1998, pp. 165–70). It is the writer who confidently asserts that, despite the fact that this worker's occupation is 'tedious, hard, and doesn't offer a wonderful future', she is 'here of her own free will' (Nike 2001, p. 26). As a reader, I must resort to imagining the voice of a Nike worker contesting this claim, challenging the denial of her moral agency and her language, arguing against the smug view of those in positions of power that 'the subordinated voluntarily serve' (Walker 1998, p. 166).

By stark contrast, the section 'Nike people', which asserts personnel as the company's most important asset and describes their diversity, opportunities for professional development and the compensation and benefits awarded to them, begins with a first-person account by a Nike employee. The rationale for this approach is explained at the outset: 'We thought the best way to introduce a section about Nike people would be to share a real story from a Nike person, and hear from her about our unique corporate culture' (Nike 2001, p. 40). The writer clearly understands the merits of 'a real story' (as opposed to a hypothetical or stereotypical one) and how, by harnessing a first-person account to represent personal experience, a subject is brought up close for the reader. The distance of the faceless, impersonal other is thus overcome. Predictably perhaps, the first-person account presented here (complete with a photo of the individual Nike employee and her partner) paints a glowing picture of Nike as a progressive and supportive employer. At the conclusion of her narrative, the employee remarks that 'so far my experience at Nike has been rewarding, challenging and unexpected. I am excited for tomorrow' (Nike 2001, p. 40). This summary remark, when set alongside that (third-person account) describing the subcontracted worker's experience (of work that is 'tedious, hard, and doesn't offer a wonderful future') produces a harsh dissonance.

In the 'Labor practices' section Nike is frank about the dilemmas raised by its pull of responsibilities, particularly between workers and their local social and economic contexts on the one hand, and the company's business interests on the other (see Nike 2001, p. 32). And the report in general demonstrates how extremely difficult it must be to make ethical decisions about labour practices, environmental sustainability and so on, in the face of market logic and shareholder demands for profitability. Such awareness notwithstanding, the report's rhetoric still seems to favour a market and profit-driven over a humanitarian or ethical impulse. For example, also in the 'Labor practices' section, an argument is mounted about why an increase in wages would disadvantage all stakeholders – even subcontracted workers who, on the face of it might initially be perceived as being obvious beneficiaries of such a move. The argument is carefully presented through paragraphs constructing a catch-22 market logic. The writer argues that increased wages would increase product costs, adversely affect the level of production and sales, and result in higher prices for consumers. The demand for products would consequently fall, and fewer units would mean lower earnings for shareholders, and also 'fewer jobs and lower earnings for Nike suppliers, employees and factory workers' (Nike 2001, p. 38).

The above examination demonstrates that, like other comparable texts, Nike's document appears to draw largely on two types of discourse in its narratives. First is the discourse of marketing or branding, which, through the production and representation of 'closed' stories, promotes its product as desirable for the consumer's integration into their aspired-for lifestyle, or for the investor's financial commitment to the corporation. Thus, through the use of marketing discourse, these two key groups of stakeholders are prioritised. Second is the discourse of ethics, which although apparently attempting to give an account of the company's moral relationships, identity and values, is subsumed by the discourses of marketing, advertising and commerce; in fact, it seems that ethics and ethical behaviour cannot be thought of or articulated otherwise. 'We run Corporate Responsibility like any other piece of the business. We have business plans, goals, action plans, timelines and measurables' (Nike 2001, p. 2). In this account, ethics and ethical relationships are 'managed' and apparently objectively measurable or quantifiable. It is evident that the public relations text is communicating on social responsibility issues that appeal particularly to *one* set of stakeholders (workers, community members, activists, concerned consumers) in a rhetorical discourse that most likely finds a far more ready understanding with *another* set of clearly *prioritised* stakeholders (shareholders, consumers and so on). In other words, what do 'business plans', 'timelines' and 'measurables' mean to Indonesian sports shoe factory workers who, if they work less than 60 hours a week in Nike contract facilities (in environments with substandard health and safety standards) struggle to survive, and who are often forced to live apart from their children and families?[21] Quoting data, statistics, rules and regulations, codes and principles adhered to, as Nike's report does, is not enough to construct an ethical and imaginative narrative. How does such language connect to people's lives, emotional and practical experiences, beliefs and values?

There is a sense, then, in which these two narrative discourses – of marketing and of ethics – have contradictory, or at least divergent, impulses. However, because marketing so often now, in its efforts to brand its products, draws on the rhetoric of human relationships, world views, and personal and social choices, in other words the language of morality, it becomes confused or conflated with ethical discourse. As a result, the rhetoric representing issues of corporate responsibility becomes absorbed into the branding process – 'freed from the corporeal world of commodities, manufacturing and products' (Klein 2001, p. 23). And people. In this scenario, the narratives of corporations' public relations texts can become almost completely obscured, and certainly alienated, from the very people and moral relationships they claim to be closely involved with and responsible to.

In a culture that demands that organisations present texts demonstrating their accountability and responsible and ethical practice, it can be conceded that they are easily tempted, even encouraged, to treat the process as a marketing exercise, and to produce self-descriptive, self-supporting documents, whose priority or focus becomes to bolster promotional initiatives. Used merely as a marketing 'ploy', however, social responsibility rhetoric proves to be a pitfall:

> the adoption of social responsibility rhetoric by corporations is a double-edged sword. On the one hand, it allows corporations to insulate themselves from pressure by the [anti-sweatshop] movement since they can point to the rhetoric as evidence that they have aligned themselves with the movement's agenda. On the other hand, beyond indicating a possible internal reconstitution of corporations' self-identity, this language provides a significant point of leverage, a form of rhetorical entrapment, for the movement to hold corporations to their 'words', and is a basis for activists to make further demands for improved production practices.
>
> (De Winter 2001, p. 111)

Perhaps, rather than viewing its use of language as 'rhetorical entrapment', Nike could exploit the opportunity that discourse offers to re-evaluate and modify both its writing and its business practices.

## *Kasky v Nike*: commerce or public debate?

De Winter's words, quoted above, were prescient. Another – potentially highly significant – dimension to the corporate social responsibility discussion in particular, and public relations practice in general, has been added by the lawsuit brought by US activist, Marc Kasky, against Nike, in which he accused the company of false advertising. The ultimately unresolved case, which passed between various California courts and an oral review by the US Supreme Court,[22] was finally concluded by an out-of-court settlement in September 2003, with Nike and Kasky agreeing that the company would donate US$1.5m to the Fair Labor Association[23] (see Nike 2003; Liptak 2003; BBC News 2003; Milchen and Kaplan 2003).

In 1998, Kasky sued Nike under California's Unfair Competition Law and False Advertising Law on behalf of the general public of the State of California (Goldstein 2003, p. 65). Kasky alleged that Nike's circulation of press releases, (paid) advertorials, letters to the editors of newspapers and to university presidents and athletics directors concerning employee pay and working conditions, particularly in South-East Asia, constituted false advertising.[24] Nike's defence was that the First Amendment (Free Speech) of the US Constitution protected the company from such claims.

Essentially, therefore, the case hinged on a debate about whether Nike's campaign of press releases, advertorials, letters and so on constituted free speech, which is protected by the Constitution, or commercial speech,[25] which is subject to government regulation and prohibits the issue of false and misleading statements. Nike contended that it was exercising its right to defend its business practices through engaging in public debate. The California Court of Appeal also held that Nike's statements 'form[ed] part of a public dialogue on a matter of public concern within the core area of expression protected by the First Amendment' (California Court of Appeal in Goldstein 2003, p. 66). However, the California Supreme Court held that Nike, as a manufacturer, distributor and retailer of sports shoes and apparel, is a commercial speaker. It also argued that Nike's statements were made to a commercial audience. Finally, the Court claimed that through a description of its labour policies, practices and factory working conditions, Nike 'was making factual representations about its own business operations' (California Supreme Court in Goldstein 2003, pp. 67–8).

The fact that the case remained unresolved at its settlement means that businesses are likely to feel tentative or reticent about writing public statements on or commentary about their practices. In Nike's case, this is undoubtedly so. In its press release following the case's settlement, the company's Vice President and General Counsel, Jim Carter, indicated that Nike, together with other corporations, media organisations and non-government organisations 'remain concerned about the impact of the California Supreme Court ruling on transparency – specifically companies who wish to report publicly on their progress in the areas of corporate responsibility'. He disclosed that, as a result of that ruling, Nike would not issue its corporate responsibility report for 2002, 'and will continue to limit its participation in public events and media engagement in California' (Nike 2003).[26]

The *Kasky v Nike* case raises some crucial questions that relate directly to the concerns of this chapter. Whether or not Nike's statements in its campaign were true or false was not addressed during any court hearing of the case, yet those statements were defended by the corporation as morally sincere. According to Thomas C. Goldstein, one of Nike's external counsel, Nike's statements 'conveyed the view that Nike does act morally because its investments produce substantial economic and political benefits for workers and because it puts its best effort toward ensuring that employees at its contract facilities are paid fairly and treated well. None of the statements at issue appeared in advertisements of Nike's products or urged consumers to buy those products' (Goldstein 2003, p. 65). Goldstein's statements reinforce the significance of Nike's intentions (its 'best effort'), and make generalised assumptions about their effects ('its investments produce substantial economic and political benefits for workers'). But surely judgements about morality can only be made in terms of the *relationships* that obtain between the parties in question, and of the impacts of different parties' actions and their implications on those relationships? And mustn't such judgements necessarily take into account the positions and the views of *all* those involved or implicated? Jim Carter's comments on transparency quoted above are important, and Nike is to be commended on its attempts to be open and self-reflective about its business practices. All the same, moving towards transparency also means giving readers the opportunity to look at issues and experiences written from different positions and reflecting different stakeholder voices, not only from the viewpoint of the writers. As Foucault's remarks, cited near the beginning of this chapter reminded us, completely transparent communication is impossible to achieve. Nevertheless, others need to write and speak themselves rather than be written or spoken for by significantly more powerful voices and in their preferred rhetorical discourses. If Nike is claiming to do the right thing, then the benefits of having others (apart from Nike-commissioned auditing agencies) endorse that through their own responsive commentary could be enormous. (And in the cases where respondents could not endorse the claims, they might offer Nike crucial direction on how to make its practices more equitable and ethical.) Of course, such a document would be unlikely to stand as a 'successful' marketing tool, but as *Kasky v Nike* has demonstrated, the confusion of marketing and moral discourses is anyway potentially fraught, particularly since the competing rhetorics draw attention to the demanding complexities of moral responsibility.

## Imaginative texts: a meaningful future for public relations texts

In its 2002 report, adidas-Salomon includes employee feedback (through direct quotation and summary) on the company's previous year's report. Several comments from employees relate to the issues concerning the company's responsibility for engaging more closely with the interests and contexts of less powerful stakeholder groups: ' "You have to divest yourself of some of your power by building a local process" ' and ' "You'd have greater legitimacy [if you included] more workers' voices" ' (adidas-Salomon 2003, p. 23). In response to this feedback the company admits that 'not all of [its] stakeholders have a voice' (adidas-Salomon 2003, p. 22).[27] It makes this observation again in its 2003 report, with the comment that 'the people who produce our products are an important part of our stakeholder community but we do not always hear their voices' (adidas-Salomon 2004, p. 14).[28]

If contemporary public relations practices are genuinely attempting to establish and extend ethical and mutually beneficial relationships with their various publics – and given the exponential rise in corporate social responsibility initiatives over recent years, we might assume that they are – they might reflect less on their capacity to engage in the polished telling and (in many cases) monotonous and monologic retelling of their preferred stories. Instead they might focus *more* (and more) attention on exchanging and negotiating different, discontinuous and open-ended stories with those publics. In other words, there needs to be a different conception of and approach to the development, function and usability of social responsibility texts.

It could, of course, be argued that given that counternarratives are circulating at the same time as a corporation's self-generated moral narrative, there is no need to shift approach. As well as being able to read a corporation's account in its social responsibility documents, some stakeholders at least have relatively easy access to contradictory accounts prepared by various activist organisations, non-government organisations and other interested parties. And yet in this scenario, the conflicting texts can remain out of touch: their dissonances may not be felt, the tangle of their often competing and sometimes incompatible claims not confronted – and the dynamic complexities of moral relationships neither acknowledged nor communicated.

By incorporating dissonant, uncensored voices, the (rarely read) texts of those who would counter or challenge a corporation's claims in its moral stories, such open, shared documents (like The Body Shop's employee stakeholder accounts, or the employee comments included in adidas-Salomon's report, referred to above) will preclude that polished finished-ness, which is anathema to a text articulating moral relationships, and extend the scope of potential contributor, reader and respondent stakeholders. Those voices could include a corporation's employees, its subcontracted workers, workers' families, the community members inhabiting the environments in and around a corporation's production facilities, activist organisations, and other groups that present different accounts, broader perspectives, or alternative views. The *evolving, dialogic text* proposed could also be used as the location at which monitoring and auditing activities and reports by independent organisations are publicised and commented on by interested individuals or groups.

Perhaps only then will corporate social responsibility documents resemble more than a studiously manufactured 'mishmash': the mess and clash of human relationships, the contradictions between capitalism and human welfare, the conflict between business and moral imperatives, obligations and responsibilities. All these will at least start the process of using texts not to distance corporations from their stakeholders but to bring them closer, even if only in closer conflict, so that new multi-authored stories may be imagined. Most importantly, such texts would lay the groundwork for discussion around why and how corporations and their stakeholders should go about developing and implementing better, more equitable, more humane business relationships.

# 5
## Being Professional by Email: Who/How are You?

In this chapter I investigate and problematise the notion of email exchange as so-called 'written conversation' in organisational contexts.[1] Drawing on interviews with users of email from two different workplace contexts, I explore the implications of this hybrid rhetorical form – email – for both professional writing and writing like a professional within and between workplaces. The senses of intimacy with and/or distance from others that email writing can either simultaneously or variously evoke implies a particular significance for the role of language in constructing subjectivity and in enabling (professionally- and personally-oriented) interaction between individuals. By reflecting on the impact of different, particularly attitudinal and situational, contexts on the processes of and approaches to writing and reading email texts, I argue that the email writer's activity of imagining (the other) in those processes becomes pressing. The chapter bases its discussion on Mark Poster's (1990, 2001) exuberant evocation of the shifting identities of the postmodern subject as mediated by digital communication technologies. It also takes particular account of Richard Lanham's (1993) advocacy of the practice of switching between 'looking at' and 'looking through' approaches to language, that is, switching between treating language as constitutive on the one hand and as instrumental on the other. Both theorists help me to articulate how we might imaginatively and ethically relate to one another through email communication in professional contexts.[2]

Unlike other forms of professional writing considered in this book, email as a communication technology in the professional environment very often explicitly obliges us to engage or interact with or respond to others *as individual subjects* through the written word (even when, as is often the case, the main focus of our interaction is work oriented). In this way, email has the potential to extend the boundaries of both the form and content of what has conventionally been defined as professional writing, particularly in workplace contexts. It is therefore, I think, an appropriate mode of writing with which to conclude this study. Zooming us back into the zone of direct interpersonal contact, an exploration of email, as writing praxis, facilitates and highlights the potential for reconciling writers and readers as human subjects. It also demonstrates how our responsibility as writers, using rhetoric as we do in particular ways and for particular ends, must work to collapse easy distinctions between public and private, 'you' and 'I', 'them' and 'us'. And it throws into relief the importance of imagining the relationship between our rhetorical intentions and the range of their possible effects.

In his article 'Email and the problems of communication' (2000), Derek Wallace explores the ambivalent attitude towards email of its users. At the conclusion of his discussion, he remarks that 'it would be a pity if people continued to jump to the conclusions encouraged by dichotomous conceptions of email (intimate/impersonal, democratic/autocratic, etc.), rather than consciously working to develop a reflexive, open and case-specific relationship with the technology'.[3] I hope that this chapter, in addition, serves to contribute to that endeavour.

## The subject of email

On a specifically operational level, the function of email could crudely be described as a technology for connecting individuals through a machine network, for the purpose of enabling them to disseminate and exchange a variety of data (in their broadest sense). However, such a description ignores both the obvious scope and the evidently ubiquitous use of email for far more than data delivery and receipt.

This chapter is concerned with exploring email as written conversation in professional contexts. In other words, my interest lies in the use of email as a substitute for face-to-face or telephone contact (that is, interpersonal exchange between embodied or disembodied subjects). This substitution takes place either because space or time preclude the possibility or viability of direct contact, or because email has become a pervasive and normative form of communication in professional contexts,[4] even when, as is often the case, correspondents share the same office, or the same office location. While email has the capacity to disseminate a host of genres – memos, letters, reports, flyers, spreadsheets, and so on – I am here interested in such forms, *only as far as* they determine relations of exchange between writers and readers. Thus, for example, the memo format and style adopted by some writers in this study is significant only insofar as it influences how, in professional contexts, writers imagine themselves and others in the process of communicating ideas, feelings, information or whatever.

Mark Poster draws on Derrida's affirmation of the significance of textuality as difference, and highlights the way in which our subjectivities have been transformed by what he calls the new 'modes of information' (see Poster 1990; 1997, pp. 45–7). Our engagement with various electronic communication systems, such as television, fax machines, VCRs, computers, the Internet, email and so on, have produced us as postmodern 'textualised agents' (see Poster 1997, pp. 38–71). This nicely represents, I think, how the identities of the writer and of the responding writer–reader are *so obviously* 'in process' through our respective texts in email communication. Indeed, email seems to require that we literally *put our selves on the line (and in our lines)* in ways that other forms of professional writing might not – even in those instances when our identities are only evident through our signatures, and even when those signatures represent an organisational rather than personal gesture. Thus, email could be said to invite and perhaps even require the conflation of the *personal* with the *professional*, the *private* with the *public*.[5] Or perhaps email communication simply exposes the illusoriness of their separateness, and thus also suggests the need for a renegotiation of the term professional. In any case, the postmodern context of electronic communication entails the reconstitution of our identities through each of our exchanges.

As email writers, we can look at ourselves as other (although this capacity will vary according to how far and in what contexts we use email as an immediate or spontaneous form of contact or response). As we write, we represent ourselves on the screen through our texts, and we can scrutinise, revise and edit those texts extensively; we can thus also scrutinise, revise and edit who and how we (would like to) appear in the text. This is never to claim that we have complete freedom in this process, or that how we appear to ourselves at a given moment in a text that we write and send to others is how we will appear to them. How we appear to ourselves may of course change (as when we look back at some of the emails we may have written and are critical of our self-representation, of *who* we were and *how* we were in that particular communication).

Even if there is broad consensus about the fact that the primary function of email in the workplace is to exchange business- or organisation-related information, I'd suggest that there is significantly less agreement about our potential roles as interacting subjects as part of that primary function. There is also, it seems to me, considerable difference of view about the status and function of language (as instrumental on the one hand, as constitutive on the other) in the preparation and exchange of emails in the professional environment. As professional writers, we need to be sensitive and responsive to this difference of view, this different approach to and use of email as written conversation in workplace contexts. In addition, we need to develop an awareness of our and others' approaches and practices, and to develop a flexibility to accommodate the needs of different writing contexts and different correspondents. Such a manoeuvre attempts to encourage a move away from what I perceive as the generating of rather limited strategies for effective email writing, such as developing email protocols or prescribing preferred formats or style for effective email use. I hope that, from what follows, a more expansive and more self-reflexive approach to email praxis may be articulated and debated, one that makes its priority the situated, subjective processes and impacts of ethical written exchange.

## Subject-ing ourselves through email

The various attitudes to email technology mentioned above resemble or parallel, I think, those expressed by individuals, in their awareness of and anxiety about the inconsistent subjectivities articulated through language itself, and for our purposes, though email writing in particular. In other words, while we may relish email as a form of communication for the control, reach and flexibility it affords us in communicating with others, we probably also resist it due to the limited control we can exert over how others might 'read' us in those communications. We are reluctant (and understandably so, particularly in professional contexts) to relinquish the idea of ourselves as expressly rational, coherent and singular identities.

In contrast to such reservations, Mark Poster clarifies his understanding of this postmodern (writing) subject almost gleefully and certainly graphically, when he describes computer writing as:

> the quintessential postmodern linguistic activity. With its dispersal of the subject in nonlinear spatio-temporality, its immateriality, its disruption of stable identity, computer writing institutes a factory of postmodern subjectivity, a machine for constituting non-identical subjects, an inscription of an other of Western culture into its most cherished manifestation. One might call it a monstrosity.
>
> (Poster 1990, p. 128)

Poster's description may sound rather radical an evocation of the subject positions under scrutiny in this chapter – email writers and readers in the professional domain. And I do think that his claims, because they remain decontextualised, need to be qualified through application to specific instances of computer writing. However, here I am interested in how the 'monstrosity', this excessive subject Poster envisages, is manifested in her/his role as a professional, by an email writer. Following Poster, if we assume that electronic communication involves a *process* of (re)constructing subjectivity and intersubjectivity, how is our subjectivity/intersubjectivity produced (actively or inadvertently) through the language, style and forms in and through which we write and are written?[6] Conversely, if we are resistant to any such notions of 'subject-ing' ourselves through email, what happens to 'us' then? What if we (or our correspondents) do regard and approach email in workplace contexts as having merely a transactional, impersonal function, or as an activity from which we, as individual subjects, are (or should be) removed? What happens to interaction then?[7]

In order to help us to understand and be responsive to these differences in attitudes to language and to our roles as email writers in professional contexts – to help us imagine our relation to the other – I think we might usefully take into account the distinction Richard Lanham (1993) draws between two broad approaches to understanding, using and interpreting language. Drawing on Richard McKeon's distinction between verbal and architectonic rhetoric, Lanham explains how the latter, architectonic rhetoric, involves what he calls 'toggling between' the two understandings of language as rhetoric: looking *at* language and looking *through* it. Looking *at* language involves using it, interpreting it self-consciously and playing games with it; looking *through* language involves using it, interpreting it unselfconsciously and acting purposively, using it as a tool. This is what Lanham calls his 'Strong Defense' argument for rhetoric, one which, he argues, 'assumes that truth is determined by social dramas, some more formal than others, but all man-made [sic]. Rhetoric in such a world is not ornamental but determinative, essentially creative' (Lanham 1993, p. 156). It is this 'creative' or constructive property of rhetoric, of language, that encourages us to look *at* it. In professional contexts, for example, this approach means that we pay close attention to (that is, we examine, critique, assess) how we construct ourselves in relation to our correspondents through email language, and how email language writes us to the other.

However, in addition, 'since truth comes to humankind in so many diverse and disagreeing forms, we cannot base a polity upon it. We must, instead, devise some system by which we can agree on a series of contingent operating premises' (Lanham 1993, pp. 187–8). These 'contingent operating premises' I would call provisionally shared understandings (understandings based on our knowledge and trust of our correspondents, or on our mutual interests, or on acknowledgement of each other's professional or personal positions, for example). Such understandings enable us to look *through* language, treating it as stable and referential, at certain times and in certain communicative contexts. In this way, we use language purposively. In professional contexts, for example, this approach means that we can exchange ideas, views and knowledge with colleagues, argue and debate, make decisions, agree on and take actions and so on. It also means that language *does* things – that emailing is a praxis with material consequences for ourselves and others, and on the social contexts in which we live and communicate.

I want to claim that it is particularly useful and important to understand rhetoric as architectonic when we email colleagues and clients in professional contexts. In so doing we can be sensitive and responsive to the ways we and our correspondents situate ourselves in relation to the function and value of the medium. This applies whether we regard email, as some writers appear to do, as an impersonal conduit for communicating – transparently and unproblematically – work-related information, ideas, questions and so on. Or whether we, as some other writers appear to do, demonstrate resistance to email as a form of interpersonal exchange, regarding it as limiting or controlling our capacity to 'be ourselves'. Or whether we, as still other writers appear to do, regard email as a medium offering us the opportunity for (re)constructing ourselves and our relationship with our correspondents, as well as for (re)constructing information, ideas, questions and so on. Of course, it is quite likely that all of us share one or more of those attitudes some or all of the time. And that flexibility is important, I think, depending on who we are, on our writing contexts, on the reasons for emailing, and on our relationships with different correspondents.

It is by looking *at* the language of email (our own and others') that we can better understand how, on the one hand, we use language self-consciously to construct ourselves as subjects and to set up (or modify) our relationships with others, and, on the other hand, how language itself constructs and positions us and our correspondent(s) as writing subjects. Conversely, it is by looking *through* email language that we can trust in the possibility of making meaningful, authentic and valuable connections with others, and acknowledge the potential for shared understandings and communicative reciprocity, both personal and professional.

We should combine or toggle between these approaches to language in the process of writing or reading a single email, concentrating more on the looking *at* or the looking *through* depending on the particular writing (or reading) context in which we are situated. Both these positions, and how or when we might toggle between them, involve making ethical judgements, judgements about our relationship to our correspondents and how the language through which we represent ourselves and are represented modifies and extends that relationship.

As we have seen, for Poster, however, it appears that electronic culture determines that language can *only* be looked *at* rather than (or as well as) *through*. According to Poster, a new understanding of the relationship between the subject and language is precisely the result of 'the combination of enormous distances with temporal immediacy produced by electronic communications', one which 'both removes the speaker from the listener and brings them together'. Now, for Poster, language 'no longer represents a reality, no longer is a neutral tool to enhance the subject's instrumental rationality: language becomes or better reconfigures reality. And by doing so the subject is interpellated through language and cannot easily escape recognition of that interpellation. Electronic communications systematically remove the fixed points, the grounds, the foundations that were essential to modern theory' (Poster 1995, p. 60). But, I would argue, the very process of (particularly ongoing) email exchange enables correspondents to produce their own (however provisional) fixed points, grounds, foundations (Lanham's 'contingent operating premises'), which does make it possible (and necessary) to look *through* as well as *at* language.

## The primary research process

As part of my investigation into email praxis, I carried out semi-structured interviews with professionals, to talk with them about their experiences of and approaches and attitudes to email use as a mode of interpersonal communication in their specific professional contexts. The aim was to draw theoretical inferences from my discussions with participants, and this explains my interweaving of their comments and email writing samples with my arguments below.

My strong sense that email communication as medium and as practice is highlighting significant questions about language, writing and subjectivity in the professional and public domains, questions that are important for reflecting on our relations with others, helped to determine my approach. Here, case study research, which involved my examination of relevant documents complemented by discussions with writer participants, serves to stimulate reflection about how and why professionals think about and use email in the ways they do. The aim of such an endeavour, however, as I have mentioned, is not to advocate one method of approaching email over another or to recommend preferred language use in specific contexts. It is rather to help foster broader options for theorising, interpreting and practising email exchange, which retain as central the ethical and imaginative relation between self and others developed through rhetoric.

My choice of participants and organisations was based on the fact that I was interested in talking to people whom I knew, and with whose environments I was familiar. I felt that with the participants knowing me, and knowing that I understood (at least to some extent) the culture of their work environments, it would make it more likely that they might talk openly, and without the need to explain or furnish a background to all their comments. Although my aim was not to undertake any kind of comparative study, I was keen to gain a range of responses, and thought this would be more likely if I were to interview professionals from quite different organisational contexts: one a university in Western Australia, and the other the West Australian office of a multinational organisation, Techniq.[8]

The first group of case study participants were three individuals who work for one of the world's largest international companies providing products and services to the oil and gas industries. All three work in the company's engineering, construction and services group, from the West Australian office. I know two of the participants – consulting engineers – because I had worked alongside them in the days when one part of the organisation had been an Australian-owned consulting engineering company. Today, Greg is the general manager of the state office. Richard holds a senior position as a consultant engineer. The third participant, Tom, was my replacement in the role of state editor, a position he retains in the current incarnation of the organisation.

The second group of case study participants are members of staff where I work, at Murdoch University (in Western Australia). Two of them are, like me, academics in humanities – Jane and Sarah, both senior lecturers. At the time of the interviews Luke, the third participant in this group and a member of the administrative staff, acted as the liaison point between and the coordinator of activities involving academics and industry professionals. (He has since moved into another position.)

As planned, I spent some time before each interview reading through and evaluating the sample emails I had been sent by each participant.

(Incidentally, each of them sent me a selection of emails, ranging from those written a couple of days before and those written several months previously. I decided not to send those earlier emails back and remind them of my request for recent emails, deciding rather the participants had felt the email trail 'history' provided was significant.) This process of going through emails cold, as it were – that is, as someone unfamiliar with the specific background to or context of an exchange, and in many cases as someone not familiar with the correspondent(s) – was at times frustrating. It made me realise how 'of the moment' our email exchanges are, however carefully planned and executed.

## Email@work

For each of the participants from Techniq email plays a significant role in the working day; all acknowledged that email communication plays a pivotal role in their organisational culture. Each of the Techniq participants also acknowledged the benefits of email: to transmit messages at speed, regardless of the time of day (particularly interstate and internationally, where time differences impose restrictions on the viability of other forms of communication); to record correspondence; to leave a trail of communication exchange; to facilitate the sharing of information. Most of these benefits, however, were also felt to play some role in what the participants variously considered are the general drawbacks of email as a mode of communication.

Richard, Greg and Tom each expressed their sense that email was overused or misused for intra-office communication: 'people are substituting email for conversation ... It needlessly uses up time', commented Richard. And Greg complained, 'it's crazy, some [internal staff] sit and email all day'. 'You get too many of the dashed things', said Tom, and Richard told how many co-workers are unnecessarily copied in on messages. Since he is aware that he 'commit[s] people to 5–10 minutes of their time' by including them in a message, he is conscious of whom he copies into his correspondence. Each of the participants also suggested that the speed of email communication imposes a considerable pressure on them to work more quickly.[9] They also talked about the substantial time involved, on a daily basis, in both writing and responding to emails. Each suggested too, in different ways, the kinds of irresistible constraints or control they feel email exerts on their working lives, and, at the same time, the ways in which they attempt to defy that control. Greg remarked that 'you're led around by the email', and his defiance of that control is to 'leave them ... I don't let [email] demand how I do things'. However, he admitted that he does then have to spend three or so hours each Saturday morning at home clearing the email backlog. Tom too commented how Saturday mornings often involved 'an email clearance operation'. Richard feels that email 'needlessly uses up time', and therefore responds to his correspondence only on an as-needs basis (often when his correspondents phone him to remind him that he hasn't responded to an email!). The number of emails in his inbox often 'gets out of hand', so that he is forced to set aside time, once a week or once a fortnight, to getting the inbox 'back in control'. (Richard and Greg mentioned how, because their email software, Outlook, is also their diary, their email is always open.) Tom described himself as 'a firefighter ... my life is a crisis here', so that he feels he always needs to check new emails as they come in.

Each of the university participants also spend a significant time each day on email correspondence – Sarah two to three hours a day, Jane one to one-and-a-half hours. Jane remarked how she generally checks her email only twice a day (she has switched off the computer's facility for checking and signalling incoming mail at frequent intervals), so that her time spent on email is organised into blocks. When working from home (which academics can sometimes do), Sarah will also switch on her email facility a couple of times a day; when she is at work the facility is continuously running. Luke, however, explained how three-quarters of his day is spent on email: 'it's the centre of everything I do ... it's the first thing I open [when I arrive at work] ... it's the last thing I close [before I go home]'. Using Outlook in combination with Microsoft Projects, Luke also uses his email as a project management tool.

Jane, Sarah and Luke all felt that email offers a range of benefits in the workplace context. The immediacy, the speed of communication exchange, the capacity to be in touch with people otherwise difficult to contact, the ability to deal with administrative matters or to send various administrative data to several people simultaneously via email were all mentioned by participants as significant advantages of the technology. Jane qualified her remarks by adding that she uses email 'primarily for relatively straightforward administrative things', since she prefers to talk to people and 'to back up' communication with her own 'body language and [oral] communication'. By contrast, as an academic who feels relatively isolated in WA in terms of her particular discipline, Sarah commented that she found the email 'an amazing tool'. It allows her to keep in touch with interstate or overseas correspondents (and to initiate contact with those with whom communication would otherwise be precluded – for example, with academics whose work she admires). She described her sense of email as offering 'a freedom' in such communication: in circumstances where she might feel tentative about disturbing her colleagues by phone to confer on intellectual matters, with email 'you're hiding behind your machine' and are afforded the potential for informal exchange. Luke believes that email allows him to have 'multiple things on the go', to better organise information, to keep track of what's going on, and to have a record of activities in progress.

Both Jane and Luke feel that a key disadvantage of email is the volume of correspondence that results from the facility in communication. 'I get so many emails' remarked Luke, and 'there's a lot of crap'. For Jane, too, 'there's an awful lot of unnecessary communication'. But for both participants this nevertheless results in their feeling pressured to respond to or act on emails quickly. Jane commented that there is an expectation in the workplace culture that email will get a response. She also believes that things could often be dealt with more quickly 'if you pop in and see someone'.

From the above comments it seems clear that attitudes vacillate between individuals' sense of control and lack of control over email technology (and by extension over their working lives and practices), their resistance to and embrace of its reach, their appreciation of its enabling flexibility and resentment of its curtailing of independence.

This fluctuating between a sense of control and lack of control can be directly linked to the belief that the language of email, removed from its embodied author, in some cases offers us an opportunity to engage productively with the other, or is inadequate to represent us *fully* or as we *intend* to be represented.[10] For example, demonstrating his privileging of the spoken word as the more controllable (and therefore, by implication, more authentic) form of communication, Luke compared email unfavourably to the telephone, describing the latter as 'a much more negotiated way of dealing with people'. Jane is aware that she is more concerned with qualifying her statements or comments in email: 'when you're writing you try to cover all the bases'. Sarah's comments echoed this sentiment, when she remarked that 'I feel quite tentative about how I come across ... I'm incredibly anxious about how I say [sic] something.' And so she tends to be self-deprecating in her emails 'as an insurance policy [against that uncertainty]', and against the lack of ownership or control over the material she writes. At the same time, however, Sarah also feels email has offered her opportunities to get to know (particularly interstate and overseas) colleagues far better than she would have been able to otherwise.

For those who feel that email generally precludes them from meaningful interpersonal exchange with their correspondents, and who are reluctant to allow themselves to be 'subject-ed' by email, the medium is treated as an impersonal mode of communication. Paradoxically, of course, attempting to avoid subject-ing ourselves, by consciously keeping personal 'stuff' out (how we are feeling, what is going on in our lives), does not produce text without a subject-writer, but simply another kind of subject (one who, in some situations, may be interpreted as cold, distant, and, in others, focused, to the point and so on). As well, the style and tone of email writing – whatever its topic – inevitably help to define the writing subject.

Thus the crude opposition between personal and impersonal, between public and private, does seem to be challenged through the practice of email rhetoric. Perhaps this is precisely because different email writers have different conceptions of the 'proper' conventions of email exchange. So isn't it each writer and reader's responsibility to imagine the other, and to write (and read) in ways that try to negotiate each other's differences and to use a rhetoric that respects those, while it also manages to develop texts that are interpretable and workable?

For Richard and Greg, email communication is an impersonal mode; both participants emphasised this point in different ways. Richard talked about how the medium of email does not help us to get to know others. And to support his conviction, he cited instances of how mistaken his assumptions have been in building up an image of someone's personality through their email writing. Greg too mentioned how, 'without exception', people are different when you meet them to how they appear in email. The idea of them built up through correspondence is contradicted by meeting them in person, according to Richard and Greg. However, it could be argued that this difference demonstrates how for each of us, our subjectivity is simply complicated by different – textual and bodily – representations.

Richard explained how he focuses on 'the message' rather than the person when he writes. He writes emails as if he is writing 'for nobody', and believes that the message will carry anywhere, independent of the person sending it. However, even the more dissemination-focused of his emails do generally appear to take implicit account of his relationship with his readers.[11] In one of Richard's emails (in quasi memo format and style), reproduced below, I have roughly edited the text removing all intersubjective references. The resulting email, it seems to me, directed at 'nobody', communicates its message inadequately, precisely because it floats free of a link between those who together would produce it as meaningful – and worthy of their attention.

Luke shares the view that emails should be impersonal: 'I don't use email much for personal things'; they 'don't come into play … I really don't like personal things in emails.' Therefore, while Luke regards email as 'a mechanism [for] keeping in contact' because it 'doesn't do anything

Subject: ENVIRO AND PLANNING WORKSHOP
~~Guys~~

For the workshop agenda ~~you will notice on the draft that we have allocated~~ one half hour <u>has been allocated</u> to each state for an overview of the current situation. ~~My thoughts are that this~~ <u>This should</u> cover:

- skills available
- type of work undertaken
- clients (industry, size, public/private)
- current business plan (strategy)

~~Could you please structure your presentations~~ <u>Presentations should be structured</u> along these lines and combine the enviro and planning activities.
~~Regards~~

Richard

to build' a personal relationship; he reiterated his sense of email as not being conducive to 'chat' or 'interaction'. Indeed, his email samples were typically brief and focused on the business at hand; no non-business material is included:

Subject: RE: In-kind

Kris the next stage is to have Meg sign a form that shows the commitments [organisation name] have agreed to make to this project. Do you have a fax number I can fax this to?

This approach may be fine in instances where we have other opportunities for (non-email) interaction, or where there exists some shared context of understanding, so that our recipients may more readily recognise the value of our exchange by imagining who is writing to us. However, Jane believes it is important to provide this context, within her emails to students and colleagues. She explained that she tries 'to invoke an ethic of friendliness' in her emails, though this was not necessarily spontaneous. She said that she didn't 'intuitively have that friendly thing', but would focus on the business at hand and then add something personal.

While continued email exchange allows us to become more familiar with our correspondents, it doesn't allow us to get to know them better, according to Richard. Greg also noted: 'I use email to communicate information. I don't use email to communicate relationships ... I can't communicate in writing on a personal level.' Greg's management style is 'person to person', he explained, because you can better gauge people's responses to what you are saying when you are face-to-face with them. With email, by contrast, he argued, 'you might get it wrong', and aware of his status as a professional and as a senior manager, he also remarked that 'you're careful with what you write'.

---

Subject: [local office] Operations for Onshore/Offshore

People,

We announced at the last toolbox meeting that there would be changes to the reporting structure of [the local office]. This email now confirms that arrangement.

This restructuring will provide our Oil and Gas people in [local office] with greater access to our global capacity and outlines a clear direction for the group. Importantly, we must ensure that we continue to work together to share technology and resources so that our respective businesses maximise the opportunities in our region. If you have any queries on the following [email, copied below], pls do not hesitate to grab me, Greg

---

Many of Greg's emails resemble the sample above: summarising actions and plans, issuing advice and directives, and so on. He sometimes abbreviates his words and writes in note form. Like Richard's emails, Greg's do address his correspondents directly or use the first-person plural; beyond that, however, there is little personal engagement.[12]

As well, for Luke, Greg and Richard the notion of the embodied subject as 'real', fully present and in control, by contrast with the textual subject as inauthentic, partial and not in control (of itself or others) is highlighted by their comments. While I would endorse the belief that, in many instances, email is a poor (and potentially damaging) substitute for face-to-face encounters, the view expressed above can also be read as misguided and simplistically intentionalist: that is, that when we have face-to-face contact the 'message' we intend to communicate is the one 'received' by our listener. Such a view takes little account of the inevitability that the interpreting subject will always interpret what we say differently (if only slightly) from the way we intend them to.

Tom's attitude towards the potential for email as a means of interpersonal exchange is completely different. It seems to me that this may be accounted for by his completely contrasting approach to language, his sense of its role in defining who he is, and his correspondingly different estimation of its value and significance. This fact cannot, of course, be unrelated to his status as a professional editor: his business is, after all, words. 'I like words ... I love words', he enthused, and his self-conscious relishing of the richness of language is easily identified in his email correspondence.

---

Subject: Good news on CP Database installation

Dear Colleagues,

The more enthusiastic among you, eager to complete your new Career Profiles on the spanking-new, state-of-the-art Career Profile database, have in most cases been dismayed to find that you have been unable to install and/or access the database. Unfortunately, your slumped shoulders, doleful faces and whingeing in the kitchens and other watering holes (to say nothing of the muffled, and occasionally unmuffled, imprecations and curses emanating from your workstations) have discouraged your less enthusiastic colleagues from even looking for the database.

But today I am the bearer of good news and the bringer of glad tidings – our IT colleagues have now overcome the problem and, with cheerful cries, delighted squeals and lightened hearts, you can now all set about installing factual information about your illustrious careers and diverse skills on the database.

[instructions follow]

The task is now complete. To open the Career Profile database, all you need to do is click on Start, then on All Programs, then on Career Profile Database and your cups of happiness will overflow. When you have mopped up the resulting mess and cleaned your keyboards you will be able to start working on your CPs.

Have fun!
Cheers,
Tom

---

The email above, like many of Tom's others, is highly performative but, while evidently more 'personal' in its approach than those above, does not necessarily demonstrate a more intimate engagement with his interlocutors. Tom described the key advantage of email as allowing him 'to be creative'. He enjoys writing emails whose distinguishing characteristics, even as they communicate work-related information, are humour, irony and sarcasm. He believes that email is a useful medium for getting to meet and to know people better: 'I meet more people every day by far through email than in the corridor.' He commented as well on how he will go to 'extra effort' in emails to people 'who are clever' and who 'like words'. In contrast, Greg suggested his suspicion of people who rely on the written word for self-creation through his comment that 'some people are very good at using the written word to make themselves look favourable'. Greg and Tom's contrasting views highlight the two significant notions of language mentioned above: as constitutive, on the one hand, and as instrumental on the other. I will go on to argue that to approach the writing of emails imaginatively and ethically we need to consider our textual relations with others with a sensitivity to both.

## Imagining the other by looking at/through language

Given the tensions or contradictions inherent in email praxis briefly outlined above, the task of imagining, particularly in making present the immaterial – in this case, our correspondents and their interpretation and use of our email texts, as well as the rhetorical and moral issues at stake in specific communication and reception processes – is particularly urgent. In the context of email writing and reading, Lanham's suggestion that we look through as well as look at language can help us in that process of imagining. Email, while not necessarily or always resembling the easy banter of some oral exchange, does always require, I would argue, the engagement (to a greater or lesser extent, whether explicitly or otherwise) of writers and readers as individual subjects in the transmission and receipt of work-related data, particularly because it is increasingly substituting for face-to-face or telephone communication. The dangers of focusing merely on 'messages' as though they float in a vacuum, and of forgetting their dynamic connection to (the subjectivity of) specific writers and readers in specific writing and reading contexts are obvious. And Richard's observation that in his workplace employee satisfaction surveys record the frequent complaint that there is 'a lack of communication ... and yet emails are running hot' indicates that readers and writers are themselves concerned about the lack of connection between colleagues.[13] Looking at language in the process of writing and reading emails helps us to imagine both *how* language creates and *what* language does: its power to construct writing and reading subjects, to define and extend an appropriate and ethical relation between them, and the contexts through which their communication produces meaning and value.

The participants in this study all appeared, in different ways and with different emphases, to focus on themselves, their correspondents and on the message, in the process of writing. It seems, however, that the interdependence of those elements and their configuration of a modified contextual space is not always recognised. For example, Tom accepted that his email writing process is involved with some concentration on presenting himself: 'I try to project my personality to [my colleagues] ... I'm trying to develop in my victims some sense of who Tom is ... I want them to know what I am.' Conversely, for Greg, a focus on self-presentation when writing an email evidently suggests inappropriate practice. He said he did not do this, but 'I think others do ... people try to make you aware of their successes through email.' For Richard, this understanding of self-representation as self-promotion is to be inferred from some colleagues' habit of copying others in on the emails they write, to spread the word that they are 'working hard'. The university participants talked about the question of self-presentation specifically in relation to their roles as professionals. Luke distinguished between internal and external correspondents in his comments, explaining that emails to industry contacts take him much longer to write, as he is concerned with looking professional and efficient, and is particular about using industry-specific language. For internal correspondence, by contrast, 'I'm much more flippant ... because you've got a much higher level of personal integration.' By contrast, Sarah sees herself as 'an academic in the whole of my life' not just in work, and for her, 'all aspects of business and [the] personal intersect'. Thus, emails written in a professional capacity have 'some kind of quirk of me in them'. She described how she 'kind of test[s] a little bit', how far she can go by putting in something personal in her emails 'to see how [her correspondents] respond'. An excerpt from one of her emails illustrates this point:

---

Subject: RE: [name of performance piece]

Dear Peter

Thanks for your reply. I really did enjoy reading your paper by the way – i hope i said that – I have the odd lapse due to placenta fog.

well, that's my excuse!
i've moved the comments into the text (at the bottom) so they can just go one after the other with the highlighted words – i hope this makes sense and can be deciphered ...

---

She noted too that she tends to be 'more experimental' with women than with men in this attitude of interspersing personal with professional matters.

Of course, it important to point out that self-referentiality when writing does not necessarily suggest solipsism,[14] although a preoccupation with (self) image rather than with imagining ourselves primarily as a relation to the other may well preclude meaningful or ethical contact with others. In both formulating the image and in the act of imagining we require the other, but in very different ways. In the first case, we need the other primarily to help us fashion the image we hope will be desirable, acceptable, reputable, attractive, good (and fixed). And our aim to make ourselves desirable, acceptable, reputable, attractive or good is largely motivated by self-interest rather than interest in the other. (Here, we are only interested in the other insofar as they can help us present an image from which we will ultimately benefit. They may benefit too, of course, but that would be an incidental outcome.) In the second case, we need the other to come to an understanding of what we (both) want, what we (both) need – at a given moment – and how we might negotiate or compromise our relative positions in that process. We can only do that by putting ourselves in each other's places: imagining the other's needs, interests, values. It doesn't mean giving up our own needs, interests or values for them (as we so often feel we are required to do when we write from subordinate or disempowered positions). In other words it doesn't mean presenting ourselves in writing as the other would have it. But it does mean acknowledging our *obligation* to be receptive to the other, to their similarly various subjectivity, and to engage with them as another unique subject towards whom we have a responsibility, and with whom we share an awareness of the contingency of our subjective position (see Poster 1995, pp. 73–4).

The intersection between the mode of communication and relative positions of writers and readers, as well as their respective use of language are also significant issues in the process of imagining, writing and reading emails. Greg and Tom both said that as they write they take into account the individual personalities of their correspondents. For Greg, 'you know the issues that individuals have ... you know how they view the world'. And while he takes this knowledge into consideration as he writes, he feels that, nevertheless, 'you might get it wrong', admitting the fallibility of what it is we (think we) know. For Richard, it is rather a question of focusing on the message (trying to keep it 'black and white') and attempting to keep it short, rather than focusing on the person. (As far as the brevity of email messages is concerned, both Richard and Greg referred to their attempts to emulate the practice of the company's senior management, whose comments in email exchanges are extremely brief.) It seems to me, however, that exclusive focus on 'the message', in other words on language's purposive function, involves the danger of misunderstanding how language constructs and modifies the context for purposeful exchange *between* individuals.

It appears we may be more aware of the constitutive function of language in those emails that we write to correspondents with whom we feel less familiar or to whom we have a different, hierarchical relation. Greg, Richard and Tom all said they used language differently depending on who their correspondents were. Greg admitted he would be more careful (as, no doubt, many of us would) about sending a message to the Vice President of the company than he would to 'the troops'. Richard described as 'sanitised' those emails that he sends to people he doesn't know well. He compared this style with the 'phone call down on paper' email to those whom he does know well. 'Absolutely' and 'Definitely' were Sarah and Luke's respective replies to the question of whether they write differently according to who their correspondents are. Sarah observed that she is 'always thinking' about her correspondents (as professionals and as individuals) as she write her emails. Luke extended his point by explaining that when he knows his correspondent well, he is happy to say he doesn't know what he is talking about; he wouldn't do that with someone he doesn't know. He also described himself as 'much more obsequious' when writing to senior executives. Where the stakes appear to be lower, then, we may well have the sense that language use can be more 'natural' or spontaneous. However, Jane was clear that difference in email writing or writing approach does not depend on who her correspondents are but on the context of writing: 'it's what the matter is that determines how something is written'.

To talk about language use in email writing, we are bound also to consider technical accuracy and the ways in which its importance is regarded or understood by different email writers and readers. For example, whoever his correspondents are, Greg tries to use what he called 'proper English ... you've got to have certain standards'. Similarly, Tom described himself as 'old-fashioned ... I don't approve of sloppiness in email writing ... I'm generally opposed to rotten English and slipping standards.' He partly explained this position through an observation about himself as a professional: 'I see myself as an advocate of better English.' While technical accuracy is not as big an issue for Luke in email writing – 'they're just typos' – he tries 'not to send spelling mistakes out'. Jane remarked that the level of her attention to technical accuracy again depends on the context of writing rather than on whom she's writing to. If Sarah is writing to a senior colleague, whom she knows 'is very good at English', she becomes anxious about her email. With other colleagues, with whom she gets on and by whom she doesn't feel judged, she can use email 'in the way I think it should be used': that is, she can be quick; she won't 'worry about it'; she'll 'get to the message'; and she'll include 'a quick hello'.

The process of imagining, of looking through as well as at language, is once again a more useful way of evaluating the significance of technical accuracy in professional contexts. I'm very doubtful whether, considered purely as a formal principle (that is, as representing some kind of objective standard for so-called proper communication), technical accuracy is of particular importance or relevance. Isn't it rather a question of considering the technology (and the pressures it may exert on us to write at speed – and therefore sometimes in error), and, as already argued, the context of the particular connection between writers, readers and message? In this case, then, the *what* and the *how*, in other words, notions of content and form in relation to language's forging connections and exchanging meanings effectively between correspondents, are inseparable. Technical accuracy can of course range from small typographical errors to substantive syntactical or grammatical mistakes – all of which may or may not inhibit the communication of ideas and information. There may, in certain situations, be perfectly good reasons why an email should be (technically) error free; in other situations such errors may matter far less, if at all. Again it is a question of being sensitive to the needs of particular writing and reading contexts, of being able to toggle between looking at and looking through language, and understanding the vital connections between the purposive and constitutive qualities of language.

The same goes, I think, for the process of revising and editing emails. The practice of redrafting an email and the extent to which such reworking is carried out is closely bound up with the process of imagining; indeed, it may be considered as the (temporal and physical) space that enables reflection on and reshaping of the self–other context of exchange. Such practice is also, of course, partly determined by the technology and its situated use, as the participants' remarks indicate. For example, Greg will spend time reflecting on, revising and editing his emails depending on how much time he has, who the email is going to and how sensitive it is. His feeling is, however, that if you already have a strong relationship with someone, how you write an email doesn't matter. For Richard, the revision process will focus on clarifying the message or the point of the email. Tom will always, unless he doesn't have the time, revise and check his emails before clicking them away. In his position he feels he can't easily afford to make a mechanical error in his writing – he is sure to have it pointed out to him. Jane feels that she spends more time than she would like to in reflecting on, revising and editing her emails before sending them. She is aware of her 'cautiousness about phrasing': 'I want to be as clear as possible … I don't want to create ambiguity and confusion.' For Sarah, the time she spends depends on whom the email is directed at. If it is to a student, she takes time to make sure her writing is perfectly clear, and if it is to an official body or to a senior colleague she will also spend time on preparing the email. In other circumstances, and as she is a touch typist, she may simply key in and send without making any checks at all. For Luke, the more correspondents his email is directed at, the longer he will spend on drafting and finalising it.

Such varying investments in preparing and editing emails before sending them can be related to the judgements we make (of ourselves and others) on the basis of our emails and our sense of how far they might represent who we are and our relation to others. Tom commented that he judges others 'a lot' based on the emails they write to him, in terms of their 'level of education', their 'literacy' and their 'courtesy'. Richard remarked that he makes judgements of others, but mainly because 'emails full of typos tend to obscure the message'. Greg, by contrast, commented that he tries not to form opinions about others based on the emails they write. And if their email only contains grammatical or typographical errors, 'I just guess they're as busy as I am.' Sarah thought she probably makes 'a lot of judgements' about people based on the emails they write. If an email is 'shoddy' or 'a mess' and it is from someone she doesn't know very well, Sarah may judge that they're under pressure, or she may judge that they're disorganised. If the email is from a friend, she doesn't, however, judge the writing or the style. Luke will only make a judgement about his correspondent if there is something 'glaring' about the email. Nevertheless, from the emails he receives, he certainly looks for a demonstration of 'an understanding of what's going on'. Jane remarked that she certainly 'get[s] impressions' from emails. The way people write, she said, 'I do take as giving me a strand' into who they are. As for making judgements based on her correspondents' technical accuracy in writing emails, Jane simply thinks they are better or worse typists than she is, or that they're 'doing things under pressure'.

We can't necessarily make definitive or reliable inferences from our correspondents' email writing according to whether they write formally, casually, completely, in slang, ungrammatically, or coherently, for example. However, we often *do* make such inferences, and are more likely to do so if we don't know them very well. That is to say we are perhaps more likely to look *at* language more closely when we aren't familiar with our correspondents, to find out 'who' they are; and we are more likely to look *through* when we are familiar with 'who' (we think) they are. Paradoxically, in the latter case, it may well be that the words we use don't matter at all (in terms of their imprecision, their mis-spelling, their clumsiness) when we are communicating with those who matter to us very much (those to whom we are personally close or whom we know well). We can – and do – imagine beyond those words, precisely because we have more to go on.

## Conclusion

There appears to be a kind of self-fulfilling prophecy at work in email praxis: our attitude to email as a technology in part determines how we use it.[15] For example, if we regard email as an impersonal medium, then that is how we tend to reproduce it. And that attitude is often repre-sented in our use of rhetoric, in the focus and in the form–content of our emails. As professional writers, our attitude to written language in general also in part influences the use to which we put email as a medium for communicating with others.

In the course of my conversation with her, Sarah explained how she finds it takes her a few emails 'to get into a rhythm' with her various correspondents.[16] She added that it takes 'four to six emails to get a sense of how [her email correspondents] want to play it'. The process of email-ing may perhaps usefully be viewed as writers and readers together establishing and then modifying their patterns of exchange. We learn 'how to play it' by paying attention not only to our own use of language and to how it might mean to others but to the ways it is used by others and how it means to us. I believe that in toggling between looking at and looking through rhetoric, we may develop both a more self-reflexive and a more imaginative, other-oriented approach to communicating by email.

As an evolving, flexible, and heavily used mode of exchange, the experience of emailing reminds us of the dangers of overestimating pre-scriptive formulations related to professional writing. Such formulations can all too easily distract us from the specific, situated processes of subject-ing ourselves in the process of connecting with others. And even the few email writers' voices interwoven through the text of this chapter give some indication of the diversity of views on and attitudes towards email. For such exchange to be productive and to generate relevant and meaningful effects we need to imagine our interlocutors, and to try to understand their different approaches to subject-ing, and we thus need to negotiate – 'to play it' – through a rhetoric that approximates all parties' needs.

Richard A. Cohen (2000) makes a compelling case for the ethical dynamics of computer-mediated communication. He rejects claims that computer-mediated communications are intrinsically good because they liberate the possibilities of multiple selves, or that they are intrinsically evil because they preclude face-to-face contact. Computer technologies, Cohen argues are, per se, neither good nor evil; it is rather human relations – ethical relations and relations of power – that determine the benefits to be derived from or the problems created by those technologies. He uses Lévinas's notion of ethics as an (asymmetrical) relation between a subject and 'the face' of the other as a key principle ('in the relation to the Face, it is asymmetry that is affirmed: at the outset I hardly care what the other is with respect to me, that is his own business; for me, he is above all the one I am responsible for'; Lévinas 1998, p. 105). Cohen extends the significance and value of the face into the sphere of writing technologies:

> In our day, the ethical dimension of human proximity transpires across the communications made possible by computers, just as human proximity takes place across phone calls, letters, artifacts. The 'face' can be a letter. The 'face' can be an email message. The computers themselves, like alphabet letters and telephones, like pencils and books, however, are neither good nor evil. The 'face' ruptures them, pierces them with the alterity of the other. By themselves, they are shadows of shadows or masks of masks.
>
> (Cohen 2000, p. 34)

Whatever the sophistication of the technologies we use, whatever the contexts in which we work, and whatever the purposes for and the genres in which we write, we need to first imagine – and to keep re-imagining – the face of the other in the words that might bring us together.

# Notes

Unless otherwise indicated, all electronic sources cited in this study were last viewed between 23 June and 29 June 2004.

## Introduction

1. Norman Fairclough (2001) describes one of the key characteristics of new capitalism as its being 'knowledge-based' or 'knowledge-driven' and thus also 'discourse-driven': 'knowledges are generated and circulate as discourses, and the process through which discourses become operationalised in economies and societies is precisely the dialectics of discourse'. In this book, my use of the term discourse is closely linked with the term rhetoric. Rhetoric consists of the specifically communicative aspects of discourse, its material functions and effects in social and individual lives, the relations of power it articulates, and its humanly transformative possibilities (see Eagleton 1983, pp. 194–217).

2. Because of its involvement with and inextricability from so many discourses, disciplines and interests, professional writing also has a baggy shape and continually shifting contours. This is clearly illustrated by Jim Henry's, *Writing workplace cultures* (2000), in which a multiplicity of writing contexts, contingencies and the shifting position of the term 'writer' are explored. Henry also examines the range of discourses with which writers in contemporary workplaces must engage (see particularly pp. 92–108).

3. See Fairclough (1995, pp. 130–66) for a critical discourse analysis of a sample range of texts developed for the university sector. This analysis serves his broader argument claiming the 'marketization' of public discourse in contemporary Britain.

4. Assuming a view of writing as a socially situated practice, James E. Porter's (1992) *Audience and rhetoric: an archaeological composition of the discourse community* argues cogently (through a historical, 'archaeological' approach to the concept of audience) for the value of an ethical relationship between writers and readers.

5. These were topics under discussion as at June 2004.

6. Norman Fairclough has developed a three-dimensional conception and method of discourse analysis, which serves to frame the scope of investigation. It consists of examining the interrelated instances of '(i) a language text, spoken or written, (ii) discourse practice (text production and text interpretation), (iii) sociocultural practice' (Fairclough 1995, p. 97). Any such investigation, this book suggests, is enhanced by integrating ethical, imaginative and rhetorical praxis.

7. I am indebted to the work of many scholars who have laid the ground on which my discussions are, in some cases directly, in others indirectly, built over the following pages. Individual chapters and the references at the end of the book naturally acknowledge those sources. However, it seems to me important to mention a few authors working in the field of writing and writing-related

given, but exactly how to go on with them, how to make them work in particular cases, and where and how to extend or modify them, may not be' (1998, p. 62).

13. Kearney's (1998) exploration of what he calls a radical hermeneutics of imagination asserts the ethical and political imperative of imagining as principle and practice in the postmodern age.

14. Young's preferred interpretation of Arendt's idea about making moral and political judgements by a process of 'enlarged thought' is 'considering the collective social processes and relationships that lie between us and which we have come to know together by discussing the world' (Young 1997, p. 59).

15. The pivotal role of rhetoric in some of the most exciting and challenging recent and current professional writing pedagogy and research is evident (see, for example, Berlin 1996; Olson and Dobrin 1994; Andrews 1992; Covino and Jolliffe 1995). Much work carried out in the fields of rhetoric and writing also emphasises their important relationship with ethics (see Katz 2003; Porter 1998; Hardin 2001).

16. See, for example, Porter (1998) and Berlin (1996) for the contributions postmodernism has made to studies in rhetoric. See Ede et al. (1995) for a detailed mapping of the congruities and incongruities of feminism and rhetoric. The article also highlights the ways in which the disciplines have transformed and continue to transform one another.

17. The brief discussion below of Derrida's notion of iterability appeared in my 2001 article 'Professional writing as ethical rhetoric: the Australian Government's response to *Bringing them home'*, *Australian Journal of Communication*, 28, 2, pp. 33–46.

## 2. The Struggle to Relate: Writers and Readers of Corporate and Public Documents

1. I use the distinguishing terms writer and reader to emphasise the primary activity in which a subject is engaged in a given situation. However, in such usage, always shadowing the writer is the reader and always shadowing the reader is the writer. The expressly hybrid term writer–reader emphasises the dynamic connection between the two activities of writing and reading.

2. The names of the consultancy and of all engineer participants have been changed.

3. Sales (2002) presents a detailed ethnographic study of aerospace engineers in the British context, exploring their attitudes to writing and their practices of developing engineering-related texts.

4. 'Duty of care requires everything "reasonably practicable" to be done to protect the health and safety of others at the workplace. This duty is placed on:

- all employers
- their employees; and
- any others who have an influence on the hazards in the workplace.

The latter includes contractors and those who design, manufacture, import, supply or install plant, equipment or materials used in the workplace' (Industry Commission, Work, Health and Safety, Report No. 47, Sept 1995,

National Occupational Health and Safety Commission, Commonwealth of Australia; available at http://www.nohsc.gov.au/OHSLegalObligations/ DutyOfCare/dutycare.htm.

5. Minor punctuation errors in the excerpt do not compromise the information's communicability.

6. Australian Standards are developed by Standards Australia, a not-for-profit organisation that facilitates 'standardization solutions'. Through its 'consensus based Standards development process', and drawing on the expertise of relevant stakeholders, it produces technical and business standards as guidelines for safe, efficient, economic, and sustainable practice (http://www.standards.org.au/).

7. Grabill and Simmons offer a detailed and persuasive account of the social construction of risk, and argue against (the artificial and reductive division of) risk assessment by 'experts' and its communication to a (passive, unengaged) public. In their view, risk communication, 'rather than a linear flow of technical information from the risk assessors to the public' becomes 'a web, a network, an interactive process of exchanging information, opinions and values among all involved parties' (2003, p. 368).

8. See Debs (1993) for a significant discussion about the impacts of corporate authority on a writer's position and voice.

9. Of course, it depends on your point of view. There are several large companies with extremely strong corporate identities who are, sometimes precisely because of this, viewed with distrust by various publics.

10. I've interchanged the terms here: corporate identity, corporate image and corporate culture or style, while realising that they are not all the same thing. See, for example, van Riel's detailed outline of the distinction between corporate identity and corporate image (1995, pp. 28–72, 73–113). Hatch and Schultz (1997) also discuss the distinctiveness of the notions of corporate identity, corporate image and corporate culture, although they also emphasise their significant interdependence: 'they are all symbolic, value-based constructions that are becoming increasingly intertwined'. For the purposes of this chapter the terms are used more or less fluidly to highlight the different ways of understanding the character, approaches and practices of the company's, its employees' and others' relation to and investment in those.

11. See Winsor's (1988) discussion of the disastrous consequences of equivocal communication exchanges between managers and engineers preceding the Challenger accident.

12. See Norlyk (2000) for a case study investigation into what happens when professional (in this instance, legal and real estate agent) discourse communities' needs clash.

13. It is as a reader, a non-Indigenous Australian citizen that I present this inevitably partial response to the Australian Conservative Government's report. Clearly, my reading indicates the resistance I sense on the part of the writer to my engagement with the argument from any other than the writer's own point of view. My position, however, is one shared by a sizeable section of the Australian community. Perhaps the strongest affirmation of the public's support for national reconciliation was evidenced by the symbolic reconciliation marches across bridges around the nation, participated in by hundreds of thousands of citizens between May and December 2000.

14. In the ten-year case *Mabo v. Queensland*, brought by Torres Strait Islander Eddy Mabo and four others, the Australian High Court recognised native title: the prior claims of Indigenous peoples to the land. This judgement invalidated the concept of *terra nullius* declared by the British colonisers in 1788.

15. Part of the Act's preamble states that 'the common law of Australia recognises a form of native title that reflects the entitlement of the indigenous inhabitants of Australia, in accordance with their laws and customs, to their traditional lands'. The Native Title Act 1993 may be accessed at http://scaleplus.law. gov.au/html/pasteact/2/1142/top.htm.

16. Augoustinos et al. (2002) also paint an informative picture of the political context surrounding the debate about reconciliation and the publication of *Bringing them home* (HREOC 1997). Their paper offers a cogent analysis of John Howard's speech at the 1997 Reconciliation Convention, and shows how its use of rhetorically self-sufficient arguments works to perpetuate racist and inequitable relations between Indigenous and non-Indigenous peoples in Australia.

17. This discursive mode of truth-telling is to be distinguished from (and preferred to) other modes: first 'an historical/juridical mode, where truth is constituted through certain academic or forensic standards'; and secondly 'a confessional mode, where truth is constituted through a Christian "wrestle of conscience" ' (Muldoon 2003, p. 188).

18. The findings of the inquiry were compiled into a large report, *Healing: a legacy of generations* (Senate Legal and Constitutional References Committee 2000). More recently, another Federal Government report has argued that, although some advances have been made, the government's approach to reconciliation is failing Indigenous peoples (see Senate Legal and Constitutional References Committee 2003).

19. Obviously, the government's submission to the Senate inquiry forms part of a complex network of texts concerning the stolen generation (in print, on the Internet, in the mass media, in public and private conversations) that had already been circulating and that (together with more recent texts) continues to circulate. And thus my remarks here are heavily influenced (even if not explicitly) by those other, myriad texts. Mailloux's remark that 'textual interpretation and rhetorical politics can never be separated ... interpretations can have no grounding outside of rhetorical exchanges taking place within institutional and cultural politics' is particularly apt in this context (Mailloux 1990, p. 133).

20. This idea resonates with Bauman's observation in relation to democracy: 'You can tell a democratic society by its never fully quelled suspicion that its job is unfinished; that it is not yet democratic enough' (Bauman 2001, p. 202)

21. For a different but not unrelated consideration of the ethics of negotiation, here in relation to discussions between parties representing native and non-native Canadians, see Govier (2001).

22. The full terms of reference are as follows:

The Senate referred the following matters to the Committee:
   (a) The adequacy and effectiveness of the Government's response to the recommendations of the report, *Bringing them home*;

    (b) After consultation and agreement with appropriate representatives of the stolen generations, to determine appropriate ways for government to:

        (i) establish an alternative dispute resolution tribunal to assist members of the stolen generations by resolving claims for compensation through consultation, conciliation and negotiation, rather than adversarial litigation and, where appropriate and agreed to, deliver alternative forms of restitution, and

        (ii) set up processes and mechanisms, which are adequately funded to:

            (A) provide counselling,

            (B) record the testimonies of members of the stolen generations,

            (C) educate Australians about their history and current plight,

            (D) help them to establish their ancestry and to access family reunion services, and

            (E) help them to re-establish or rebuild their links to their culture, language and history

    (c) Effective ways of implementing recommendations of the *Bringing them home* report including an examination of existing funding arrangements;

    (d) The impact of the Government's response to recommendations of the *Bringing them home* report, with particular reference to the consistency of this response with the aims of the Council for Aboriginal Reconciliation; and

    (e) The consistency of the Government's response to recommendations of the *Bringing them home* report with the hopes, aspirations and needs of members of the stolen generations and their descendants.

    (Senate Legal and Constitutional References Committee 2000, pp. 1–2)

23. References to the term in the Federal Government report are as follows: 'the treatment of separated Aboriginal children was essentially lawful and benign in intent', Executive Summary iii; 'essentially benign intent of governments' (Herron 2000, p. 6); 'essentially benign intent of government policy and subsequent indigenous child separations' (Herron 2000, p. 9); 'benign intentions of the policy and of the people involved' (Herron 2000, p. 12). Robert Manne has been a particularly vocal critic of the claim that the removals of Indigenous children were altruistically motivated. He presents convincing evidence that the policy of removal was, before the Second World War, driven by a programme of eugenics, one intent on 'breeding out' the 'problem' of the half-caste (Aboriginal–European) in Australia. After the war, the policy was driven by the welfarist objective of cultural assimilation (see Manne 1998, 2001).

24. Compare Muldoon's explanation of the way in which, in South Africa's Truth and Reconciliation Commission proceedings, 'a clear distinction was drawn between the "forensic truth" that is established through rigorous procedures of verification and the "social truth" that is established through interaction, discussion and debate' (Muldoon 2003, p. 194).

25. Manne's essay, 'In denial: the stolen generations and the Right', examines the ways in which the government's view on the (non-)existence of the stolen generation has been bolstered by a host of right-wing critics and

journalists. This campaign, argues Manne, has brought about 'a growing atmosphere of right-wing and populist resistance to discussions of historical injustice and the Aborigines' in Australia (Manne 2001, p. 104).

26. For details of the progress on this project, see the National Library of Australia's website, *Bringing them home* oral history project, available at: http://www.nla.gov.au/oh/bth/. For details of the book, *Many voices: reflections on experiences of Indigenous child separation*, written as a result of the project, see the National Library of Australia's website, Gateways, at: http://www.nla.gov.au/ntwkpubs/gw/60/p01a01.html.

27. By eliding the moral dimension of the stolen generation's voices, the government's submission perpetuates the coloniser's view of the colonised and the Indigenous people as lacking the moral capacity or judgement to articulate their own pain in a bid to begin the process of healing and self-determination (see also Bauman 1993, pp. 120–1).

## 3.  Public Information: Up for Debate or Up for Sale? Writing via the Internet

1. Keane, however, is all too aware of the other side of this story: 'it is common knowledge that three-quarters of the world's population (now totalling 6 billion) are too poor to buy a book; that a majority have never made a phone call in their lives; and that only 5 per cent currently have access to the Internet' (Keane 2003, p. 140).

2. Through this chapter I use 'writers' as an umbrella term to refer to the originators of Internet texts, or to those with whose name a text is chiefly associated, or whose authority a text represents. I favour the term 'readers' (over 'users', for example) to emphasise the interpretive process integral to accessing and making sense of Internet texts.

3. Tim Jordan teases out Jaron Lanier's now often rehearsed statement that 'information is alienated experience' (Jordan 1999, pp. 194ff.).

4. See, for example, Coleman and Gøtze (2001); Griffiths (2002); Hacker and van Dijk (2000); Kamarck and Nye (2002); OECD (2003a); OECD (2001); Maarek and Wolfsfeld (2003); Tsagarousianou et al. (1998).

5. Here I use Nancy Kaplan's definition of the term, as 'multiple structurations within a textual domain ... Such documents consist of chunks of textual material (words, video clips, sound segments or the like), and sets of connections leading from one chunk or node to other chunks. The resulting structures offer readers multiple trajectories through the textual domain' (Kaplan 1995, p. 13).

6. Of course my argument is informed by the excellent work carried out by a number of scholars in relation to the framework and architecture of Internet and computer technology, to issues of regulation and legislation of Internet content and its use, and to related cultural, ideological and political questions. See, for example, Catinat and Vedel (2000); Dutton (1999); Holmes (1997); Jordan (1999); Kearns (2002); OECD (2003); Porter (1999); Porter (1997); Poster (2001); Warschauer (2002).

7. See Poster for a discussion of democracy, and of the Internet as the contemporary public sphere (2001, pp. 171–88).

8.  It must be in governments' interests to support e-democracy activities since, as Griffiths also points out, governments may be concerned by the 'dispersal of political power, resulting from the widespread distribution of information through non-traditional channels' such as the Internet. It is thus incumbent on democratic governments to use technology 'to stabilise social and political relations. Increased information circulated from government about government to citizens is being seen increasingly as not only a response to a democratic citizen right, but also as engendering a citizen's responsibility to participate, in orderly ways, in political life' (Griffiths 2002).

9.  Porter effectively highlights the role of rhetoric (of writing) as an enabling or disabling technology: 'In its design a particular rhetoric can be a strategy either for domination or for democratization. The rhetoric that constructs the audience as a passive receiver of the message determined by the author and that talks only to the rhetor about strategies for changing the audience over to his point of view is a rhetoric of domination. The rhetoric that constructs the audience as an interlocutor, as a source of knowledge, and as a necessary participant in the construction of discourse is a rhetoric of democratization' (Porter 1998, pp. 67–8).

10. See also Johnson-Eilola (1997).

11. For a thoughtful and provocative discussion on agency and politics in the technological age, see Feenberg (1999).

12. Statistical information about my visit to the site will be collected, but this will include no personal information about me.

13. In this case, I treat the writer as produced by as well as producer of the text of information.

14. For a discussion of reciprocity in terms of broadcast and online communities, see David Holmes (1997, pp. 26–45). Part of Holmes's argument consists in developing the idea that Internet technology 'facilitates reciprocity with very low levels of recognition' of socially shared meanings (p. 37).

15. By November 2002, RAWA.org had counted 4,800,000 hits (Bickel 2003).

16. For a discussion of Internet-mediated political interactivity and the White House, see Hacker (2000, pp. 105–29). For an analysis of the White House Internet site that draws on the ideas of the political scientist Murray Edelman, see Andrew Chadwick (2003, pp. 43–64).

17. This is known as e-government rather than e-democracy. Mary Griffiths describes it as referring to 'relations of top/down power – governing populations through use of on-line information and services' (Griffiths 2002). In the USA, the government's official web portal is FirstGov (firstgov.gov); in Australia, the whole-of-government portal is Access to the Information and Services of the Australian, Federal, State, Territory and Local Governments (www.gov.au), although there are an additional three key access points: Access to Australian Commonwealth Information (www.fed.gov.au), Commonwealth Government Online Directory (www.gold.gov.au) and Government Services for Australians (www.australia.gov.au).

18. For examples of a few such initiatives in Europe and Australia, see Coleman and Gøtze (2001, pp. 36–45) and OECD (2003a, pp. 93–128). For government initiatives in the USA see egov (http://www.whitehouse.gov/omb/egov/gtoc.htm).

19. Foss suggests that three kinds of judgement are harnessed in evaluating an image using a rhetorical approach. The first involves the critic's interpretation of the function of 'the physical data of the image'. The second involves 'an assessment of how well that function is communicated' and the various 'stylistic and substantive' elements in the image that support the function. The third kind of judgement involves 'scrutiny of the function itself – reflection on its legitimacy or soundness, determined by the implications and consequences of the function' (Foss 1994, pp. 216–17).

20. My reading and analysis of Bush's site took place on 28 April 2004.

21. The photographs are changed regularly: they are always shots of the Oval Office, but taken from different angles and of different individuals.

22. As the page Oval Office History (available through a hypertext link on the president's home page) explains, the office itself is 'a symbol of the presidency'. During the presidency of George Washington, two offices in the White House were each modified to create bowed ends. Washington would stand in the middle of the room and his guests would form a circle around him. 'With no one standing at the head or foot of the room, everyone was an equal distance from the president. The circle became a symbol of democracy.'

23. The photograph was taken on 20 January 2003. This image is interchanged with other Oval Office shots on a regular basis.

24. Gardiner's comments are made in the context of his discussion about Mikhail Bakhtin and the ethics of the self–other relation using the metaphors of perception.

25. This photo of a meeting between President Bush and some of his staff was taken on 20 September 2001, before the president's address to Congress following September 11.

26. My reading and analysis of Howard's site took place on 29 April 2004.

27. This is presumably not unconnected to the relation between legislative and executive branches of Australian government. (The head of government must be an elected member of parliament to be eligible for selection as party political leader, and then to assume the role of prime minister, should that party win an election.) Compare the president of the USA who is directly elected by the national electorate.

28. However, readers are informed that if an email is sent, no personal response will be received. The survey consists largely of questions requiring tick box answers. There is also a space for readers to make general comments.

29. Thomas Meyer refers to this naturalising process as 'the main theatrical strategy of the politics of image'. In a discussion of image-making in mediated politics, he argues that 'the images that are supposed to make good the candidates' claims to personify desired qualities, and so enhance their credibility, allegedly come from "natural" situations that have not been contrived for public effect' (Meyer 2002, p. 69).

30. It could be pointed out that this is an unfair comparison, that local government sites perform a different function, are properly far more focused on particular communities and are more directly accountable to specific publics than national government sites. This, of course, is true. Nevertheless, both types of site do perform the function of 'face' of government, and it is in this spirit that the comparison is made.

31. The USA and Australia, given the size and range of government operations, necessarily have separate sites for services.
32. Cynics would suggest that this is a cheap public relations ploy designed to make the council appear responsive. It would be interesting to discover local residents' opinions of the service.
33. See also Mary Griffiths (2002).
34. The text referred to was available in 2003. During the process of manuscript revision in 2004, the text had been replaced by a far less 'risky' account of Shell's approach to issues.
35. Compare the 2003 pages described with Shell's currently different approach to key issues: go to www.shell.com, click on 'About Shell' and follow the prompts.
36. The inverted commas here of course indicate a direct quotation from Shell. However, I was aware, as I keyed them in, that those commas also carry a trace of irony: when a corporation, institution or industry is most commonly known as a commercial entity, its most earnest (and perhaps justified) claims as a moral citizen are likely to be regarded by some as motivated by economic expedience.

## 4. Challenging Unreliable Narrators: Writing and Public Relations

1. I treat corporate social responsibility as a component of public relations. Compare Cynthia E. Clark (2000), who treats public relations and corporate social responsibility as separate disciplines and professional realms. She nevertheless argues that by acknowledging the similarities between them (specifically those relating to communication approaches and methods) researchers and practitioners can gain further insights into both corporate social responsibility and public relations.
2. I need to point out that the choice of Nike as a case study was made on the basis of its public visibility and the availability of diverse and variously mediated (particularly web-based) narratives about it, which would be accessible to readers. The choice is not intended to suggest Nike as necessarily any 'better' or 'worse' than other – large or small – corporations (see also Birch and Glazebrook 2000, pp. 49–50).
3. For example, see Clare Duffield's (2000) sceptical view of multinational corporations' approaches to their contract workers' rights, wages and conditions of work.
4. See, for example, McDonald's House Charities, available at: http://www.rmhc.com/; Philip Morris Companies Inc.'s philanthropic activities, available at: http://www.philipmorris.com/philanthropy/philanthropy_main.asp; GlaxoSmithKline's community investment programmes, available at: http://www.gsk.com/community/about.htm.
5. As Lyotard remarks: 'Our master is capital. Capital makes us tell, listen to and act out the great story of its reproduction, and the positions we occupy in the instances of its narrative are predetermined' (Lyotard 1989, p. 140).
6. However, note Penman's worry about the diminished opportunity for ethical engagement without physical contact/interaction (2000, p. 93).

7.  See Kevin Moloney (2000), who focuses on public relations in the UK context as socially pervasive practice. Moloney argues for a reconceptualisation of the profession so that, among other changes, the concentration of public relations activities in the hands of big business and powerful political and media institutions are more equitably distributed to include traditionally less powerful stakeholders and groups.

8.  See Shell's site at http://www2.shell.com/home/Framework and click on the TellShell hyperlink.

9.  See Sharon Livesey (2001) for a discussion of the discourses of sustainability and their struggle with other (predominantly economic and rationalist) discourses in the evolving rhetoric of the Royal Dutch/Shell Group.

10. And see Holtzhausen's (2000) use of Lyotard's notion of the differend. In her development of a postmodern approach to public relations, Holtzhausen rejects the idea that consensus and symmetry between practitioners and publics are either realisable or desirable goals.

11. Of course, one comment cannot and should not be read as representative of widespread employee dissatisfaction. The quote rather serves to demonstrate The Body Shop's willingness to have other voices written into and read from its texts.

12. See also Perkins and Blyler's discussion on the importance of professional communication 'taking a narrative turn' (1999, particularly pp. 10–28).

13. See Oxfam Community Aid Abroad's discussion of and involvement in the campaign on this issue at http://www.caa.org.au/horizons/may_2002/srilank_milk.html.

14. See Mark Currie's discussion of the applications of narratology in studying contemporary culture (Currie 1998, pp. 96–113).

15. See McSpotlight's site, http://www.mcspotlight.org/case/trial/story.html, for an activist version of this case. No information from the corporation's perspective on the case could be found on McDonald's website.

16. See Greenpeace's website at http://www.greenpeace.org/ and Amnesty International's at http://www.amnesty.org/.

17. See the McSpotlight site at http://www.mcspotlight.org/ and Oxfam Community Aid Abroad's NikeWatch at http://www.caa.org.au/campaigns/nike/. Another activist site that must not escape mention here is the US academic, David Boje's, Academics studying Nike at http://cbae.nmsu.edu/~dboje/nike/nikemain1.html. Not only does the site provide a cornucopia of texts documenting a history of Nike's policies and practices, from an activist perspective, but it carries links to several important related resources.

18. See the site at http://www.prwatch.org/index.html.

19. In this chapter, I have worked off a hard-copy version of the report, obtained from Nike. However, the report can also be downloaded from http://www.nike.com/nikebiz/nikebiz.jhtml?page=29.

20. In his development of what he calls 'a configural theory' for the design or writing and the critical reading of images, Carlos Salinas argues that images should be theorised as configurations, 'as designed/written artifacts, rhetorically figured, representing particular ideologies and values, and projecting their make[r]'s ethos' (Salinas 2000, Abstract). He offers an astute reading of Nike's 1997–98 website to concentrate his discussion, and makes a detailed critique of the company's representations of its labour practices.

21. For a detailed account of Nike and adidas-Salomon's subcontract worker conditions in Indonesia, see Connor, *We are not machines* (2002).
22. For a detailed background to the case, and its movement through different courts, see Goldstein (2003, particularly pp. 65–70).
23. The Fair Labor Association (FLA) is a non-profit coalition of industry, non-government, and tertiary sector groups. The organisation exists to promote compliance with international labour standards and to improve working conditions around the world (www.fairlabor.org). The FLA has been criticised by various activist groups for its failure to effect full-scale improvements in labour conditions and wages for workers.
24. See Goldstein (2003, pp. 65–6) for details of Kasky's allegations.
25. The California Supreme Court defined ' "commercial speech" to cover everything said by anyone "engaged in commerce", to an "intended audience" of potential ... customers" or "persons (such as reporters ...)" likely to influence actual or potential customers that conveys factual information about itself "likely to influence consumers in their commercial decisions" ' (in Goldstein 2003, pp. 70–1).
26. In 2003, Nike released the first issue of *Nike responsibility*, an e-newsletter. In that issue's editorial, the Nike Corporate Responsibility Team comments that, with the settlement of the court case, 'we are introducing new tools for dialogue with our stakeholders'; the newsletter and the company's corporate responsibility website (www.nike.responsibility.com) are two such tools. From the three issues of the newsletter produced thus far (June 2004), there is a significant focus on Nike's implementing of and involvement in several large-scale community-based initiatives around the world. While the level of the company's investment in such activities is undoubtedly impressive, the function of the newsletter appears to be exclusively self-promotional. Evidence of 'stakeholder dialogue' is not, so far, in evidence.
27. The company goes on to report its 2002 launch of what it calls 'stakeholder dialogues' – consultation meetings with key stakeholders in the regions of its outsourced labour activity (Asia, the Americas and Europe) (adidas-Salomon 2003, p. 22).
28. This latest document does contain an appraisal of adidas-Salomon's reporting processes by business-focused corporate social responsibility organisation, CSR Network Ltd (adidas-Salomon 2004, p. 15), as well as summaries of stakeholder dialogues held with workers, non-government organisations and other groups in the course of 2003 (see adidas-Salomon 2004, pp. 13–17). However, a more diverse range of voices, quoted in context rather than summarised in abstraction, is yet to be recorded.

## 5. Being Professional by Email: Who/How are You?

1. See Sims (1996) for a study interested in the resemblances between email communication and oral discourse. See also Judith Yaross Lee (1996) for a discussion on email as a new hybrid form that draws on written and oral discourses and allows authors and responding readers to be embodied in their electronic texts.
2. See Rooksby (2000, p. 68) for an exploration of empathy in computer-mediated communication. Rooksby argues that 'empathy is ... essential for

*ethically engaged communication*, even though it does not guarantee success-ful information-transmission, however broadly this last term is interpreted'.

3. Similarly, Spears et al. (2002) critique simplistic judgements about computer-mediated communication technologies, and argue that interaction through cyberspace does not necessarily result in less 'social' processes and that issues of power are not necessarily dissolved. They argue for more context-specific analyses, which are both socially and technologically grounded.

4. Nevertheless, because of rapid changes influencing Internet technology (and email as part of that technology), claims made about the Internet, as Poster (2001, p. 19) suggests, need to be tentative and/or hypothetical.

5. And see Poster's discussion of this conflation in his exploration of the new meaning of the 'public sphere' that emerges with the Internet (Poster 2001, pp. 171–88).

6. See Jordan for further discussion on online markers of identity (2002, pp. 120–8).

7. Rooksby (2000, p. 113) argues that unless the writers of computer-mediated communication make an effort to elicit empathy from their readers, then they are 'at risk of leaving their experiences invisible, and their selves mis-understood'.

8. The names of the company, of all interview participants and proper names in emails cited have been changed.

9. In a related discussion, Jones considers the impact of Internet technology on our sense of time. He argues that 'the Internet's insertion into modern life represents a further displacement, or divergence, between our sense of "lived" time (the time that passes according to our senses, the time of "being") and our sense of "social" or "functional" time (the time that we sense as a form of obligation, or as time for "doing", for "capturing" ...)' (1997, p. 13).

10. See also Wallace (2000), who refers to the work of John Durham Peters and his argument that 'technologies will never solve the differences in intention and reception amongst socially and therefore differentially positioned inter-locutors'.

11. Wallace (2000) argues that email used for dissemination of information is not the negative obverse of email used for dialogue. He claims that 'if email is encouraging widespread dissemination of information which could have been held back (and arguably would have been held back in large organisa-tions lacking email's facilitative qualities), then the workforce will be better informed, and hence more able – and more inclined! – to engage in dia-logue'. It seems to me that such generalised claims may be difficult to sus-tain about email genres, given that those genres are fluid, and that the contexts of their circulation and reception will influence their specific func-tions and effects.

12. There is the sense here too that a particular attitude towards email, for ex-ample, its treatment as an impersonal medium, is reinforced and perpetuated by the way it is used. In the same vein, Jane remarked that in an institution, '[email's] overall effect can be distancing'. This can be an advantage too, she pointed out, as email allows you to 'keep your distance' if you wish.

13. See also Waldvogel (2001).

14. Foster warns against 'a particular danger' in computer-mediated communi-cation: 'solipsism, or the extreme preoccupation with and indulgence of

one's own inclinations is potentially engendered in the technology' (1997, p. 26).

15. Minsky and Marin (1999) make a similar observation in their study of university faculty members' use of email in a North American university.

16. Compare Kolb, who refers to the rhythm of email exchange in his reflections on the ways in which computer-mediated communication can allow us to 'be and communicate together' (1996, p. 25).

# References

All electronic sources referenced below were last viewed between 23 June and 29 June 2004.

adidas-Salomon (2003), *Behind our brand: social and environmental report 2002*, at http://www.adidas-salomon.com/en/sustainability/reports/default.asp.

adidas-Salomon (2004), *Staying focused: social and environmental report 2003*, at http://www.adidas-salomon.com/en/sustainability/reports/default.asp.

Alcoa (2003), 'Health fears unfounded', media release, Alcoa, Western Australia, 25 August, at http://www.alcoa.com/australia/en/news/releases/20030825_Health_fears_unfounded.asp.

Andrews, R. (ed.) (1992), *Rebirth of rhetoric: essays in language, culture and education*, Routledge: London and New York.

Arendt, H. (1968), 'The crisis in culture: its social and political significance', in *Between past and future: eight exercises in political thought*, The Viking Press: New York, pp. 197–226.

Augoustinos, M., Lecouteur, A. and Soyland, J. (2002), 'Self-sufficient arguments in political rhetoric: constructing reconciliation and apologizing to the Stolen Generations', *Discourse and Society*, 13,1, pp. 105–42.

Australian Broadcasting Corporation (3 April 2000), *The 7.30 report*, Kerry O'Brien interview with Senator John Herron, Minister for Aboriginal and Torres Strait Islander Affairs, at http://www.abc.net.au/7.30/stories/s115694.htm.

Bakhtin, M.M. (1981), *The dialogic imagination*, ed. M. Holquist, trans. C. Emerson and M. Holquist, University of Texas Press: Austin, Texas.

Bakhtin, M.M. (1984), 'Toward a reworking of the Dostoevsky book' [1961], in *Problems of Dostoevsky's poetics*, ed. and trans. C. Emerson, *Theory and history of literature*, Volume 8, University of Minnesota Press: Minneapolis, pp. 283–302.

Bauman, Z. (1993), *Postmodern ethics*, Blackwell Publishers: Oxford.

Bauman, Z. (2001), *The individualized society*, Polity Press: Cambridge.

BBC News (2003), 'Nike settles "free speech" court case', BBC News UK Edition website, 13 September 2003, at http://news.bbc.co.uk/go/pr/fr/-/1/hi/world/americas/3106930.stm.

Benhabib, S. (1992), *Situating the self: gender, community and postmodernism in contemporary ethics*, Polity Press: Cambridge.

Benhabib, S. (1999), 'Sexual difference and collective identities: the new global constellation', *Signs: Journal of Women in Culture and Society*, 24,2, pp. 335–61.

Berlin, J. (2003), *Rhetorics, poetics and cultures: refiguring college English studies*, Parlor Press: West Lafayette, IN.

Bernhardt, S.A. (2002), 'Active practice: creating productive tension between academia and industry', in B. Mirel and R. Spilka (eds), *Reshaping technical communication: new directions and challenges for the 21st century*, Lawrence Erlbaum Associates: Mahwah, NJ and London, pp. 81–90.

Bickel, B. (2003), 'Weapons of magic: Afghan women asserting voice via the Net', *Journal of Computer-Mediated Communication*, 8,2, at http://www.ascusc.org/jcmc/vol8/issue2/bickel.html.

Birch, D. and Glazebrook, M. (2000), 'Doing business – doing culture: corporate citizenship and community', in S. Rees and S. Wright (eds), *Human rights, corporate responsibility: a dialogue*, Pluto Press: Annandale, NSW, pp. 41–52.

Bizzaro, P. (2004), 'Research and reflection in English studies: the special case of creative writing', *College English*, 66,3, pp. 294–309.

Blake, N. (1997), 'Truth, identity and community in the university', in R. Barnett and A. Griffin (eds), *The end of knowledge in higher education*, Cassell: London, pp. 151–64.

Blumler, J.G. and Coleman, S. (2001), *Realising democracy online: a civic commons in cyberspace*, IPPR/Citizens Online Research Publication no. 2, March, at www.citizensonline.org.uk/pdf/realising.pdf.

Britt, E.C., Longo, B. and Woolever, K. (1996), 'Extending the boundaries of rhetoric in legal writing pedagogy', *Journal of Business and Technical Communication*, 10,2, pp. 213–38.

Catinat, M. and Vedel, T. (2000), 'Public policies for digital democracy', in K.L. Hacker and J. van Dijk (eds), *Digital democracy: issues of theory and practice*, Sage Publications: London, pp. 184–208.

Chadwick, A. (2003), 'Murray Edelman', in C. May (ed.), *Key thinkers for the information society*, Routledge: London and New York, pp. 43–64.

Christensen, L.T. (1997), 'Marketing as auto-communication', *Consumption, Markets and Culture*, 1,3, pp. 197–302, at http://www.crito.uci.edu/noah/CMC%20Website/CMC%20PDFs/CMC1_3.pdf.

Clark, C.E. (2000), 'Differences between public relations and corporate social responsibility: an analysis, *Public Relations Review*, 26,3, pp. 363–80.

Clark, G. (1998), 'Writing as travel or rhetoric on the road', *College Composition and Communication*, 49,1, pp. 9–23.

Clendinnen, I. (2001), 'Who's telling this story', *The Australian Review of Books*, March, pp. 11–12.

Clyne, M. (2002), 'Saving us from them', *M/C: a Journal of Media and Culture*, 5,5, at http://www.media-culture.org.au/mc/0210/Clyne.html.

Cohen, R.A. (2000), 'Ethics and cybernetics: Lévinasian reflections', *Ethics and Information Technology*, 2, pp. 27–35.

Coleman, S. (2001), 'E-politics: democracy or marketing?', *E-Government Bulletin*, 100, June, at http://headstar.com/egb/issues/June2001.txt.

Coleman, S. and Gøtze, J. (2001), *Bowling together: online public engagement in policy deliberation*, Hansard Society, London, at http://www.bowlingtogether.net.

Commonwealth Government (1997), '*Bringing them home*: government initiatives', tabled in Parliament (out of session), 16 December, Canberra, ACT, at http://www.atsia.gov.au/media/reports/index.htm.

Community Arts Network (2004), Welcome page, at http://www.communityarts.net/canwelcome.php.

Comprone, J.J. (1993), 'Generic constraints and expressive motives: rhetorical perspectives on textual dialogues', in N.R. Blyler and C. Thralls (eds), *Professional communication: the social perspective*, Sage Publications: Newbury Park, London and Delhi, pp. 92–108.

Connor, T. (2002), *We are not machines*, Oxfam Community Aid Abroad, at http://www.caa.org.au/campaigns/nike/reports/machines/.

Couture, B. (1998), *Toward a phenomenological rhetoric: writing, profession and altruism*, Southern Illinois University Press: Carbondale and Edwardsville.

Covino, W.A. and Jolliffe, D.A. (eds) (1995), *Rhetoric: concepts, definitions, boundaries*, Allyn and Bacon: Boston, MA.

Currie, M. (1998), *Postmodern narrative theory*, Palgrave: Basingstoke.

Daymon, C. (2000), 'On considering the meaning of managed communication: or why employees resist "excellent" communication', *Journal of Communication Management*, 4,3, pp. 240–52.

De Winter, R. (2001), 'The anti-sweatshop movement: constructing corporate moral agency in the global apparel industry', *Ethics and International Affairs*, October 15,2, pp. 99–115.

Debs, M.B. (1993), 'Corporate authority: sponsoring rhetorical practice', in R. Spilka (ed.), *Writing in the workplace: new research perspectives*, Southern Illinois University Press: Carbondale and Edwardsville, pp. 158–70.

DeLuca, K. (1999), 'Articulation theory: a discursive grounding for rhetorical practice', *Philosophy and Rhetoric*, 32,4, pp. 334–48.

Derrida, J. (1988), *Limited Inc.*, Northwestern University Press: Evanston, IL.

Devitt, A.J., Bawarshi, A. and Reiff, M.J. (2003), 'Materiality and genre in the study of discourse communities', *College English*, 65,5, pp. 541–58.

Dozier, D.M. and Lauzen, M.M. (2000), 'Liberating the intellectual domain from the practice: public relations, activism and the role of the scholar', *Journal of Public Relations Research*, 12,1, pp. 3–22.

Driskill, L. (2003), 'Understanding the writing context in organizations', in T. Peeples (ed.), *Professional writing and rhetoric: readings from the field*, Longman: New York, pp. 105–21.

Duffield, C. (2000), 'Multinational corporations and workers' rights', in S. Rees and S. Wright (eds), *Human rights, corporate responsibility: a dialogue*, Pluto Press: Annandale, NSW, pp. 191–209.

Dutton, W.H. (1999), *Society on the line: information politics in the digital age*, Oxford University Press: Oxford.

Eagleton, T. (1983), *Literary theory: an introduction*, Basil Blackwell: Oxford.

Ede, L., Glenn, C. and Lunsford, A. (1995), 'Border crossings: intersections of rhetoric and feminism', *Rhetorica*, 13,4, pp. 401–41.

Edmonds, P. (2004), 'Respectable or risqué: creative writing programs in the marketplace', *TEXT*, 8,1, at http://www.gu.edu.au/school/art/text/.

Erickson, K.V. (2000), 'Presidential rhetoric's visual turn: performance fragments and the politics of illusionism', *Communication Monographs*, 67, pp. 138–57.

Eubanks, P. (1999), 'Conceptual metaphor as rhetorical response: a reconsideration of metaphor', *Written Communication*, 16,2, pp. 171–99.

ExxonMobil (2004), *2003 Corporate citizenship report: summary*, at http://www.exxonmobil.com/corporate/Citizenship/Corp_citizenship_report_archive.asp.

Fairclough, N. (1995), *Critical discourse analysis: the critical study of language*, Longman: London.

Fairclough, N. (2001), 'The dialectics of discourse', *Textus*, 14,2, pp. 231–42, at http://www.ling.lancs.ac.uk/staff/norman/download.htm.

Feenberg, A. (1999), *Questioning technology*, Routledge: London and New York.

Foss, S.K. (1994), 'A rhetorical schema for the evaluation of visual imagery', *Communication Studies*, 45,3–4, pp. 213–24.

Foster, D. (1997), 'Community and identity in the electronic village', in D. Porter (ed.), *Internet culture*, Routledge: London, pp. 23–37.

Foucault, M. (1984), 'What is an author?', in P. Rabinow (ed.), *The Foucault reader*, Pantheon: New York, pp. 101–20.

Foucault, M. (2000), 'The ethics of the concern for the self as a practice of freedom', in *Ethics: subjectivity and truth*, ed. P. Rabinow, trans. R. Hurley and others. *Essential works of Foucault 1954–1984*, vol. 1, Penguin: Harmondsworth, pp. 281–301.

Freed, R.C. (1993), 'Postmodern practice: perspectives and prospects', in N.R. Blyler and C. Thralls (eds), *Professional communication: the social perspective*, Sage Publications: Newbury Park, London and Delhi, pp. 196–214.

Gardiner, M. (1999), 'Bakhtin and the metaphorics of perception', in I. Heywood and B. Sandywell (eds), *Interpreting visual culture: explorations in the hermeneutics of the visual*, Routledge: London, pp. 57–73.

Gelber, K. (2003), 'A fair queue? Australian public discourse on refugees and immigration', *Journal of Australian Studies*, 77, pp. 23–35.

Gilligan, C. (1982), *In a different voice: psychological theory and women's development*, Harvard University Press: Cambridge, MA and London.

Goldstein, T.C. (2003), '*Nike v Kasky* and the definition of "commercial speech" ', *Cato Supreme Court Review*, pp. 63–79 at http://www.cato.org/pubs/scr2003/commercialspeech.pdf.

Govier, T. (2001), 'Trust, acknowledgement, and the ethics of negotiation', in Law Commission of Canada, *Speaking truth to power: a treaty forum*, Minister of Public Works and Government Services Canada, pp. 95–112, at http://www.lcc.gc.ca/en/ress/part/200103/traites.pdf.

Grabill, J. and Simmons, M. (2003), 'Toward a critical rhetoric of risk communication: producing citizens and the role of technical communicators', in T. Peeples (ed.), *Professional writing and rhetoric: readings from the field*, Longman: New York, pp. 360–82.

Graycar, R. (1998), 'Compensation for the stolen children: political judgments and community values', Forum: stolen children: from removal to reconciliation, *UNSW Law Journal*, at http://austlii.law.uts.edu.au/au/other/unswlj.OLD/forum/1998/vol4no3/graycar.html.

Green, L. (2000), 'Relating to Internet "audiences" ', *M/C: a Journal of Media and Culture*, 3,1, at http://media-culture.org.au/0003/internet.txt.

Griffiths, M. (2002), 'Australian e-democracy?: its potential for citizens and governments', Presentation at Innovative e-Government for Victoria, 26 March, at www.egov.vic.gov.au/Documents/eDemocracy1.doc.

Hacker, K.L. (2000), 'The White House computer-mediated communication (CMC) system and political interactivity', in K.L. Hacker and J. van Dijk (eds), *Digital democracy: issues of theory and practice*, Sage Publications: London, pp. 105–29.

Hacker, K.L. and van Dijk, J. (eds) (2000), *Digital democracy: issues of theory and practice*, Sage Publications: London.

Hardin, J.M. (2001), *Opening spaces: critical pedagogy and resistance theory in composition*, State University of New York Press: Albany, NY.

Harper, G. (2003), 'A state of grace?: creative writing in UK higher education, 1993–2003', *TEXT*, 7,2, at http://www.gu.edu.au/school/art/text/.

Hassett, M. (1995), 'Constructing an ethical writer for the postmodern scene', *Rhetoric Society Quarterly*, 25, annual edition, pp. 179–95.

Hatch, M.J. and Schultz, M. (1997), 'Relations between organizational culture, identity and image', *European Journal of Marketing*, 31,5/6, pp. 356–65, Academic Research Library, Proquest Direct, http://proquest.umi.com/pqdweb.

Heath, R.L. (2000), 'A rhetorical perspective on the values of public relations: crossroads and pathways towards concurrence', *Journal of Public Relations Research*, 12,1, pp. 69–91.

Henry, J. (2000), *Writing workplace cultures: an archaeology of professional writing*, Southern Illinois University Press: Carbondale and Edwardsville.

Herndl, C.G., Fennell, B.A. and Miller, C.R. (1991), 'Understanding failures in organizational discourse: the accident at Three Mile Island and the Shuttle Challenger disaster', in C. Bazerman and J. Paradis (eds), *Textual dynamics of the professions: historical and contemporary studies of writing in professional communities*, University of Wisconsin Press: Madison, WI, pp. 279–305.

Herron, J. (2000), *Senate Legal and Constitutional References Committee: Inquiry into the stolen generation*, Federal Government submission, March, Canberra, ACT.

Holmes, D. (ed.) (1997), *Virtual politics: identity and community in cyberspace*, Sage Publications: London.

Holtzhausen, D.R. (2000), 'Postmodern values in public relations', *Journal of Public Relations Research*, 12,1, pp. 93–114.

Howard, J. (1997), Reconciliation Convention Opening Ceremony speech, Australian Reconciliation Convention, Melbourne, at http://www.austlii.edu.au/au/other/IndigLRes/car/1997/3/speeches/opening/howard.html.

Human Rights and Equal Opportunities Commission (1997), *Bringing them home: report of the national inquiry into the separation of Aboriginal and Torres Strait Islander children from their families*, Human Rights and Equal Opportunities Commission: Sydney. Report also available from Australian Legal Information Institute website, http://www.austlii.edu.au/au/special/rsjproject/rsjlibrary/hreoc/stolen/.

Johnson-Eilola, J. (1997), 'Just information: the politics of decontextualization in technical communication', paper presented at Conference on College Composition and Communication, Phoenix, AZ, 13 March, at http://www.clarkson.edu/~johndan/read/just/welcome.html.

Jones, S.G. (1997), 'The Internet and its social landscape', in S.G. Jones (ed.), *Virtual culture: identity and communication in cybersociety*, Sage: London, Thousand Oaks, CA and New Delhi.

Jordan, T. (1999), *Cyberpower: the culture and politics of cyberspace and the internet*, Routledge: London and New York.

Jordan, T. (2002), 'Technopower and its cyberfutures', in J. Armitage and J. Roberts (eds), *Living with cyberspace: technology and society in the 21st century*, Continuum: New York, pp. 120–8.

Kamarck, E.C. and Nye, Jr, J.S. (2002), *Governance.com: democracy in the information age*, Brookings Institution Press: Cambridge, MA.

Kaplan, N. (1995), 'E-literacies', *Computer-Mediated Communication Magazine*, 2,3, 1 March, at http://www.ibiblio.org/cmc/mag/1995/mar/hyper/Literacies_624.html.

Katz, S.B. (2003), 'The ethics of expediency: classical rhetoric, technology, and the holocaust', in T. Peeples (ed.), *Professional writing and rhetoric: readings from the field*, Longman: New York, pp. 183–201.

Keane, J. (1997), 'Eleven theses on communicative abundance', version of keynote address at inaugural meeting of the Amsterdam School of Communications Research, University of Amsterdam, 18 September, at http://home.wmin.ac.uk/csd/Staff/jk.htm.

Keane, J. (2002), 'Whatever happened to democracy?', a public lecture delivered for the Institute for Public Policy Research, 27 March, at http://home.wmin.ac.uk/csd/Staff/jk.htm.

Keane, J. (2003), *Global civil society?*, Cambridge University Press: Cambridge.

Kearney, R. (1998), *Poetics of imagining: modern to postmodern*, Edinburgh University Press: Edinburgh.

Kearns, I. (2002), *Code red: progressive politics in the digital age*, IPPR, London.

Kingston University (2002), *The Body Shop employee stakeholder survey 2000: summary report*, Centre for Stakeholding and Sustainable Enterprise, Kingston University: Kingston, Surrey, at http://www.thebodyshop.com/web/tbsgl/images/tbs_employee_stakeholder_survey_2000.pdf.

Kingston, M. (2004), Webdiary, *Sydney Morning Herald*, at http://www.smh.com.au/news/opinion/webdiary/index.html.

Klein, N. (2001), *No logo*, Flamingo: London.

Kolb, D. (1996), 'Discourse across links', in C. Ess (ed.), *Philosophical perspectives in computer-mediated communication*, State University of New York Press: New York, pp. 15–26.

Krauth, N. (2000), 'Where is writing now?: Australian university creative writing programs at the end of the millennium', *TEXT*, 4,1, at http://www.gu.edu.au/school/art/text/.

L'Etang, J. (1996), 'Public relations and rhetoric', in J. L'Etang and M. Pieczka (eds), *Critical perspectives in public relations*, Thomson International Business Press: London, pp. 106–23.

L'Etang, J. (1997), 'Public relations and the rhetorical dilemma: legitimate "perspectives", persuasion, or pandering?', *Australian Journal of Communication*, 24,2, pp. 33–53.

Lanham, R.A. (1993), *The electronic word: democracy, technology and the arts*, University of Chicago Press: Chicago and London.

Lee, J.Y. (1996), 'Charting the codes of cyberspace: a rhetoric of electronic mail', in L. Strate, R. Jacobson and S.B. Gibson (eds), *Communication and cyberspace: social interaction in an electronic environment*, Hampton Press Inc.: Cresskill, NJ, pp. 275–95.

Leitch, S. and Motion, J. (1999), 'Multiplicity in corporate identity strategy', *Corporate Communications: an International Journal*, 4,4, pp. 193–200, Academic Research Library, Proquest Direct, http://proquest.umi.com/pqdweb.

Lévinas, E. (1987), *Collected philosophical papers*, Martinus Nijhoff Publishers: Dordrecht.

Lévinas, E. (1998), 'Philosophy, justice, and love', *Entre nous: thinking of the other*, trans. M.B. Smith and B. Harshav, Columbia University Press: New York, pp. 103–21.

Liptak, A. (2003), 'Free speech: Nike move ends case over firms' free speech', Reclaim democracy.org, first published *New York Times*, 13 September, at http://ReclaimDemocracy.org/nike/nyt_nikesettles.html.

Livesey, S.M. (2001), 'Eco-identity as discursive struggle: Royal Dutch/Shell, Brent Spar, and Nigeria', *Journal of Business Communication*, 38,1, pp. 58–91.

Lyotard, J.-F. (1988), *The differend: phrases in dispute*, trans. George Van Den Abeele, University of Minnesota Press: Minneapolis, MN.

Lyotard, J.-F. (1989), 'Lessons in paganism', in *The Lyotard reader*, ed. Andrew Benjamin, Basil Blackwell Ltd: Oxford, pp. 122–53.

Maarek, P.J. and Wolfsfeld, G. (2003), *Political communication in a new era: a cross-national perspective*, Routledge: London and New York.

Mailloux, S. (1990), 'Interpretation', in F. Lentricchia and T. McLaughlin (eds), *Critical terms for literary study*, University of Chicago Press: Chicago, pp. 121–34.

Manne, R. (1998), 'The stolen generation', *Quadrant*, 42,1–2, pp. 53–63.

Manne, R. (2001), 'In denial: the stolen generations and the Right', *The Australian Quarterly Essay*, 1, Schwartz Publishing Pty Ltd: Melbourne.

McDonald's (2002), *McDonald's social responsibility report*, at http://www.mcdonalds.com/corp.html.

McGee, M.C. (1990), 'Text, context, and the fragmentation of contemporary culture', *Western Journal of Communication*, 54, pp. 274–89.

McQuillan, M. (2000), 'Introduction – aporias of writing: narrative and subjectivity', in M. McQuillan (ed.), *The narrative reader*, London: Routledge, pp. 1–33.

Meech, P. (1996), 'Corporate identity and corporate image', in J. L'Etang and M. Pieczka (eds), *Critical perspectives in public relations*, Thomson International Business Press: London, pp. 65–81.

Meyer, T. (2002), *Media democracy: how the media colonize politics*, Polity Press: Cambridge.

Milchen, J. and Kaplan, J. (2003), 'Saving corporations from themselves?', Reclaim democracy.org, 27 June, at http://ReclaimDemocracy.org/nike/nike_court_case_oped_6272003.html.

Miller, C.R. (1984), 'Genre as social action', *Quarterly Journal of Speech*, 70 (May), pp. 151–67.

Miller, C.R. (1994), 'Rhetorical community: the cultural basis of genre', in A. Freedman and P. Medway (eds), *Genre and the new rhetoric*, Taylor and Francis: London, pp. 67–78.

Minsky, B.D. and Marin, D.B. (1999), 'Why faculty members use e-mail: the role of individual differences in channel choice', *Journal of Business Communication*, 36,2, pp. 194–205.

Mirel, B. and Spilka, R. (eds) (2002), *Reshaping technical communication: new directions and challenges for the 21st century*, Lawrence Erlbaum Associates: Mahwah, NJ and London.

Moloney, K. (2000), *Rethinking public relations: the spin and the substance*, Routledge: London and New York.

Muldoon, P. (2003), 'Reconciliation and political legitimacy: the old Australia and the new South Africa', *The Australian Journal of Politics and History*, 49,2, pp. 182–96.

Nike Inc. (2001), *Corporate responsibility report 2001*, at http://www.nike.com/nikebiz/nikebiz.jhtml?page=29.

Nike Inc. (2003), 'Nike, Inc. and Kasky announce settlement of Kasky v. Nike First Amendment case', media release, 12 September, at http://www.nike.com/nikebiz/news/pressrelease.jhtml?year=2003&month=09&letter=f.

Norlyk, B. (2000), 'Conflicts in professional discourse: language, law and real estate', in A. Trosborg (ed.), *Analysing professional genres*, John Benjamins Publishing Company: Amsterdam and Philadelphia, pp. 163–73.

OECD (2001), *Citizens as partners: information, consultation and public participation in policy-making*, OECD, Paris, at http://www1.oecd.org/publications/e-book/4201131E.PDF.

OECD (2003), 'Engaging citizens online for better policy-making', *Policy Brief*, March, OECD, Paris, at http://www.oecd.org/dataoecd/62/23/2501856.pdf.

OECD (2003a), *Promise and problems of e-democracy: challenges of online citizen engagement*, OECD, Paris.

Olson, G.A. and Dobrin, S.I. (eds) (1994), *Composition theory for the postmodern classroom*, State University of New York Press: Albany, NY.

Ornatowski, C.M. (2003), 'Between efficiency and politics: rhetoric and ethics in technical writing', in T. Peeples (ed.), *Professional writing and rhetoric: readings from the field*, Longman: New York, pp. 172–82.

Oxfam Community Aid Abroad (2002), 'The price of milk in Sri Lanka', *Horizons*, 2,2, June, pp. 14–15.

Paré, A. (2002), 'Keeping writing in its place: a participatory action approach to workplace communication', in B. Mirel and R. Spilka (eds), *Reshaping technical communication: new directions and challenges for the 21st century*, Lawrence Erlbaum Associates: Mahwah, NJ and London, pp. 57–80.

Parliament of Australia (1998), 'The role of the Senate', Senate brief no. 10, at www.aph.gov.au/senate/pubs/briefs/brief10.htm.

Peeples, T. (ed.) (2003), *Professional writing and rhetoric: readings from the field*, Longman: New York.

Penman, R. (2000), *Reconstructing communicating*, Lawrence Erlbaum Associates: Mahwah, NJ.

Perkins, J.M. and Blyler, N. (1999), *Narrative and professional communication*, Ablex Publishing Corporation: Stamford, CT.

Petelin, R. (2002), 'Managing organisational writing to enhance corporate credibility', *Journal of Communication Management*, 7,2, pp. 172–80.

Phelps, L.W. (1990), 'Audience and authorship: the disappearing boundary', in G. Kirsch and D.H. Roen (eds), *A sense of audience in written communication*, Sage: Newbury Park, CA, pp. 153–74.

Porter D. (ed.) (1997), *Internet culture*, Routledge: New York and London.

Porter, J.E. (1992), *Audience and rhetoric: an archaeological composition of the discourse community*, Prentice Hall: Englewood Cliffs, NJ.

Porter, J.E. (1993), 'The role of law, policy, and ethics in corporate composing: towards a practical ethics for professional writing', in N.R. Blyler and C. Thralls (eds), *Professional communication: the social perspective*, Sage Publications: Newbury Park, London and Delhi, pp. 128–43.

Porter, J.E. (1998), *Rhetorical ethics and internetworked writing*, Ablex Publishing Corporation: Greenwich, CT and London.

Porter, J.E. (1999), 'Public rhetorics and the corporate takeover of electronic writing', paper delivered at the Conference on College Composition and Communication, Atlanta GA, March, at http://www.rhetoric.msu.edu/writing_takeover.html.

Porter, J.E., Sullivan, P., Blythe, S., Grabill, J.T. and Miles, L. (2000), 'Institutional critique: a rhetorical methodology for change', *College Composition and Communication*, 51,4, pp. 610–42.

Poster, M. (1990), *The mode of information: poststructuralism and social context*, Polity Press in association with Basil Blackwell: Cambridge.

Poster, M. (1995), *The second media age*, Polity Press: Cambridge.

Poster, M. (1997), 'Textual agents: history at "the end of history" ', in *Cultural history and postmodernity: disciplinary readings and challenges*, Columbia University Press: New York, pp. 38–71.

Poster, M. (2001) *What's the matter with the Internet?*, University of Minnesota Press: Minneapolis and London.

Rooksby, E. (2000), 'Style and ethical relations in computer-mediated communication', PhD dissertation, Murdoch University, Western Australia.

Sales, H.E. (2002), 'Engineering texts: a study of a community of aerospace engineers, their writing practices and technical proposals', PhD dissertation, University of Birmingham, England.

Salinas, C. (2000), 'Toward a critical rhetoric of images: design/writing within a corporate web site', doctoral dissertation, Purdue University, West Lafayette, Indianapolis, at http://communication.utsa.edu/salinas/research/research. html.

Sanders, W. (2002), *Journey without end: reconciliation between Australia's Indigenous and settler peoples*, discussion paper no. 237, Centre for Aboriginal Economic Policy Research, Australian National University, at http://www.anu.edu.au/caepr/Publications/DP/2002_DP237.pdf.

Senate Legal and Constitutional References Committee (2000), *Healing: a legacy of generations: the report of the inquiry into the Federal Government's implementation of the recommendations made by the Human Rights and Equal Opportunities Commission in Bringing them home*, Commonwealth of Australia, at http://www.aph.gov.au/senate/committee/legcon_ctte/stolen/report/contents.htm.

Senate Legal and Constitutional References Committee (2003), *Reconciliation: off track*, Commonwealth of Australia, at http://www.aph.gov.au/senate/committee/legcon_ctte/reconciliation/report/report.pdf.

Sims, B.R. (1996), 'Electronic mail in two corporate workplaces', in P. Sullivan and J. Dautermann (eds), *Electronic literacies in the workplace: technologies of writing*, NCTE and Computers and Composition: Urbana, IL, pp. 41–64.

Spears, R., Postmes, T., Lea, M. and Wolbert, A. (2002), 'When are net effects gross products? The power of influence and the influence of power in computer-mediated communication', *Journal of Social Issues*, 58,1, pp. 91–107.

Spilka, R. (1990), 'Orality and literacy in the workplace: process- and text-based strategies for multiple-audience adaptation', *Journal of Business and Technical Communication*, 4, pp. 44–67.

Spilka, R. (ed.) (1993), *Writing in the workplace: new research perspectives*, Southern Illinois University Press: Carbondale and Edwardsville.

Stanworth, K. (2002), 'In sight of visual culture', *Symploke*, 10,1–2, pp. 106–17.

Steiner, C.J. (2001), 'How important is professionalism in corporate communication?', *Corporate Communications*, 6,3, pp. 150–6.

Suchan, J. (1998), 'The effect of high-impact writing on decision-making within a public sector bureaucracy', *Journal of Business Communication*, 35,3, July, pp. 299–328.

Suchan, J. (1995), 'The influence of organizational metaphors on writers' communication roles and stylistic choices', *Journal of Business Communication*, 32,1, January, pp. 7–29.

Sullivan, P.A. and Porter, J.E. (1993), 'Remapping curricular geography: professional writing in/and English', *Journal of Business and Technical Communication*, 7, pp. 389–422.

Sullivan, P.A. and Porter, J.E. (1997), *Opening spaces: writing technologies and critical research practices*, Ablex Publishing Corporation: Greenwich, CT.

Taylor, A. (1999), 'The ghost and the machine: creative writing and the academic system', *TEXT*, 3,1, at http://www.gu.edu.au/school/art/text/april99/taylor. htm.

The Body Shop (2003), *Values reporting: individual stakeholder accounts for employees*, Littlehampton, West Sussex: The Body Shop, at http://www.thebodyshop.com/web/tbsgl/library.jsp.

Tsagarousianou, R., Tambini, D. and Bryan, C. (eds) (1998), *Cyberdemocracy: technology, cities and civic networks*, Routledge: London and New York.

van Riel, C.B.M. (1995), *Principles of corporate communication*, Prentice Hall: London.

Vercic, D., Van Ruler, B., Butschi, G. and Flodin, B. (2001), 'On the definition of public relations: a European view', *Public Relations Review*, 27,4, pp. 373–87.

Waldvogel, J. (2001), 'Email and workplace communication: a literature review' Language in the workplace Occasional Papers 3, School of Linguistics and Applied Language Studies: Victoria University of Wellington, at http://www.vuw.ac.nz/lals/publications/pdfs/op3.pdf.

Walker, M.U. (1998), *Moral understandings: a feminist study in ethics*, Routledge: New York.

Wallace, D. (2000), 'E-mail and the problem of communication', *M/C: a Journal of Media and Culture*, 3,4, at http://www.api-network.com/mc/0008/email.html.

Warschauer, M. (2002), 'Reconceptualizing the digital divide', *First Monday*, 7,7, July, at http://www.firstmonday.dk/issues/issue7_7/warschauer/index.html.

Watson, D. (2003), *Death sentence: the decay of public language*, Random House Australia Pty Ltd: Milsons Point, NSW.

*Weekend Australian* (2001), 'O'Donoghue sheds some tears of regret', 24–25 February, p. 1, p, 4.

Weisser, C.R. (2002), *Moving beyond academic discourse: composition studies and the public sphere*, Southern Illinois University Press: Carbondale and Edwardsville.

Williams, R. (1965), *The long revolution*, Penguin: Harmondsworth.

Winsor, D.A. (1988), 'Communication failures contributing to the Challenger accident: an example for technical communicators', *IEEE transactions on professional communication*, 31,3, pp. 101–7.

Winsor, D.A. (1990), 'Engineering writing/writing engineering', *College composition and communication*, 41,1, pp. 58–70.

Woods, C. and Skrebels, P. (1997), 'Students and an undergraduate program in professional writing and communication: altered geographies', *TEXT*, at http://www.gu.edu.au/school/art/text/oct97/woods.htm.

Young, I.M. (1997), *Intersecting voices: dilemmas of gender, political philosophy and policy*, Princeton University Press: Princeton, NJ.

Zorn, T.E. (1998), 'Educating professional communicators: limiting options in the new academic "marketplace" ', *Australian Journal of Communication*, 25,2, pp. 31–44.

# Index